Compiled by R M Clarke

ISBN 1 85520 6633

BROOKLANDS BOOKS LTD.
P.O. BOX 146, COBHAM,
SURREY, KT11 1LG. UK
sales@brooklands-books.com

www.brooklands-books.com

ACKNOWLEDGEMENTS

Both of our books on early Cadillacs recently went out of print, they covered the years 1949-1969 and ran to 100 pages each. Due to the great interest in these early years, especially the 1957 and 1958 finned models, we have doubled the coverage of these years and increased the page count to 128. The more flamboyant 1959 models are covered in our new publication *Cadillac Performance Portfolio 1959-1966*.

Our books are printed in small numbers and now with over 400 titles are one of the main reference works for those that indulge in the hobby of automobile restoration. We exist because firstly there is a need by enthusiasts for this information and secondly because the publishers of the world's leading motoring journals generously support us by allowing us to include their copyright articles. We are indebted in this instance to the management of *Autocar, Car Life, Classic American, Hop Up, Modern Motor, Motor, Motor Age, Motor Life, Motor Trend, Motorsport, Popular Mechanics, Popular Science, NZ Classic Car, Science and Mechanics, Special Interest Autos* and *Wheels*.

We are also indebted to Tony Beadle, the motoring journalist, for his observations below and also for generously supplying our front cover photograph.

R.M. Clarke

The name Cadillac has always represented the ultimate in luxury motoring. Automobiles bearing the famous coat of arms of French explorer Antione de la Mothe Cadillac were also regarded as being manufactured to the highest specification, with a quality of workmanship that few others could match. Performance was usually a secondary consideration.

That all changed with the introduction of the 1949 Cadillac models, thanks to a new generation of high-compression, overhead valve V8 engines. The modern, postwar design featured lighter construction, a shorter stroke and better breathing than before, which added up to 160 horsepower from 331 cubic inches. While the power output figures might seem nothing to write home about these days, it was sufficient to enable a Cadillac to reach 60mph in only 13 seconds - a quick time over fifty years ago.

Being at the forefront of engine development in this manner enabled Cadillac to establish a reputation for performance that would last for many years to come. Cadillac engines became the choice of racers because they were thought to be more carefully assembled at the factory, using closely matched precision components to generate superior horsepower numbers.

Throughout the Fifties, Cadillac engine power output grew in parallel to the ever higher tailfins on the cars themselves. By 1958, the standard 365 cubic inch V8 was delivering 310bhp - almost double that of a decade earlier. There was also an optional 335 horsepower Eldorado engine with triple two-barrel carburettors available. And, although by the late '50s a Cadillac was undoubtedly bigger, heavier and more ornate than its predecessors, its zero to 60mph time had been cut to 11 seconds.

However, such were the improvements being made by other manufacturers, Cadillac was no longer ahead of the field. A spokesman for the company justified this situation by stating: "We aren't building cars for drag racing. We feel our cars offer all the performance their drivers need - and can use with safety."

While Cadillac might have been overtaken in the race for greater pace, it retained its pre-eminence where quality was concerned. In other words, although some cars might be slightly faster, only a Cadillac could deliver the performance with such luxury and style.

Tony Beadle

CONTENTS

Page	Title	Source	Date		
4	1948 Cadillac 61 Drive Report	*Special Interest Autos*	May		1999
12	The 1948 Cadillac	*Motor Age*	Feb		1948
13	The High-compression Cadillacs Introduction	*Motor*	Mar	2	1949
16	The 1949 Cadillac - Car of the Year	*Motor Trend*	Nov		1949
18	The 1949 Cadillac V-8 Retrospect	*Motor Trend*	Apr		1975
22	Convertible Converts - Series 62	*Classic American*	Aug		1997
25	The Cadillac V-8 Series 62 Touring Sedan Road Test	*Autocar*	Mar	22	1950
28	Cadillac - Series 62 Sedan Motor Trails	*Motor Trend*	Nov		1951
31	Cadillac Series 62 Saloon Road Test	*Autocar*	Nov	9	1951
34	Road Testing the 50th Anniversary Cadillac - Series 62	*Motor Trend*	Sept		1952
38	America's Most Powerful Car - Series 62	*Popular Science*	Mar		1953
40	Testing the Cadillac Series 62 Road Test	*Science and Mechanics*	Oct		1952
43	Cadillac - Car of the Year	*Motor Trend*	Feb		1953
47	Sectioned Cadillac	*Hop Up*	May		1953
50	Cadillac - America's Favorite Luxury Car	*Motor Trend*	May		1953
54	'54 Cadillac	*Motor Trend*	July		1954
57	Cadillac: El Camino, Park Avenue & La Espada	*Motor Life*	Apr		1954
58	Murphy's Law - 1953 Coupe de Ville	*NZ Classic Car*	Feb		2001
62	Hello Norma Jean - 54 Series 62 Convertible	*Classic American*	Aug		1992
65	Cadillac Series 62 Sedan	*Motor Life*	Aug		1954
67	'55 Cadillac - Full Details	*Motor Trend*	Jan		1955
69	Better than the Best!	*Modern Motor*	Sept		1955
70	The 1955 Cadillac	*Car Life*	Feb		1955
72	Cadillac Fleetwood 60 Special Road Test	*Motor Life*	May		1955
74	Cadillac Specials	*Car Life*	May		1955
75	A New Cadillac for 1956 - Eldorado Brougham	*Motor Life*	Sept		1955
76	Caddie Coupe	*Wheels*	Nov		1955
77	The 1956 Cadillac	*Motor Life*	Dec		1955
78	A Barris Bonanza	*Motor Trend*	Dec		1955
80	1956 Cadillac Consumer Analysis	*Car Life*	June		1956
82	The Cadillac 60 Special Road Test	*Motorsport*	May		1956
85	The 1957 Cadillac	*Motor Life*	Dec		1956
86	Cadillac Engineering	*Motor Life*	Dec		1956
87	Eldorado Brougham for '57	*Motor Life*	Feb		1957
88	Cadillac	*Motor Trend*	Jan		1957
90	1957 Cadillac Consumer Analysis	*Car Life*	May		1957
94	1957 Cadillac 62 Four-door Hardtop Road Test	*Motor Life*	May		1957
96	Buying a Cadillac for Economy? - 60 Research Report	*Motor Trend*	June		1957
98	'57 Cadillac Eldorado Brougham Retrospect	*Motor Trend*	Nov		1992
101	Nothing But the Best - '58 Series 62 Convertible	*Classic American*	Oct		1994
104	Dream "Caddie" is Out	*Modern Motor*	Sept		1957
106	Cadillac Drive Report	*Motor Trend*	Jan		1958
108	1958 Cadillac Consumer Analysis	*Car Life*	May		1958
112	1958 Cadillac 62 Four-door Hardtop Road Test	*Motor Life*	July		1958
114	Soft Top, Hard Work! - '58 Series 62 Convertible	*Classic American*	Oct		1997
118	Upscale Cadillac - Fleetwood Sixty Special '58	*Special Interest Autos*	Mar		2001
126	1958 Cadillac Test Data - Analysis & Opinions	*Popular Mechanics*	July		1958

1948 Cadillac 61
The First Shall Be Last

by Arch Brown
photos by Bud Juneau

IT isn't very often that one encounters a totally original, 50-year-old automobile that is still in really presentable condition. We found this one, of all places, at a Vintage Chevrolet Club meet. It's a 1948 Cadillac Sixty-One coupe, popularly known as a "sedanet." This model, as Cadillac aficionados are aware, represented the least expensive car in the entire Cadillac line, with a base price of just $2,728. But of course the "bottom of the line" at Cadillac still represents a distinctly upscale automobile. And its original price tag, though a bargain by just about anyone's standards, was $431 (19 percent) higher than the corresponding Buick Roadmaster — which of course was a luxurious machine in its own right.

One might think of the 1948 line as both the Alpha and the Omega at Cadillac. All but the out-sized Fleetwood Seventy-Five models bore a completely redesigned body that year, representing GM's first really new postwar styling effort. Thus the "Alpha" designation. And on the other hand, the monobloc, flathead V-8, which dated from 1936, represented the "Omega," for it was making its final appearance for '48. When 1949 rolled around there would be a brand new V-8, featuring over-square design, high compression and overhead valves.

Which, by the bye, takes nothing away from the venerable Cadillac flathead, which, in combination with the Hydra-Matic transmission, had given an excellent account of itself during wartime, powering first the M-5 light tanks (two engines, two transmissions per unit), and by 1944 the M-24 light tank. Cadillac's durability and reliability were put to the most rigorous of tests during the war, and they passed with flying colors.

At 364.6 cubic inches, the 1948 engine is slightly larger than the forthcoming 1949 mill, though it doesn't have quite the performance potential of its successor. But on the other hand, it has been our experience that the flathead is both smoother and quieter than 1949's overhead valve job. And if its 150 horsepower is ten short of that of the later engine, we found it to be more than adequate for the job of propelling this two-ton-plus automobile. We don't run any races with our driveReport subjects, obviously, but General Motors proving grounds records show this model with a top speed of 93.3 miles per hour; and according to the same source, the run from rest to 60 mph is made in 16.3 seconds. By 1948 standards, these are rather impressive figures, and Cadillac's claim of lively acceleration was certainly borne out during our test drive.

This, by the way, despite the fact that the engine in our driveReport car is obviously tired. The odometer registers something over 22,000 miles, doubtless on its second trip around the clock, and as best we have been able to determine, the heads have never been off. Owner Doug Dauterman tells us that when he first acquired the car "it smoked like Humphrey Bogart," though no such problem was encountered during our test drive.

We started and stopped the engine several times in the course of Bud Juneau's photo session, and it never failed to fire at the first turn. Steering seems a little heavy, now that we're all accustomed to the ease of a power assist; yet the wheel turns more easily than that of a good many cars of the immediate postwar era. Nor is it excessively slow: Just four turns of the big wheel are required to take it from lock-to-lock, giving the Cad remarkably good maneuverability for a car of this size and weight.

The transmission surges, as the early HydraMatics always do, as it changes from gear to gear. This is particularly noticeable in the shift from First to Second, which represents a jump in ratio from 3.97 to 2.55. But if the driver's foot doesn't lay too heavily upon the accelerator, the action of the transmission is comparatively smooth thereafter. Once in fourth gear, the Cadillac glides along in near-silence; and then when the accelerator is punched, the Hydra-Matic down-shifts to third speed for quicker acceleration. We found the Cad to be an exhilarating car to drive, despite its considerable heft.

These old Cadillacs provide a marvelously smooth ride, but the shocks in this particular car are clearly worn out, which makes it impossible for us to give a fair evaluation of the Cad's potential in that respect. In the turns, the car leans more heavily than one might wish; and there's a floating situation when a dip is encountered. But despite the handicap posed by the poor shocks, we experienced no loss of control in our limited test drive.

The brakes are powerful, as befits a heavy car. Owner Doug Dauterman recently had them completely overhauled, but they still have a mild but discon-

Top: All-new front end styling still carried traditional Cadillac appearance. **Above left:** "Sombrero" wheel covers were carried over from earlier cars. **Right:** It wouldn't be a Cadillac without the V and traditional crest. **Below left and right:** Tailfins were a styling sensation when introduced and began a Cadillac tradition. Flip-up taillamps were another Caddy trademark. **Bottom:** Sleekest of the '48 line was also the cheapest at $2,728. f.o.b.

1948 Cadillac 61

Above: Caddy script accents front fenders. *Below left:* Flip-up taillamp/gas filler actually originated on earlier cars and was a carryover for '48. *Right:* All-new styling gave a modern yet conservative look except for the fins. *Bottom:* Another assurance of quality. *Facing page:* Handling is typical of big, heavy US cars of the time.

certing tendency to pull to the left. To date, Doug has been unable to determine the cause.

The parking brake is more effective than most, but it is nevertheless prudent to "lock" the transmission when the car is parked. The technique here is to kill the engine while the transmission quadrant is in the "Lo" position, then move the lever to Reverse, which immobilizes the Cadillac. The transmission quadrant is typical of all the early General Motors automatics: N - D - L - R. This layout was useful for rocking the car out of mud or snow, but over the years it occasionally led to difficulties, and in a few cases, reportedly, to tragedy. The problem was that drivers accustomed to the three-speed manual shift (as nearly all of us were, in 1948) tended to pull down on the transmission control lever, expecting to engage Low gear, only to find that the transmission had been shifted into Reverse. Eventually, of course, the quadrant was standardized, just as the three-speed floor-shift pattern had been standardized in 1928.

Leg room is ample in front, and knee room is adequate to the rear, despite the fastback design. This represents a trade-off, however, for in order to provide an acceptable level of space, the rear seat backrest is positioned nearly vertically. This, we think, could be an invitation to big-time discomfort on a long trip. Rearward visibility has never been a strong point with fastback cars, but the window in this car is big enough to give the driver a fairly good over-the-

1948 Cadillac Prices, Weights and Production

	Price	Weight	Production
Series Sixty-One, 126-inch wheelbase			
Sedanet (club coupe), 5 passenger	$2,728	4,068	3,521
Sedan, 4-door, 5-passenger	2,833	4,150	5,081
Chassis only	n/a	N/A	1
TOTAL PRODUCTION, SERIES SIXTY-ONE			8,603
Series Sixty-Two, 126-inch wheelbase			
Sedanet (club coupe), 5-passenger	2,912	4,125	4,764
Sedan, 4-door, 5-passenger	2,996	4,179	23,997
Convertible coupe, 5-passenger	3,442	4,449	5,450
Chassis only	N/A	N/A	2
TOTAL PRODUCTION, SERIES SIXTY-TWO			34,213
Series Fleetwood Sixty-Special, 133-inch wheelbase			
Sedan, 4-door, 5-passenger	3,820	4,356	6,561
Series Fleetwood Seventy-Five, 136-inch wheelbase			
Sedan, 5-passenger	4,779	4,875	225
Sedan, 7-passenger	4,999	4,878	499
Business sedan, 9-passenger	4,679	4,780	90
Imperial sedan, 7-passenger	5,199	4,959	382
Business Imperial, 9-passenger	4,868	4,839	64
Chassis only (163-inch wheelbase)	N/A	N/A	2
TOTAL PRODUCTION, SERIES FLEETWOOD 75			1,261
GRAND TOTAL, 1948 MODEL YEAR PRODUCTION:			50,638
TOTAL 1948 CALENDAR YEAR PRODUCTION:			66,209

shoulder view from the inside mirror.

Seat cushions are soft, almost like living room sofas. Personally, we'd prefer something a little firmer, but perhaps this is part of the Cad's luxury image. The upholstery must have been covered throughout most of the Cadillac's life, for it appears almost new. Similarly, the woodgraining on the window sills is in excellent condition. Doug Dauterman has been told that the original owner would not permit his passengers to rest their elbows on the window sills. Neither would he permit smoking in the car. The woodgraining on the dash could use a bit of attention, presumably as the result of sunburn, but otherwise the interior is in amazingly good shape.

The instrument panel is one of the most attractive ever devised. In Dick Langworth's words, it is "dominated by a huge, ornate drum-type housing for the speedometer, minor gauges and controls." Langworth goes on to explain, with obvious regret, that "this lasted only a year, because it was complicated and costly to produce."

The Cadillac's exterior finish looks better than anyone would have a right to expect, after 50 years. The paint is worn thin on the crown of the right front fender, and a faded spot on the right door

1948 Luxury Club Coupes Compared

	Cadillac 61	Lincoln	Packard Super 8
Base price	$2,728	$2,533	$2,665
Wheelbase	126"	125"	120"
Overall length	214"	218.0625"	204.625"
Overall width	79"	77.83"	77.47"
Overall height	67.5"	67.125"	64.0625"
Front track	59"	59"	59.594"
Rear track	63"	60.6875"	60.72"
Weight (lb.)	4,068	3,915	3,790
Engine	V-8	V-12	Straight-8
Displacement (cu. in.)	346.4	292.0	327.1
Compression ratio	7.25:1	7.20:1	7.00:1
Horsepower @ rpm	150/3,400	125/3,600	145/3,600
Torque @ rpm	253/1,600	214/1,600	266/2,000
Valve configuration	L-head	L-head	L-head
Carburetor	Dual downdraft	Dual downdraft	Dual downdraft
Clutch	Dry plate	Dry plate	Dry plate
Outside diameter	10.5"	10"	10.5"
Standard transmission	3-speed	3-speed	3-speed
Optional transmission	HydraMatic	Overdrive	Overdrive
Final drive ratio (standard)	3.77:1	4.22:1*	3.90:1**
Steering	Recirc. ball	Worm/roller	Worm/roller
Ratio	21.3:1	22.5:1	26.2:1
Braking area (sq. in.)	208.0	184.0	171.5
Drum diameter	12"	12"	12"
Tire size	8.20/15	7.00/15	7.00/15
Stroke/bore ratio	1.286:1	1.304:1	1.214:1
Crankshaft revs per mile	2,650	3,038	2,808
Horsepower per c.i.d.	.433	.428	.443
Weight (lb.) per h.	27.1	31.3	26.1
Weight per c.i.d.	11.7	13.4	11.6

Above: 1948 marked the last year of the venerable 348 flathead, which had proven itself in peace and war. *Above right:* Original sales agreement for driveReport car. *Below left:* Great-looking instrument cluster design was used only in '48. *Right:* Bin-style glove compartment is placed logically in middle of dash. *Facing Page:* Fastback sacrifices trunk space for style. Original tools are still in their factory-supplied bag.

1948 Cadillac 61

gives evidence of a minor repair somewhere along the way. Otherwise, the finish is almost as good as it appears here in Bud's photographs.

We were moderately surprised to find that this is not a heavily optioned automobile. In so many cases, during the early postwar years, dealers—who literally had customers standing in line, awaiting the opportunity to purchase a new car—tended to load each new automobile with options in order to increase their profit margin. The list of extras on this car is short, but well chosen: HydraMatic transmission, radio with antenna, "sombrero" wheel covers, white sidewall tires, day/night (flip-type) mirror, left outside mirror, and—oddly enough—a single backup light. Most of us are accustomed to thinking of backup lights in pairs, but they didn't necessarily come that way in 1948.

It's all a matter of personal preference, of course, but the 1948 Cadillac "eggcrate" grille, taller and narrower than the 1949 edition and bolder than the '41, has always had a special appeal for this writer. But the styling feature that provoked the most comment when these cars were introduced was the little fins that rode atop the rear fenders. The inspiration for these fins, which became the industry's major fad during the 1950s, can be traced back to 1940, when GM styling director Harley Earl sent several members of his staff to Selfridge Field, near Detroit, for a look at the new Lockheed P-38 Lightning fighter plane, the twin-tailed hotshot that the Germans dubbed "Der Gabelschwanzteufel," or "Two-Tailed Devil." So intrigued was this group of stylists that, according to Walter M. P. McCall, they "went back to their drawing boards and translated some of the Lightning's radical features into styling concepts for possible cars of the future." This accounts not only for the fins, but also for the simulated air scoops on the leading edge of the rear fenders of our featured Cadillac.

(Truthfully, as Bill Mitchell, head stylist at Cadillac when our driveReport car was developed, once commented to journalist Dick Langworth, the original fin was "merely a humped-up taillight, really, it wasn't a fin at all." But the fins, or whatever they were, provided Cadillac with as clear an identity from the rear as it had when viewed from the front. Langworth quotes GM Chairman Alfred Sloan as saying to Cadillac General Manager Jack Gordon, "Jack, now you have a Cadillac in the rear as well as in the front.")

So our driveReport Cadillac was a trail-blazer in terms of styling.

And, by the bye, the left-side fin is hinged, revealing a small, illuminated compartment in which the gasoline filler cap is hidden. A clever touch, and a convenient one.

There's an interesting sidelight concerning the body shell used by the 1948 Series Sixty-One, Sixty-Two and Fleetwood Sixty-Special Cadillacs, as well as the Oldsmobile Ninety-Eight. Known officially as the GM "C" body, it had originally been intended as the corporate "B" body. In a 1993 letter to this writer, the late Richard H. Stout, a General Motors stylist when these cars were built, explained, "This is why wheelbases on the new jobs were the same as the old B-body and three inches shorter than the previous ones. GM simply did not have time to get a C-body done, so this was rechristened C from B. Cadillac had to be first with some all new stuff." (During 1942-47 the Sixty-One had employed the then current B-body on a 126-inch wheelbase, while the Sixty-Two used the larger C-body on a 129-inch chassis. For 1948, both models employed the 126-inch wheelbase, fitted with the new B-cum-C body. A stretched version was employed for the Fleetwood Sixty-Special.)

Thanks to delays caused apparently by re-tooling for the new body, the 1948 Cadillacs weren't introduced until March of that year. Long before that, prospective buyers had been standing in line, awaiting their chance to buy a new Cadillac; and of course the new model

specifications

illustrations by Russell von Sauers, The Graphic Automobile Studio

© copyright 1999, Special Interest Autos

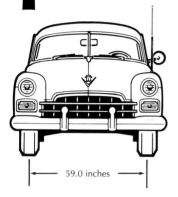
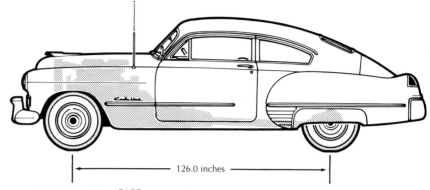

59.0 inches — 126.0 inches

1948 Cadillac 61

Price $2,728 f.o.b. factory, with standard equipment
Options on dR car HydraMatic transmission, radio with antenna, white sidewall tires, left outside mirror, day/night mirror, backup light

ENGINE
Type 90-degree L-head V-8
Bore x stroke 3.5 inches x 4.5 inches
Displacement 346.4 cubic inches
Compression ratio 7.25:1
Horsepower @ rpm 150 @ 3,400 (gross)
Torque @ rpm 283 @ 1,600 (gross)
Taxable horsepower 39.2
Valve configuration L-head
Valve lifters Hydraulic
Main bearings 3
Fuel system 1.25-inch dual downdraft carburetor, camshaft pump
Lubrication system Pressure
Cooling system Centrifugal pump
Exhaust system Single
Electrical system 6-volt battery/coil

TRANSMISSION
Type HydraMatic 4-speed automatic planetary
Ratios: 1st 3.97:1
2nd 2.55:1
3rd 1.55:1
4th 1.00:1
Reverse 3.74:1

DIFFERENTIAL
Type Hypoid
Ratio 3.36:1
Drive axles Semi-floating

STEERING
Type Saginaw recirculating ball
Turns lock-to-lock 4
Ratio 25.6:1 gear
Turning diameter 45 feet 7 inches

BRAKES
Type 4-wheel internal hydraulic
Drum diameter 12 inches
Effective area 208 square inches

CHASSIS & BODY
Construction Body-on-frame
Frame Channel section steel with central X-member
Body construction All steel
Body type Sedanet (fastback club coupe)

SUSPENSION
Front Independent A-arms, coil springs, torsional stabilizer bar
Rear Rigid axle, semi-elliptic longitudinal springs
Shock absorbers Lever hydraulic
Tires 8.20/15 4-ply
Wheels Pressed steel, drop-center rims

WEIGHTS AND MEASURES
Wheelbase 126 inches
Overall length 214 inches
Overall width 79 inches
Overall height 66.75 inches
Front track 59 inches
Rear track 63 inches
Min. road clearance 8 inches
Shipping weight 4,068 pounds

CAPACITIES
Crankcase 7 quarts
Cooling system 26 quarts
Fuel tank 20 gallons

CALCULATED DATA
Horsepower per c.i.d. .433
Weight per hp 27.1 pounds
Weight per c.i.d. 11.7 pounds
P.S.I. (brakes) 19.6
Stroke/bore ratio 1.286:1
Crankshaft rev/mile 2,650

PERFORMANCE
Top speed 93.3 mph
0-60 mph 16.3 seconds

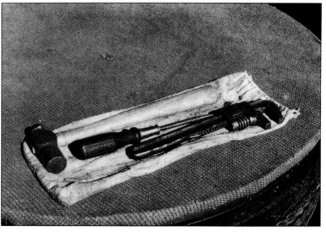

1948 Cadillac 61

brought an increase in demand. By year's end, Cadillac's total production totaled 66,209 cars. The total for the somewhat abbreviated model year came to 50,638 units.

It's interesting to note that while Cadillac's 1948 calendar year production represented an eleven percent increase over 1941, previously the division's all-time record. Meanwhile, output at all the other GM divisions actually fell. Specifically, Pontiac's volume was down by ten percent, Buick's by 13 percent, Oldsmobile's by 16 percent and Chevrolet's by 17 percent. It would be

1948

If 1998 was a less-than-felicitous time for Republicans, consider how they must have felt 50 years earlier, during the year when our driveReport Cadillac was built.

To refresh the reader's memory, that was the year when President Harry S. Truman pulled one of the great political upsets of all time by beating New York Governor Thomas E. Dewey in the race for the United States Presidency. Dewey's election had seemed assured, partly because Truman, who had inherited the presidency upon Franklin Roosevelt's death, had never been particularly popular; and partly because there were two "third party" candidates in the running, both of them representing spin-offs from the Democratic party. Former Vice President Henry A. Wallace was running to Harry Truman's left on the Progressive ticket, while South Carolina Governor J. Strom Thurmond rivaled Truman on the right as the candidate of the States Rights or "Dixiecrat" party. (And yes, this is the same Strom Thurmond who, at age 96, is still serving, at this writing, as the most senior member of the United States Senate.)

So certain of the results were the pundits, and nearly everyone else for that matter, that *Life* magazine had already gone to the printers with a photograph of "President Dewey" on the cover. But, in the end, Dewey captured only 16 states with 189 electoral votes against Truman's 28 states and 304 electoral votes.

And speaking of Franklin Roosevelt, on April 12th the third anniversary of his death was observed in London with the unveiling by his widow of a statue in Grosvenor Park. The entire Royal Family, as well as Winston Churchill, were on hand for the occasion.

Back in Washington, DC, Congress passed the Foreign Assistance Act, establishing the Economic Co-operation Administration, popularly known as the "Marshall Plan" after General George C. Marshall, President Truman's Secretary of State, who had originally proposed it. The purpose was to rehabilitate the economies of post World War II European nations in order to create stable conditions in which free institutions could survive. Under the direction of former Studebaker president Paul G. Hoffman, $12 billion worth of economic aid was distributed over the next four years, in one of the most generous—and most successful—undertakings in the nation's history.

Of course, life had its brighter side. At the movies, Americans saw *Hamlet*, featuring Laurence Olivier; *Easter Parade*, starring Judy Garland; and *Treasure of the Sierra Madre*, with Humphrey Bogart and Walter Huston. And Jane Wyman, still married to Ronald Reagan in those days, won an Oscar for her role in *Johnny Belinda*, co-starring Lew Ayres.

And then, there were poignant moments, such as Babe Ruth's final public appearance, at the debut of the biographical motion picture *The Babe Ruth Story*. Three weeks later the Babe was dead, the victim of cancer. Still, all-in-all it was a happy time. The world was at peace, at least for the moment, and the economy was booming.

By way of illustrating how far recorded music has come in a comparatively short time, it was on June 21, 1948, that Dr. Peter Goldmark of the Columbia Broadcasting System demonstrated his "long-playing" (33 rpm) recordings. Until that time, phonograph turntables revolved at 78 rpm, limiting most of them to about a three-minute run. Of course, in the years that followed, Goldmark's triumph has been topped twice, first by tapes and more recently by CD's—with, we are told, more technological advances yet to come!

It wasn't a particularly outstanding year for popular music, perhaps because a number of the great songwriters, such as Jerome Kern and George Gershwin, were gone. Still, there were some good songs. Frank Loesser's "Once in Love with Amy," forever to be associated with Ray Bolger, and Cole Porter's "So In Love" come to mind, along with Sammy Cahn and Jule Styne's "It's Magic," a number made famous by Doris Day.

A three-cent stamp carried a first-class letter in those days; and the US Post Office issued 29 distinct versions of it during 1948, honoring American historical events and noted Americans. Among those whose likeness appeared on these stamps were Elizabeth Cady Stanton, Carrie Chapman Catt and Lucretia Mott, pioneers in the cause of women's suffrage; Francis Scott Key, author of our national anthem; Clara Barton, founder of the American Red Cross; and the scientist Dr. George Washington Carver, the first African American ever to be so-honored.

Detroit, of course, was still enjoying the remnants of the post-war "seller's market." Ever since the end of World War II, demand for new cars had far exceeded the supply. And more than any other make, it was the Cadillac that was in demand. So much so, in fact, that dealers were confronted with the problem of customers who bought new Cadillacs at the government-imposed ceiling price, and then re-sold them on the "gray market" at an inflated figure.

Dealers fought back as best they could, often displaying considerable ingenuity in the process. Our driveReport Cadillac serves as case-in-point, for upon taking delivery of it, the original purchaser was required to sign an agreement stipulating that the car would not be sold or otherwise disposed of for a period of six months from the date of sale, without giving the dealer the option of re-purchasing the vehicle at the original purchase price, less sales tax and license fee. (A copy of this agreement appears on page 22.) Whether such a contract would stand up in court is debatable, of course; but this "Repurchase Option Agreement" serves to illustrate how seriously the dealers viewed the problem.

But still, new Cadillacs were rolling out of the factory in greater numbers than ever before in the division's history, and customers were literally standing in line, awaiting the opportunity to buy them. Nor was there any haggling over price. So when complaints were heard, they rarely came from Cadillac dealers.

The automobile industry had endured some very lean years. But by 1948, happy times had returned. Especially at Cadillac.

naive, however, to suggest that these figures accurately portrayed customer demand at that time. Critical materials, including sheet metal, were still in somewhat short supply during 1948; and there can be little doubt that General Motors executives, with an eye on the bottom line, were particularly generous in their allocations to the division that returned the highest per-unit profit.

(A similar pattern can be observed at Buick, by the way. There, the Roadmaster series represented 37.5 percent of the division's 1948 production, compared to just 4.2 percent during the 1941 model year.)

Cadillac fielded four distinct series of automobiles for 1948, down from six during the 1941 season. The '48s were late in arriving, having been introduced during March of that year, but surely they were worth the wait.

The entry-level Series Sixty-One was available in either of two body types, the coupe shown here and a four-door sedan.

Next up was the Sixty-Two, similar to the Sixty-One but featuring a somewhat higher level of equipment and trim, as well as a higher (by $184) price tag. It was offered in the same two body types, plus a smart convertible coupe.

For those who could afford it and had enough garage space to house it, there was the sumptuously trimmed and lavishly equipped Fleetwood Sixty-Special. Built on a 133-inch chassis and fitted with a stretched version of the new General Motors "C" body, it measured 225 21/32 inches bumper-to-bumper. Thus it was nearly a foot longer (as well as over $800 more costly) than the Sixty-Two.

And at the top, there was the Fleetwood "75" series, built on a 136-inch wheelbase and featuring styling that differed little from the 1941 version. These were Cadillac's most prestigious, as well as most expensive, cars, though they were only fractionally longer than the Sixty-Special. This series would have to wait until 1950 to be restyled, but so impressive were these warmed-over pre-war models that nobody really cared. Several variations were offered, ranging from a nine-passenger Business Sedan, intended primarily for the funeral trade, to a glamorous seven-passenger Imperial Sedan representing, at $5,199, the very acme of the Cadillac line.

We mentioned the HydraMatic transmission. Although it was an option, for which an extra $174 was charged, it was fitted to 97 percent of all new 1948 Cadillacs. (By 1952, the year after the Sixty-One was dropped from the line, the automatic would become standard issue for both the Sixty-Two and the Fleetwood Sixty-Special.)

Clubs and Specialists

Cadillac-LaSalle Club, Inc.
PO Box 1916
Lenoir, NC 28645-1916
828-757-9919; 828-757-0367 FAX
E-mail:cadlasal@twave.net
For Cadillac and LaSalle collectors and enthusiasts. 6,200 members with regions in 23 states.

Cadillac Drivers Club
5825 Vista Ave.
Sacramento, CA 95824
916-421-3193

Cadillac Past
14 Dudley Rd.
Billerica, MA 01821
508-667-0075

Ed Cholakian Enterprises, Inc.
12811 Foothill Blvd.
Sylmar, CA 91342
800-808-1147; 818-361-1147
818-361-9738 FAX
Specializing in Cadillac parts from 1940 to 1958.

F.E.N. Enterprises
PO Box 1559
Wappingers Falls, NY 12590
914-462-5959

Justin Hartley
17 Fox Meadow Lane
West Hartford, CT 06107-1216
860-523-0056; 860-604-9950 cellular
860-233-8840 FAX
Specializing in reprinted Cadillac shop manuals for all years through 1995.

Ted Holcombe Cadillac Parts
2933 Century Lane
Bensalem, PA 19020
215-245-4560

Honest John's Caddy Corner
PO Box 741-2271
Justin, TX 76247
940-648-3330

Kanter Auto Products
76 Monroe St.
Boonton, NJ 07005
800-526-1096

McVey's
5040 Antioch, Suite E
Merriam, KS 66203
913-722-0707

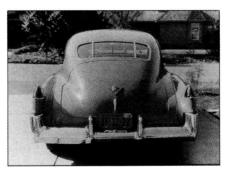

Best-equipped among the 1948 Cadillacs were the Fleetwood Seventy-Fives and the Sixty-Two convertibles, both lines being supplied with hydro-electric powered windows and seats. The latter feature was also furnished at no extra cost with the Sixty-Specials.

But for sheer value in a luxurious, high-quality, high-performance automobile, nothing, in 1948, could beat the $2,728 Cadillac Sixty-One sedanet. Don't you wish you could buy a new one just like it, at that price? ✌

Facing Page: Dashboard has a highly contemporary appearance. **This page, left:** *High quality fit and materials throughout the interior.* **Below left:** *One of the very best aspects of the car.* **Below:** *AAA badge is another original touch on the Caddy.*

Acknowledgments and Bibliography

Automotive Industries, *March 15, 1948*; Hendry, Maurice D., Cadillac: The Complete History *(Fourth edition)*; Kowalke, Ron (ed.), Standard Catalog of American Cars, 1946-1975; Langworth, Richard M., Encyclopedia of American Cars, 1940-1970; Langworth, Richard M., "Of Tail Fins and V-8's," Automobile Quarterly, Volume XIII, No. 3; Lamm, Michael, "Two Very Important Cars," Special Interest Autos #11; McCall, Walter M.P., 80 Years of Cadillac-LaSalle.

Our thanks to Charles Carroll, Chico, California; Tom Dauterman, Chico, California; Bud Juneau, Brentwood, California. Special thanks to Doug Dauterman, Chico, California.

Most unusual design feature of the new Cadillac is the odd, fin-like extension that forms the trailing edge of each of the rear fenders.

The 1948 CADILLAC

This year's model features completely re-designed bodywork and follows the trend toward integrated body and fenders.

THE bodywork on the Cadillac for 1948 has been completely redesigned, although mechanically the car remains unchanged from last year.

Preserving the Cadillac identity, the new car is longer, lower and wider. The front fenders sweep rearward from the headlights, in an unbroken line, to the rear fenders, and form part of the body itself.

The radiator grille, now made up of only two rather heavy horizontal chrome bars crossed by seven vertical bars of stainless steel, is lower and wider than that on last year's model. The headlamps are recessed in the upper part of the fenders, and parking and directional lamps are recessed directly below them. If fog lights are desired, a triple function lamp assembly is available to replace the one mentioned above.

The rear fenders are unusual in that they are turned up at the rear to form vertical fins that house the flush tail-lights and directional lights.

The front bumpers are heavier for added protection and follow the contours of the fenders closely. The broad hood slopes downward to a greater degree than on last year's model, affording increased road visibility, while the hood side panels are integrated with the top panel and blend into the fenders.

Window and windshield posts are narrower for increased visibility and the windshield and rear window are now made of curved glass. Push button window and front seat control is standard equipment on the Series 60 Special, Series 75, and convertibles. It is optional on other models.

The interiors have been redesigned and now provide increased seat width and leg room. All driving instruments are grouped together in a compact cluster above the steering column, and a new steering column jacket completely conceals the steering and gear shift columns behind the instrument panel extension. An unusual feature of the panel itself is that its lower edge is carried downward and forward to the front edge of the toe-board, providing a completely finished and enclosed front compartment.

As stated above, the Cadillac has undergone few mechanical changes. Some modifications in the suspension have been made, however, such as re-location of the rear shock absorbers and the addition of a new type of compression bumper. The steering ratio has been changed, as has the caster adjustment, to accomodate the new low pressure tires.

Hydra-Matic Drive will continue to be available as optional equipment on all models. The reverse control, according to Cadillac, has been improved so as to afford smoother, quicker shifting.

The engine, in all models, is the familiar 150 hp V-8, with $3\frac{1}{2}$ x $4\frac{1}{2}$ in. bore and stroke and 346 cu. in. piston displacement. Hydraulic tappets are a standard feature.

The Cadillac line is divided into four series, the 61, 62, 60-S and 75. The 61 and 62 are mounted on a 126 in. wheelbase, while the 60-S measures 133 in. and the 75 $136\frac{1}{4}$ in.

Five, seven and nine-passenger bodies are available in these series, including a convertible coupe in the Series 62.

BIGGEST AND BEST.—Heading the Cadillac range is the Model 75, a long-wheelbase car available with 7- or 9-seater coachwork which retains such conventional features as rubber-covered running-boards.

The High-compression Cadillacs

America's Quality Car Redesigned to Incorporate a New Overhead-valve V8 Engine Developing 160 b.h.p.

PIONEERS in the production of new engines strong enough to withstand eventual use with ultra-high-compression ratios and promised high-octane fuels are General Motors Corporation. Since the London Motor Exhibition in October all cars in their most expensive range, the Cadillacs, have been redesigned to incorporate an overhead-valve V8 engine, which also appears in substantially modified form in certain Oldsmobile models.

A sectioned view of this engine has already appeared in "The Motor," and the arrival of fuller specifications makes it clear that it incorporates a great many characteristically modern features. It has been designed to meet present-day needs for fuel economy without sacrifice of performance, and to be light and compact with a view to installation in low cars.

Space saving has its root in the cylinder dimensions of the 90-degree V8 engine, the cylinders of which have a stroke-bore ratio of 0.95 instead of the 1.28 of the unit hitherto produced. In conjunction with this change in cylinder shape, connecting rods have been shortened to $6\frac{5}{8}$ ins. and the overall piston length to $3\frac{1}{6}$ ins., piston skirts being cut away on the non-thrust carrying faces to provide clearance for the crankshaft counterbalance weights.

The wedge form of the combustion chambers is evident in the sectioned drawing of the engine, and the location of the sparking plug gives the flame spread from a large towards a smaller volume, which makes for smooth running. For the U.S. market, a compression ratio of 7.5 to 1 is used, giving the notably high brake mean effective pressure of 142 lb. per sq. in. on the high-octane premium-price fuels now available. Future models will probably have an even higher compression ratio, but cars exported to countries where only low-grade fuel is supplied have the compression ratio lowered to 6.7 to 1.

Carburation is by a $1\frac{1}{4}$-in. twin-choke Carter down-draught unit, drawing air via an oil-bath filter and equipped with an

TWO-PEDAL.—Fitting of the optional Hydra-Matic 4-speed fully automatic transmission eliminates the clutch pedal, leaving only the dip switch to be operated by the driver's left foot.

CONTINUITY.—Running-boards which appear only on long-wheelbase models are blended into the line of protective chrome strips on front mudguards and rear-wheel covers.

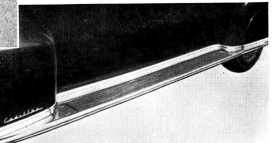

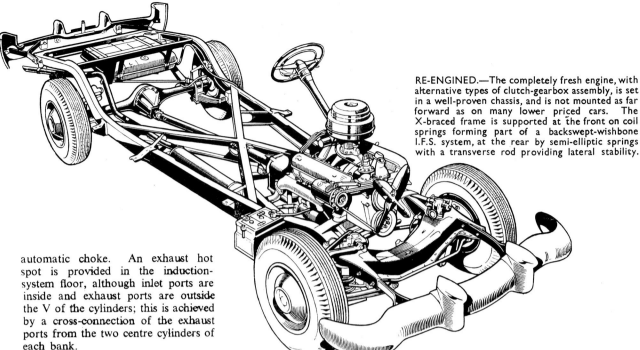

RE-ENGINED.—The completely fresh engine, with alternative types of clutch-gearbox assembly, is set in a well-proven chassis, and is not mounted as far forward as on many lower priced cars. The X-braced frame is supported at the front on coil springs forming part of a backswept-wishbone I.F.S. system, at the rear by semi-elliptic springs with a transverse rod providing lateral stability.

automatic choke. An exhaust hot spot is provided in the induction-system floor, although inlet ports are inside and exhaust ports are outside the V of the cylinders; this is achieved by a cross-connection of the exhaust ports from the two centre cylinders of each bank.

Rigidity is a characteristic of the new engine, the crankshaft with its $2\frac{1}{4}$-in.-diameter crankpins being supported in five main bearings of $2\frac{1}{2}$-in. diameter. Crankcase and cylinder blocks form a single casting, in which the gear-driven five-bearing camshaft runs.

Alternative transmissions are offered by Cadillac, the orthodox one being a combination of $10\frac{1}{2}$-in. single-dry-plate clutch and three-speed synchromesh gearbox. For those who prefer two-pedal control, there is the General Motors Hydra-Matic transmission available.

Automatic Transmission

Part one of this automatic transmission takes the form of a fluid coupling, a species of automatic clutch which has long been known in this country as the "fluid flywheel." An interesting detail is that, although such a coupling is often expected to cushion the transmission, in this application it is supplemented by a torsionally springy coupling, such as is usually incorporated in the centre of a modern dry-plate clutch.

Part two of the Hydra-Matic transmission is a four-speed epicyclic gearbox. Three gear trains are provided, two of which, when used separately or together, provide the three indirect gears or can be locked solid for direct drive, the remaining gear train being for reversing. The operation of the gearbox is in automatic response to speed and load, so that on gentle running the engine revs. are kept low, but with hard use of the throttle the engine is allowed to attain the speed at which its full power is developed. To quote an example, on full-throttle acceleration the upward change from third to

PLAINER PLUMBING.— The number of flexible hoses in the main cooling water circuit is cut down to two, by this neat assembly of pump, thermostatic by-pass, and cross-pipes inter-linking the cylinder blocks and heads.

top gear will only take place when a speed of approximately 65 m.p.h. is attained, and third gear will be re-engaged if a gradient slows the car below 60 m.p.h. On very light throttle, however, top gear will come into action so soon as the car speed exceeds 18 m.p.h., and be held until the speed has sunk as low as 14 m.p.h. unless the throttle is opened.

The chassis in which this power unit is installed may be regarded as very typical of good modern U.S. practice without being in any sense revolutionary. It is X-braced and has channel-section longerons of $6\frac{5}{8}$ ins. maximum depth, the whole being downswept between the axles to give a low floor level. Exhaust piping and the propeller shaft pass through the X-bracing structure,

RAKISH.—The combination of two-door coupé body and series 62 chassis make one of America's fastest production cars.

CADILLAC DATA

Model	Series 61, 62, 60S	Series 75
Engine Dimensions:		
Cylinders	V8	V8
Bore	97 mm.	97 mm.
Stroke	92 mm.	92 mm.
Cubic capacity	5,440 c.c.	5,440 c.c.
Piston area	91.3 sq. ins.	91.3 sq. ins.
Valves	Pushrod, o.h.v.	Pushrod, o.h.v.
Compression ratio	7.5 to 1	7.5 to 1
Engine Performance:		
Max. b.h.p.	160	160
at	3,800 r.p.m.	3,800 r.p.m.
Max. b.m.e.p.	142 lb./sq. in.	142 lb./sq. in.
at	1,800 r.p.m.	1,800 r.p.m.
B.h.p. per sq. in. piston area	1.75	1.75
Peak piston speed, ft. per min.	2,290	2,290
Engine Details:		
Carburetter	Carter 1¼ in. dual d/d	Carter 1¼ in. dual d/d
Ignition	Delco-Remy coil	Delco-Remy coil
Plugs: make and type	14 mm. AC, type 48	14 mm. AC, type 48
Fuel pump	Mechanical	Mechanical
Fuel capacity	16½ gallons	16½ gallons
Oil capacity	8¼ pints	8¼ pints
Cooling system	Pump and fan	Pump and fan
Water capacity	3¾ gallons	3¾ gallons
Electrical system	Delco-Remy, 6 volt	Delco-Remy, 6 volt
Battery capacity	115 amp.-hours	115 amp.-hours
Transmission:		
Clutch	Fluid coupling or Long single dry plate 10½ in. dia.	Fluid coupling or Long single dry plate 11 in. dia.
Gear ratios with hydra-matic transmission:		
Top	3.86	3.77
3rd	4.87	5.47
2nd	8.85	9.93
1st	12.83	14.40
Rev.	14.46	16.23
Gear ratios with synchro-mesh gearbox:		
Top	3.77	4.27

Model	Series 61, 62, 60S	Series 75
Transmission—contd.:		
2nd	5.76	6.63
1st	9.00	10.20
Rev.	9.00	10.20
Prop. shaft	Open	Open
Final drive	Hypoid bevel	Hypoid bevel
Chassis Details:		
Brakes	Bendix hydraulic	Bendix hydraulic
Brake drum diameter	12 ins.	12 ins.
Friction lining area	220 sq. ins.	233 sq. ins.
Suspension:		
Front	Coil and wishbone, i.f.s.	Coil and wishbone, i.f.s.
Rear	Semi-elliptic leaf	Semi-elliptic leaf
Shock absorbers	Piston type, Delco	Piston type, Delco
Wheel type	Steel disc	Steel disc
Tyre size	8.20 × 15	7.50 × 16
Steering gear	Saginaw recirculating ball	Saginaw recirculating ball
Dimensions:		
Wheelbase	10 ft. 6 ins.	11 ft. 4¼ ins.
Track:		
Front	4 ft. 11 ins.	4 ft. 10½ ins.
Rear	5 ft. 3 ins.	5 ft. 2½ ins.
Overall length	17 ft. 11 ins.	18 ft. 9¾ ins.
Overall width	6 ft. 7 ins.	6 ft. 10½ ins.
Overall height	5 ft. 3¾ ins.	5 ft. 8½ ins.
Ground clearance	7¼ ins.	8¼ ins.
Turning circle	46¼ ft. (over bumpers)	49 ft. (over bumpers)
Dry weight	36 cwt.	41¾ cwt.
Performance Data (Hydra-matic transmission):		
Piston area, sq. ins. per ton	50.6	43.7
Brake lining area, sq. ins. per ton	122	112
Top gear m.p.h. per 1,000 r.p.m.	25.2	23.25
Top gear m.p.h. at 2,500 ft./min. piston speed	104	96.5
Litres per ton-mile, dry	3,600	3,360

the shaft being a single tubular unit taking drive from a rear extension of the gearbox to the hypoid axle.

Front suspension is independent, by coil springs and unequal backswept wishbones, and there is an anti-roll torsion bar. At the rear, 2-in.-wide semi-elliptic leaf springs take the drive and braking loads, but a transverse rod is provided to give lateral location of the chassis.

All springs are damped by Delco shock absorbers of double-acting hydraulic pattern. Bendix hydraulic brakes operate in 12-in.-diameter steel-faced cast-iron drums, and 56 per cent. of braking effort is applied to the front wheels, braking areas being generous by U.S. standards.

Coachwork styles are based upon two-door coupé, four-door sedan and two-door convertible bodies for the normal-wheelbase chassis, plus bodies seating five, seven or nine people for mounting on the long 75-series chassis. There are, however, quite wide variations in interior and exterior finish details as between the 61, 62 and 60S series cars, which cater for either conservative or advanced tastes. All bodies are of Fisher steel construction, equipped with such items as lamps which light up automatically when doors or luggage locker are opened. On certain models, hydraulic push-button control is applied to windows, front-seat adjustment and folding coupé top.

Perhaps the most striking recognition feature of recent Cadillac models, including those with the now-obsolete side-valve engine, is the tail-fin motif on each rear mudguard. Tail lamps are formed in these fins, and one lamp hinges up to reveal the fuel filler. Visible modifications on the 1949 o.h.v. models are a slightly lengthened bonnet and a new, low, full-width radiator grille.

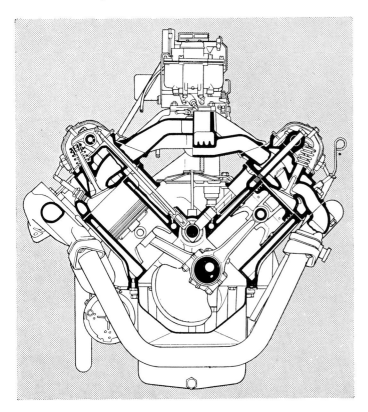

POWER SECTION.—Economy is the main claim for the new engine, high compression ratios being acceptable with the carefully designed combustion chamber, in which are overhead valves operated by hydraulic tappets, pushrods and rockers. Lighter than the side-valve V-8 it supersedes, the new engine is of enlarged cylinder bore and shortened piston stroke. Cross passages interlink the exhaust systems to provide a hot-spot beneath the dual downdraught carburetter.

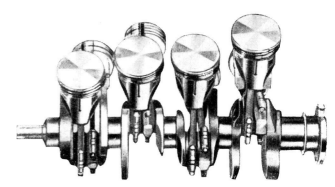

MECHANISM.—Visible in this photograph are the sturdy 4-throw 5-bearing crankshaft, the side-by-side big end bearings, and the slipper pistons whose skirts are cut away to clear the crankshaft counterweights at bottom dead centre.

CAR OF THE YEAR

THE 1949 CADILLAC

by John Bond

NOTE: *In this article, automotive enthusiast John Bond was asked to describe his idea of the most advanced of the 1949 models. Before making his selection, he considered all models, ranging from the Jeepster through the Lincoln, and gave serious thought to the engine, appearance, and handling characteristics. His final choice may be subject to controversy, but definitely has merit.—Editor*

CHOOSING an outstanding "car of the year" for certain years past may be difficult, but for 1949 the selection is narrowed down to three most worthy of consideration: Ford, Oldsmobile, and Cadillac.

While the Ford has an entirely new chassis and body, plus many mechanical changes, it offers nothing new or outstanding from an engineering viewpoint, since it now falls in line with conventional design practice established by competitors before the war.

The Cadillac was chosen in preference to the Olds because, while both have outstanding new V-8 engines which are similar, they are not by any means the same. The Cadillac, with 10 per cent more piston displacement than the Olds, develops 18.5 per cent more bhp and weighs a few pounds less.

This new engine by Cadillac is not the so-called Kettering engine, which was a small six of 180 cubic inches. The Kettering six was a square engine (equal bore and stroke), had seven main bearings, used a simple combustion chamber shape about like the last Buick Six of 1930, looked externally very similar to the current 216.5 cubic inch Chevrolet, and was even heavier than the Chevrolet. While the Cadillac was developed concurrently with the GM Research 12.5 to 1 compression engine, it is considerably different.

The 1949 Cadillac powerplant, with a cylinder bore of 3.8125 inches and a stroke of only 3.625 inches, is unique in that this gives it a stroke-bore ratio of 0.95:1. (Most engines have a smaller bore than stroke.) The large bore permits large valves in relation to the total piston displacement with resultant good specific output, or bhp per cubic inch. The short stroke makes the engine lighter and more compact as well as giving lower piston speeds.

Cadillac's change-over from "L" head to overhead valve type of design accomplishes two desirable goals. First, the overhead valve engine is recognized as a definite must for getting the most potential advantage from higher octane fuels—provided, of course, that such fuels become available at economic prices. It is not possible to increase compression ratio in "L" head engines to much over 8:1, even with better fuel, because volumetric efficiency falls off at

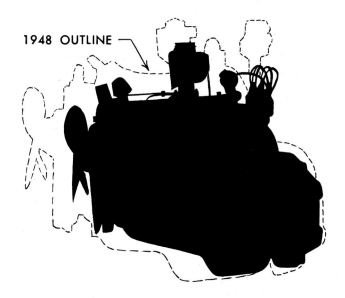

COMPARISON of 1948 and 1949 engine sizes shows reduction in size of later model. Weight has also been decreased 220 lbs.

high speeds with consequent peak bhp loss. Even more important, engine roughness sets in at this point. This engine roughness, which stems from the combustion process itself, can be more easily controlled with an OHV (overhead valve) type head. The second reason for adaption of an overhead valve engine has to do with thermal efficiency. With less surface area in the combustion chamber of an overhead valve engine, more of the heat energy of the fuel is utilized to produce power, and less is lost to the cooling system.

The new Cadillac is the first evidence in the U. S. of a trend toward OHV engines, a trend noticeable even before the war in Europe. In Europe since the war, not one of the large number of new or redesigned engines is a side valve ("L" head) engine. A General Motors executive recently stated to the press that all GM cars would have OHV engines in the near future. (Only the Pontiac 6 and 8, and Oldsmobile 6 are left.)

On the other hand, there have been, since the war, new "L" head engines by Willys (the 6), Hudson 6, Lincoln V-8, and redesigns by Ford (6 and 8) and Packard. Hudson's President E. A. Barit recently made the statement that they could go to 9.2:1 compression ratios with only minor changes to their present "L" head designs. Such

ALBERT H. ISAACS

a statement is somewhat premature from the standpoint that fuels requiring compression ratios beyond the practical range of "L" head engines are probably a long way off. The cost of producing 100 octane gasoline is not only very high, but it is a waste of our dwindling petroleum reserves.

Aside from the technical considerations already discussed, perhaps the only real test of the worth of a new car or engine is the net gain or loss to the purchaser. With an increase of 10 bhp, the Cadillac now develops 160 bhp with the engine stripped, or 133 bhp "as installed," with all accessories. This increase in power, together with a very noteworthy decrease in engine weight of 220 pounds (including saving in cooling system), results in a noticeable improvement in acceleration performance. The increase in compression ratio, though only from 7.25 to 7.50, is an automatic guarantee of reduced fuel consumption. Actually, as a result of reduced engine friction and improved thermal efficiency, the average user should get about two miles per gallon better mileage with the new model.

Perhaps an even more important advantage of the new OHV Cadillac engine to its owner is its increased durability.

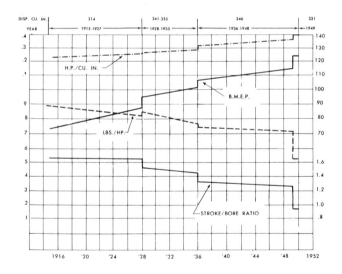

TRENDS in design characteristics of Cadillac V-8 engines

Cadillac engineers have done a thorough job of development work toward improved stamina in every part of the engine. To give just one example, in a paper read before the Society of Automotive Engineers describing the new engine, photographs were shown of engine bearings after test runs at 4250 rpm or an equivalent of 108 mph. (Of course, the car will not actually travel that fast on the road.) The 1948 engine, with 4.50 inch stroke, was run 131 hours at this speed. The bearings could be described as being in fair condition, and good for many more hours of running. However, they would certainly be replaced if encountered by a competent mechanic in the field. On the other hand, the bearings from the new short stroke engine were in perfect condition after 541 hours at the same speed, or more than four times the test period on the long stroke engine.

Automobile engines are not subject to the annual external sheet metal changes for the benefit of providing a new-appearing model. The new Cadillac OHV powerplant is brand new, and can normally be expected to be continued with little change for a period of at least seven years. By looking ahead, Cadillac engineers have designed an engine which can easily and economically have its compression ratio increased to anything up to 12:1, with assurance to the owner that he can take full advantage of future fuels, with no harmful effects.

Finally, it is encouraging to see a new model offered with no readily visible styling changes, thus reversing the usual "face-lifting" trend, along with using the original model engine.

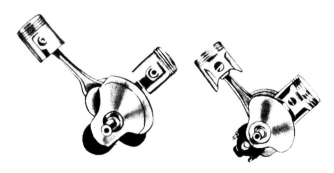

THOMAS J. MEDLEY

COMPARISON of 1948 and 1949 crankshaft and piston assemblies—major factor in weight reduction and added acceleration

When George and Doris Braunstein went looking for a new car to supplement their Jaguar XKE, they came back disappointed. While their budget was set for a sub-compact, apparently that wasn't what they really wanted, because when they spotted an ad for a 1949 Cadillac Series 61 fastback they went to look at it. A thousand dollars later, they owned it.

The original owner had guided that Caddy through 90,000 miles when the Braunsteins bought it. They liked it for its looks, its ride and the engine. We're not about to fault their logic, because those are the same reasons Motor Trend named the 1949 Cadillac as its first Car of the Year.

Our award was for more models than just the fastback, of course, with sedans, coupes and convertibles also spread across the Series 61, Series 62, Series 60 Special and Series 75 lines. For the most part, it was the amount of chrome that distinguished one model from the other, but they all led from the chunky chrome grille, along the slightly bulby fender lines to sweep up and over the tiny tail fins. Those taillight bumps were cute then, a logical ending to a design that has to be considered graceful if bulgy, before tail fins were carried to wretched excess in the late Fifties and early Sixties. The fins continue today, though happily in a more subdued form.

Those fins weren't just a figment of some designer's imagination. Their origins run back to 1940, when General Motors' Styling Chief, Harley Earl, took a few young stylists to Selfridge Field outside Detroit to look at P-38 fighters. A good designer who knows the history of the car can point out other bits of that same airplane that made it to the 1948 model, that first-of-the-finned Caddys. And if you have never seen a P-38 arcing toward the sun or lifting out of a dive, don't snicker.

A Cadillac release of the times said, "The entire Cadillac line for 1949 reflects fresh beauty in every detail, from the massive front grille to the famous up-sweep of the rear fenders. A longer hood line with ornament moved forward increases the apparent length of the car." Later, they would increase "...the apparent length of the car..." by actually increasing the length of the car.

Even now, when so many interiors are finally settling back into reasonableness, leaving the chrome clutter of a few years ago, the 1949 Cadillac's insides look simple. The seats were done in a very plain heavy gauge wool broadcloth. The instrument panel was set straight ahead, visible through the white plastic-rimmed steering wheel, the radio was off to the right, with the

RETROSPECT
1949 Cadillac V-8
BY JOHN LAMM

clock still farther away and all but invisible to the driver. The radio speaker was hidden behind a series of vertical chrome strips, something seen in probably every car at one time or another in the Forties and Fifties. No doubt the dash was hard and unforgiving in an accident, but it still lacked all the sharp protrusions and solid knobs that would later prod the government into legislating interior safety standards.

That was mostly window dressing, though, because most automobiles had hood ornaments and bulges and massive grilles in 1949. Only Cadillac had the high compression, overhead valve, 160-horsepower V-8. Oldsmobile had a similar engine, but it was smaller and less powerful.

Cadillac claimed that the V-8 had been under development for 12 years, a period stretched out by a four-year halt for World War II. The new V-8 was the latest in a Cadillac progression that began in 1914 with what was one of this country's first V-type engines.

It was the overhead valves that made the difference. John Bond, who would later start Road and Track magazine, wrote our 1949 Car of the Year story and explained why Cadillac made the switch to overhead valves—"Cadillac's changeover from ''L'' head to overhead valve type of design accomplishes two desirable goals. First, the overhead valve engine is recognized as a definite must for getting the most potential advantage from higher octane fuels [developed from wartime technology] provided, of course, that such fuels become available at economic prices. It is not possible to increase compression ratio in ''L'' head engines to much over 8:1, even with better fuel, because volumetric efficiency falls off at high speeds with consequent peak horsepower loss. Even more important, engine roughness sets in at this point... The second reason for adaptation of an overhead valve engine has to do with thermal efficiency. With less surface area in the combustion chamber of an overhead valve engine, more of the heat energy of the fuel is utilized to produce power, and less is lost to the cooling system."

Bond then noted that the Cadillac engine was "...the first evidence in the U.S. of a trend toward OHV engines..." He then turned soothsayer and wrote, "The cost of producing 100 octane gasoline is not only very high, but it is a waste of our dwindling petroleum reserves."

This engine, which caused one copywriter to tag it a "...creative masterpiece—a totally new, far finer version of the traditional Cadillac V-type engine..." had a displacement of 331 cubic inches. The "high compression" that produced the euphoria among the press was 7.50:1—mild compared even to today's emasculated 8.2:1 ratio Cadillacs, but hot stuff in 1949. Enough so that in 1950, Briggs Cunningham took two Cadillacs to the 24-hour race at LeMans (one a fairly stock machine, the other a rebodied car nicknamed "Le Monstre") and placed them tenth and eleventh, the stock machine finishing ahead of the special. There are even stories that the drivers of the stock Caddy raced around listening to the radio. Warmed-over versions of the V-8 were stuffed into the famous, if somewhat frightening, Cad Allard J2 sports car.

The new Cadillac V-8 meant more than just high compression and greater horsepower. It was the break, the step out of the pre-war formative era into, shall we say, modern times. Caddy's engine was not only more powerful, but lighter and more compact than its near-half ton predecessor. The 12-year-old flathead V-8 had scaled in at 992 pounds, while the new kid was 771 pounds. There were "slipper pistons" that allowed the engineers to lighten the entire bottom end of the engine. Five main bearings were added in place of the traditional three that allowed the crankshaft to twist and wobble. The engine was oversquare, with the wider bore and shorter stroke

Despite Briggs Cunningham and the soothing effects of hindsight, few will remember the 1949 Cadillac for its fine handling. Yet, Braunstein's wife has little trouble guiding the big car through traffic. Both like the car's smooth ride. The idea for the first tail fins (actually in 1948) came from P-38 fighter planes of World War II.

Underneath that ancient-looking air cleaner and tiny carburetor the first modern high compression V-8. It wasn't just the overhead valves they had been seen many times before but the compactness and light weight of the Caddy engine that made it memorable.

keeping piston speed, friction, heat and bearing loads down. Nothing about the engine was necessarily revolutionary or mind-boggling, it just put all the new thinking together. And the men who did it seem to have profited from it (among other things, of course). The division General Manager, Jack Gordon, became president of General Motors in 1958 and Harry Barr, chief engineer in charge of engine design and development, became GM's engineering vice president. And we've all heard of the man who was Cadillac's chief engineer at the time—recently retired GM President, Ed Cole.

Now that was all well and good for 1949, but what is the engine like in 1975? As you remember, George Braunstein bought this month's Retrospect car with 90,000 miles on it. After wheeling through another 30,000, he decided to restore the car. He did the engine himself and reports that after 120,000 miles, the engine was "in excellent condition." He did all the usual rebuild tasks, replacing the bearings, the valves and pistons after having the bore opened up a bit.

The Hydra-matic transmission was rebuilt and Braustein replaced all the usual wear-out pieces in the suspension such as the king pins, shackles and bushings. He also replaced the shock absorbers, though he swears the huge originals were still in decent working condition. The only difficult piece to find for the restoration was the replacement broadcloth for the upholstery. He finally found that in Great Britain.

Why all the effort for a 1949 Cadillac? First, both Braunsteins liked the car, its ride and the safety they felt inside. He likes to call it "such an honest car," an opinion formed by the condition of the car after the number of miles it has endured. "The car," he claims, "is now part of the family."

The second reason should appeal to any driver—money. Braunstein paid $1000 for the car about three years ago, has since put $2000 in the restoration and has been offered as much as $5000 for it. It sounds like a case in point from our Classic Comments column, so perhaps we should dub this the Robert J. Gottlieb-mobile.

Braunstein isn't about to stop now. When it became obvious that his E-Type coupe was dying, he searched out a 1949 Cadillac convertible. It is being rebuilt from the ground up and should be ready by autumn. ■

RETROSPECT

RETROSPECT

1949 Cadillac   Owned by George Braunstein
Photographed for *Motor Trend* by John Lamm

Convertible
CONVER

Words & Photographs:
Paul Trunfull

It's everyone's dream, isn't it? A classic American convertible for posing during the summer months. And they don't come much better than a 1950 Cadillac Series 62 rag top – just like the one photographed here. We meet the proud owners, husband and wife Roy and Joan Smith

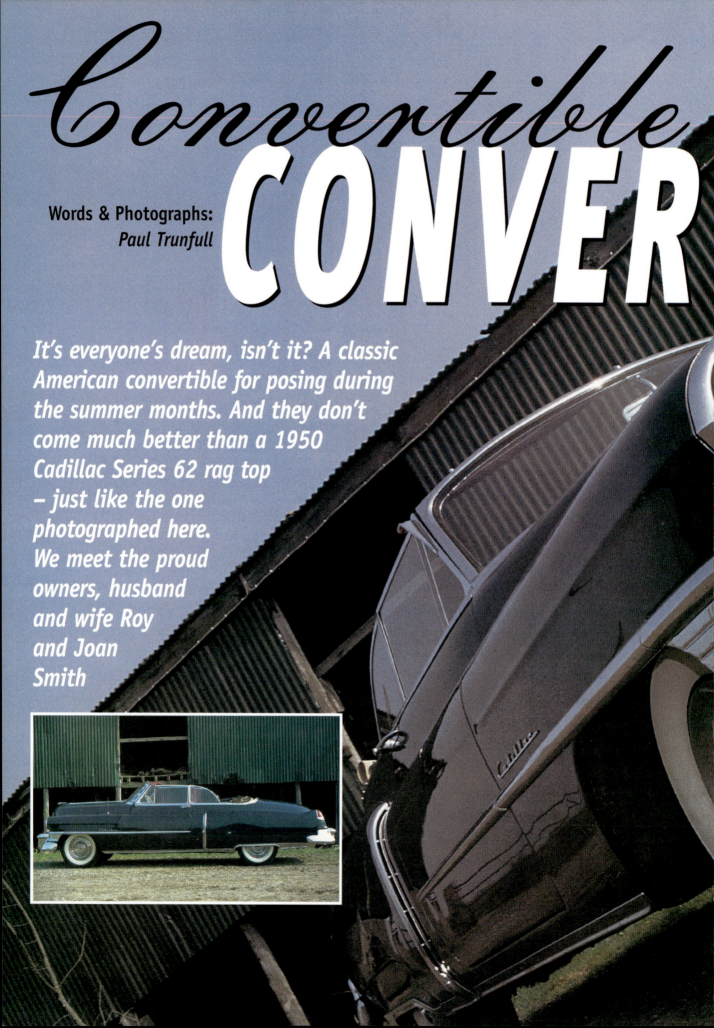

TS!

IN THE WINTER OF 1995, American car fanatics Roy and Joan Smith decided to buy a convertible for use during the following summer. Well, that's perfectly understandable, don't you think? And the car they had set their hearts on was a 1957 Chevrolet Bel Air convertible, a model that would go beautifully with their own '57 Bel Air hard top, a car previously featured in *Classic American*. But finding exactly what you want isn't always easy, particularly when it's a very specific forty-year-old rag top.

Roy obviously kept an eye on all the small ads, eventually coming across one that intrigued him. It read: 'Cadillacs for sale, Coltrain style'. He could not resist making the inevitable 'phone call.

One of the Cadillacs turned out to be a 1973 model, the other a 1950 Series 62 Convertible and well within the price range that Roy and Joan were thinking of.

It turned out that the owner of the Cadillacs, one Andrew McKenzie, bought the Series 62 while on vacation in Florida. The car's first known owner had been a Richard T Miller of Clearwater, Florida, who subsequently sold the car to Warren Berliner of Dania, Florida. Sadly, little else is known of the Caddy's early history.

Andrew McKenzie made good use of his newly acquired Series 62 Cadillac throughout his vacation, finally shipping her back to this side of the pond once his holiday was over. That was back in 1989.

It was when Andrew eventually decided to sell his beloved '50 Cadillac in 1995 that Roy Smith saw the car advertised and, after a few minutes

Convertible CONVERTS!

speaking with Andrew, decided that he simply had to view this magnificent machine.

When the Caddy was rolled out of its garage, Roy stood speechless and all thoughts of that '57 Chevy Convertible went straight out of his head. Roy knew he just had to have the car but his wife, Joan, was not quite so sure – a quick chat was called for. Roy was even thinking of offering his '57 hard top in part exchange but Joan soon put the brakes on that notion. After another careful look at the Caddy, a deal was done and Roy and Joan finally had their summer runabout – or so they thought!

On the way back home to Kent, the Cadillac's brakes almost failed – a rather hair-raising experience, to say the least. Once the car was sitting safely on the drive, Roy started to check over the rest of it in greater detail than he had before. He flicked the switch for the power hood and nothing happened. He tried the windows and, again, nothing moved. Roy also noticed there was a wire hanging loose underneath. Clearly the electrics were in need of some prompt attention, so into Roy's garage the Caddy went.

Roy started work on the brakes first of all. These were completely stripped and fully reconditioned, including replacement of all the pipework and the master cylinders.

Next on the list was a careful check of all the wiring which, as Roy had suspected, was in a pretty bad way. Roy called in auto electrical specialist Steve Smith to check out the entire wiring loom, his advice being to cut out all the wiring from the firewall back. Another problem was that the car's hydraulic pump (for operating the power hood, power windows and so on) had been wired as a 12 volt unit instead of a six volt system, which had obviously done the pump no good at all.

Roy decided to have the hydraulic pump reconditioned, but sadly it turned out to be beyond saving. A new replacement was sourced in the States, this costing a massive £400 all in.

Before Steve started renewing all the Cadillac's wiring, Roy gave the car's floorpan a newly painted 'factory fresh' finish. He also fitted the new hydraulic pump.

Steve returned to the scene and, with the wiring finally sorted, it was time to test

'He hit a switch and got covered in hydraulic fluid'

the whole electrical system. He hit a switch and got covered in hydraulic fluid, sprayed up from the connecting pipework. This was duly replaced and it was time for another test. This time, up went the hood! (As did the windows, and even the power operated driver's seat was now working.)

Roy's attention then turned to the engine, thinking it would probably be in need of a full service. Everything went fine until the engine's sump plug was removed – no oil came out! Roy

FACT FILE
MAKE & MODEL: 1950 Cadillac Series 62 Convertible
PRICE WHEN NEW: $3654
PRODUCTION RUN: 6986
ENGINE: 331cu.in. V8
POWER OUTPUT: 160bhp @ 3800rpm
TRANSMISSION: Hydra-Matic four-speed column shift
SUSPENSION: Independent Hypoid semi-floating; rear leaf springs; telescopic shock absorbers
BRAKES: Drums all round

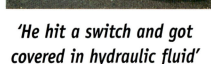

then stuck his finger in the hole and was greeted with what felt like jelly. The sump was quickly removed and Roy discovered no less than two inches of sludge in the bottom. With all this cleaned out and the whole engine treated to a new set of gaskets, the Caddy's powerplant was soon purring like a kitten once again.

The engine in Roy's Series 62 is Cadillac's 331cu.in. V8, producing a reasonable 160bhp at 3800rpm ('Not quite enough', insists Roy). Fuel is fed via a single twin-downdraft carburettor. The Cadillac's transmission is the ultra-smooth four-speed Hydra-Matic, with column shift.

Braking is handled by drums all round and, surprisingly, there is no servo assistance. Similarly, the steering is not power assisted, which makes it rather heavy at parking speeds, although it is quite positive and responsive for a car of this age.

The Cadillac's interior is very much as it left the factory, apart from a new set of carpets. The seats and the door panels are finished in original red leather tuck 'n' roll. The front bench seat splits in half to allow access to the rear.

When the hood is down, it is stowed neatly behind the rear seat, helping to keep wind noise and buffeting to an absolute minimum, even in the rear, making the Cadillac one of the most pleasurable top-down convertibles for both driver and passengers.

Roy's Cadillac was fitted from new with an 'all weather ventilation system', a set-up that even included ducts in the doors to allow the door glass to be defrosted. There was also a heater fitted under the front seat, enabling the driver to balance the heat in the upper and lower cabin.

The wheels on Roy's car are still the original factory items, fitted (of course) with Cadillac wheel discs. These are wrapped in Centennial whitewall tyres.

By the time you read this, Roy may finally have got round to taking Joan out for a ride in their Cadillac. Joan says: 'The only time I've been in the car so far was when I helped Roy to bleed the brakes!'. That looks set to change though, with both Roy and Joan spending hoping to spend the rest of the summer attending as many American car shows and meets as possible. But I wonder who will be driving which car? CA

The CADILLAC V.8 S.62

High Performance, Extremely Quiet Running and Automatic Gear Changing are Prominent Features of One of America's Finest Cars

ALMOST invariably, cars road tested by "The Motor" are submitted by the manufacturers concerned or by their agents, but in the case of the Cadillac V.8 about to be reviewed this is not so. The car in question is the private property of a well-known American enthusiast, Briggs S. Cunningham, Esq., who for personal reasons has had it maintained in Europe and who was kind enough to make it available for road test purposes. The car tested had rather more than 7,000 miles on the odometer and during this period had received regular but strictly routine attention. For practical reasons it was necessary to take the maximum speed figures immediately before, and the acceleration and fuel consumption figures, directly after, a journey to Turin and it is therefore possible that the figures quoted in the accompanying data panel are slightly inferior to those that would have been recorded by a works-tuned car. Even as they stand they indicate performance of an extremely high order, and a one-way timed speed of over 100 m.p.h. has been recorded by only one other closed car during the whole of the post-war series of "The Motor" Road Tests. But, startling as some of the figures appear, it is in other respects that the latest V.8 Cadillac makes the greatest impact upon the European observer.

Cadillac lends a certain majesty which is not always present with this type. The figures for overall width, length and weight tell their own story, and they are matched by one of the largest engines in world production, with a capacity of 5.4 litres, and 160 b.h.p. at the moderate engine speed of 3,800 r.p.m. The engine is notable for a stroke/bore ratio under unity and the use of overhead valves in conjunction with a cylinder head design which permits a very high compression ratio, although on the car tested the figure is limited to 7.5 : 1 for use in conjunction with 80 octane fuel. This drives the car through a fluid flywheel and a four-speed epicyclic gear box in which the ratio employed is automatically chosen by a control which tastes both engine speed and throttle opening.

The Cadillac is a vehicle manifestly intended to cover long distances at a high cruising speed whilst demanding the absolute minimum of effort from the driver and imposing the smallest possible distraction upon the passengers. Outstanding overall silence both in respect of mechanical noise, and also the equally important and often neglected aspects of road noise and wind roar, is perhaps the major virtue which is noticed in ordinary

IMPRESSIVE SIGHT.—One of the largest cars in the world, the Cadillac S.62 has a well-balanced appearance which is here excellently depicted.

It will be remembered that the chassis design is conventional in the sense that it has an X-braced frame, a hypoid rear axle with semi-elliptic rear springs, independent front suspension using the conventional unequal length wishbones, and open coil springs. The full-width body of envelope form would have been considered entirely heterodox immediately after the war but although it is now sufficiently established as to cause little comment, the sheer scale effect of the running and conversation in ordinary tones can be maintained at between 80 and 90 m.p.h. on a speedometer which is only 4 per cent. fast at these speeds.

The combination of high acceleration with a comfortable cruising speed of not much less than 100 m.p.h. naturally results in exceedingly high overall speeds, and 60 miles in the hour may be considered normal on reasonably straight roads.

As can be seen from the data panel, fuel economy is excellent in the upper part of the speed range, nearly 12 m.p.g. being available at a steady 80 m.p.h. and 14 m.p.g. at a level 70 m.p.h. On long runs on part throttle the car will achieve 17 m.p.g. overall but it is only fair to add that, if full use is made of the acceleration and hill climbing in English conditions, there is a considerable worsening of the consumption, which may drop to below 10 m.p.g.

Fully Automatic Transmission

Before analysing the acceleration times one must remark upon the characteristics of the transmission and the kind of performance which is offered on the road. To take an extreme case, the car can be held at rest on the brakes with the throttle wide open with 100 per cent. slip in the fluid flywheel. On releasing the brakes, the fluid flywheel will play the part of an ordinary clutch and the speed will rise to 14 m.p.h. in first gear after which a speed-responsive governor will feed hydraulic pressure to the second-gear band and in this ratio 30 m.p.h. will be achieved. At this speed, a corresponding mechanism engages third gear on which the speed will rise to 66 m.p.h., whereupon top gear is enjoyed. Provided the engine is working on full throttle, there will be downward gear changes at approximately the same speeds under conditions of steadily increasing gradient and hence it is, for example, impossible to use full throttle and top gear between 10 and 30 m.p.h., for the mere act of opening the throttle fully inevitably engages a low ratio in this condition. The driver has, however, some control over the gear situation. Firstly, on light throttle openings the higher ratios will be engaged at very considerably lower speeds and one may for instance accelerate between 40 and 60 m.p.h. in top on part throttle in 12 seconds as compared with the 7.5 seconds achieved with full throttle and the automatically engaged third speed. Additionally there is a mechanical control which bars the engagement of third and fourth speeds and thus, by moving a lever to a position marked

"LO," the engine may be used as a brake either when approaching a corner on the flat or for descending a long mountainous gradient.

From the foregoing description it will be seen that one cannot set out the acceleration figures in the normal terms of times taken on top gear, third gear, etc.; one must rather regard the transmission as an entity in which the infinitely variable torque converter is approached through the medium of four automatically engaged steps. The advantages of such a transmission are self-evident for there is neither clutch pedal nor clutch and except for abnormal conditions such as engine braking or reverse there is no need to touch a gear lever.

These advantages are won at slight cost. There is a definite increase in engine noise and "fuss" on full throttle as a result of the engine running up into the upper part of the speed range although the gears themselves are exceedingly quiet and the engagement thereof almost imperceptible when changing up. The absence of synchronisation between engine and tail shaft speed when changing down can produce a jerk which would bring a reprimand to a professional driver and a feeling of shame to the experienced amateur if a modicum of skill is not exercised. Very high stopping power is obtained with abnormally low pedal effort, but this is derived from a substantial servo effort in the shoes themselves which in turn leads to somewhat abrupt braking at low speeds in traffic and to a loss of poise in the car as a whole if the brakes are applied hard at high road speeds.

For a car which weighs nearly two tons, the steering is remarkably light and the fact that the wheel needs nearly five turns between one full lock and the other must be related to the very big angle through which the front wheels are turned, and to the exceedingly large lock which makes the car easy to handle in traffic and far more simple to park than one would imagine upon a mere study of its dimensions. The car is obviously not designed to corner in sports fashion but it handles accurately on bends with the slow response characteristic of the under-steering car which puts rapid high-speed manœuvring out of the question.

The suspension system has obviously been designed to cope with two extreme conditions. It gives almost complete freedom from body movement on really smooth roads, the slight and infrequent irregularities of which are absorbed almost without notice. By reason of the stiff chassis and body structure, and the very large wheel movement permitted, exceedingly rough roads can be attacked at speeds in the environ of 40 or 50 m.p.h. with, again, but little effect upon the overall stability, the state of the road surface chiefly being deduced by increase in noise. On the wavy surfaces typical of neglected British main roads, the car is somewhat less satisfactory and, between 70 and 80 m.p.h., body movement of considerable frequency and magnitude can be built up.

Carrying Capacity

The latest V.8 Cadillac is particularly suitable for long-distance motoring, not only for technical reasons but also because the body accommodation is suitable for this purpose. The rear luggage locker is of exceptional capacity, and, as three persons could be comfortably carried for any required number of miles on the front seat, the whole of the rear of the body (which will also seat three if required) can be kept free for additional stowage of personal luggage. There is also a considerable flat area between the back of the rear seat and the rear window which can be used for carrying small parcels, and a locker in the facia panel which will serve as a receptacle for maps, guide books, and the like. Less commendable is the fact that if only two persons are aboard, a passenger on the front seat notices the lack of an armrest and definitely feels the need for sideways support whilst, on this particular model, the general equipment of the car may well be thought excessively austere. One ashtray is provided, and that available to the rear seat passengers only. There is no under-scuttle accommodation for small parcels and the dark brown finish of the facia panels and window cappings may be thought more suitable for a utility car than for a make which ranks as one of the world's best. Similarly, the cloth upholstery is far from first-class quality, and there is an entire absence of the attention to personal comforts varying from ladies' mirrors and powder cases to cocktail cabinets and picnic trays which are normal to the European car of the highest class.

In fairness it should be stated that the Cadillac range offers a progression from the Spartan to the Athenian taste, and that the particular car reviewed was among the lower priced of nine models. Viewed in this light the car offers astonishing value for money. It has a performance which few makes can rival, even fewer surpass, a general silence of running (including low wind noise) which many will consider unbeaten, and an ease in driving which must be a great asset when very long mileages are attempted.

TWO-PEDAL DRIVE.—This illustration shows the complete absence of clutch pedal characteristic of the Hydra-Matic transmission, also the rubber seal in the air conduit which gives de-misting to the driver's side windows in addition to the windscreen.

CLEAR SPACE.—By mounting the spare wheel vertically at the side of the luggage locker it may be removed without disturbing the large amount of luggage which can be stowed under lock and key.

The Motor Continental Road Test No. 2C/50

Make: Cadillac **Type:** Series 62 Touring Sedan
Makers: Cadillac Motor Car Division, Cenneral Motors Corpn., Detroit, Mich., U.S.A.

Dimensions and Seating

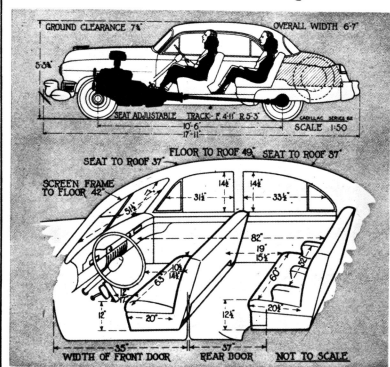

Test Conditions

Dry, cold, little wind, 80 octane fuel. Maximum speed recorded on Aeltre-Jabbeke Autostrada.

Test Data

ACCELERATION TIMES

	Top	Hydra-Matic
10–30 m.p.h.		3.6 secs.
20–40 m.p.h. see text		4.6 secs.
30–50 m.p.h.		6.1 secs.
40–60 m.p.h.	12.0 secs.	7.5 secs.
50–70 m.p.h.	14.0 secs. part throttle	8.8 secs.
60–80 m.p.h.	16.2 secs.	13.1 secs.

ACCELERATION TIMES Through Gears
- 0–30 m.p.h. ... 5.1 secs.
- 0–40 m.p.h. ... 7.8 secs.
- 0–50 m.p.h. ... 11.6 secs.
- 0–60 m.p.h. ... 15.8 secs.
- 0–70 m.p.h. ... 20.7 secs.
- 0–80 m.p.h. ... 31.7 secs.
- Standing quarter-mile ... 20.0 secs.

FUEL CONSUMPTION
- 24.0 m.p.g. at constant 30 m.p.h.
- 23.5 m.p.g. at constant 40 m.p.h.
- 21.0 m.p.g. at constant 50 m.p.h.
- 18.0 m.p.g. at constant 60 m.p.h.
- 14.0 m.p.g. at constant 70 m.p.h.
- 11.5 m.p.g. at constant 80 m.p.h.
- Overall consumption for 136 miles, 8 gallons, equals 17.0 m.p.g.

HILL CLIMBING (at steady speeds)
- Max. speed on 1 in 20 ... 84 m.p.h.
- Max. speed on 1 in 15 ... 79 m.p.h.
- Max. speed on 1 in 10 ... 70 m.p.h.
- Max. speed on 1 in 5 ... 45 m.p.h.

BRAKES AT 30 m.p.h.
- 0.95 g. retardation (= 31.6 ft. stopping distance) with 90 lb. pedal pressure.
- 0.75 g. retardation (= 40 ft. stopping distance) with 50 lb. pedal pressure.
- 0.35 g. retardation (= 86 ft. stopping distance) with 25 lb. pedal pressure.

MAXIMUM SPEEDS
Flying Quarter-mile
- Mean of four opposite runs ... 99.7 m.p.h.
- Best time equals ... 101.1 m.p.h.

Speed in Gears
- Max. speed in 3rd gear ... 66 m.p.h.
- Max. speed in 2nd gear ... 30 m.p.h.
- Max. speed in 1st gear ... 14 m.p.h.

WEIGHT
- Unladen kerb weight ... 37¼ cwt.
- Front/rear weight distribution ... 52/48
- Weight laden as tested ... 40¾ cwt.

INSTRUMENTS
- Speedometer at 30 m.p.h. ... accurate
- Speedometer at 60 m.p.h. ... 3% fast
- Speedometer at 80 m.p.h. ... 4% fast
- Distance recorder ... 4% fast

In Brief

Price $3,040 ex works (£1,086 at £1 = $2.80). Not available in United Kingdom.
Capacity ... 5,420 c.c.
Unladen kerb weight ... 37¼ cwt.
Fuel consumption ... 17.0 m.p.g.
Maximum speed ... 99.7 m.p.h.
Maximum speed on 1 in 20 gradient ... 84 m.p.h.
Acceleration,
10–30 m.p.h. in Hydra-Matic 3.6 secs.
0–50 m.p.h. through gears 11.6 secs.
Gearing 25.2 m.p.h. in top at 1,000 r.p.m.
104 m.p.h. at 2,500 ft. per min. piston speed.

Specification

Engine
- Cylinders ... V.8
- Bore ... 96.84 mm.
- Stroke ... 92.07 mm.
- Cubic capacity ... 5,420 c.c.
- Piston area ... 91.3 sq. in.
- Valves ... Push rod o.h.v.
- Compression ratio ... 7.5/1
- Max. power ... 160 b.h.p.
- at ... 3,800 r.p.m.
- Piston speed at max. b.h.p. 2,290 ft. per min.
- Carburetter ... Carter
- Ignition ... Delco-Remy
- Sparking plugs ... A.C. 46.5
- Fuel pump ... A.C.
- Oil filter ... Floating intake

Transmission
- Clutch ... Fluid coupling
- Top gear ... 3.77
- 3rd gear ... 4.87
- 2nd gear ... 8.85
- 1st gear ... 12.83
- Propeller shaft ... Open
- Final drive ... Hypoid bevel

Chassis
- Brakes ... Bendix hydraulic servo
- Brake drum diameter ... 12 ins.
- Friction lining area ... 220 sq. in.
- Suspension:
  - Front ... Coil and wishbone I.F.S.
  - Rear ... Semi-elliptic leaf
- Shock absorbers ... Delco telescopic
- Tyres ... 8.00 x 15

Steering
- Steering gear ... Saginaw
- Turning circle ... 45 ft.
- Turns of steering wheel, lock to lock ... 4¼

Performance factors (at laden weight as tested)
- Piston area, sq. in. per ton ... 45
- Brake lining area, sq. in. per ton ... 108
- Specific displacement, litres per ton-mile 3,200

Fully described in "The Motor," March 2, 1949.

Maintenance

Fuel tank: 16½ gallons. **Sump:** 8½ pints. **Gearbox and differential:** 20 pints. **Rear axle:** 4 pints. **Radiator:** 29 pints (3 drain taps). **Chassis lubrication:** By grease gun every 1,000 miles to 22 points, plus 2 generator oil cups. **Ignition timing:** 32 deg. b.t.d.c. full advance. **Spark plug gap:** 0.033 in. **Contact breaker gap:** 0.0125. **Valve timing:** I.O. 19 B.T.D.C., I.C. 83° A.B.D.C., E.O. 53° B.B.D.C., E.C. 49° A.T.D.C. **Tappet clearances:** Zero Lash tappets. **Front wheel toe-in:** 1/32 in.: 3/32 in. **Camber angle:** minus 3/8 in. plus 3/8 in. **Castor angle:** minus ¾ in.: plus ⅛ in. **Tyre pressures:** Front 24 lb., rear 24 lb. **Brake fluid:** Delco. **Battery:** Delco 6-volt 115 amp./hour at 20-hour rate. **Lamp bulbs:** 6 volt; Headlight 43-35 watt; parking and signal lamps 21-3 CP; stop and tail lamp 21-3 CP; instrument cluster 2 CP; dome light (except 6267) 15 CP; instrument panel clock light 2 CP; courtesy lamps 7523-33 1 CP; licence plate light 3 CP; trunk compartment light 2 CP; directional signal indicator 1 CP; glove compartment light 2 CP; beam indicator 1 CP.

Ref. US/55/50

Cadillac MOTOR TRIAL

BORGESON SAYS, HERE'S A CAR THAT GIVES REAL ECONOMY WHETHER YOU WANT IT OR NOT

by Griff Borgeson

THERE'S NO getting away from it—General Motors is the design and sales genius of today's auto industry. Chevy is tops in sales; Pontiac has fine performance along with quiet, tasteful styling; Olds is the answer for most people who want jackrabbit performance at a moderate price; Buick, brazen as a bird of paradise, is one of the most desired cars in the world. Finally, there's Cadillac, everybody's dreamboat, probably the most coveted, most sold, and therefore most successful luxury car in the industry's long history. To complete the picture, GM looks ahead to mass desires of next year and of a decade from now—there are enough experimental features in Le Sabre, stylewise and machinerywise, to create a dozen radically-superior passenger cars tomorrow. And there's the XP-300. GM is both a super-shrewd judge of public taste and a daring pioneer—a rare but fortunate combination.

We need never have put the Cadillac through a Motor Trial to have arrived at these conclusions. In New York or Dallas, Chicago or Beverly Hills, people who have "arrived" acquire Cadillacs almost automatically. The Caddie is the badge of success. The big question is, "Why should it be so? There are other cars, equally fine." That's the point: GM has hit the bull's eye of the luxury target at which it was aiming with a degree of accuracy that can only mean skill—not chance.

We of MOTOR TREND research—Walt Woron, Dick van Osten, and I—have been familiar with Cadillac excellence for a long time. It's a story stretching back to 1900 when that unsung genius, Henry M. Leland, originated the make. He had learned the art of making interchangeable parts at the old Samuel Colt's arms works back in the last century. He applied his knowledge to the building of cars and amazed the world in 1906 with a remarkable demonstration. Before the Royal Automobile Club in England, three Cadillacs were torn down, the parts scrambled, three cars reassembled and successfully road tested. This was the first step in bringing the automobile within the economic reach of the general population. It also implied workmanship of superior quality and established the Cadillac tradition of excellence which survives today.

With a vast backlog of reader requests for a Cadillac Motor Trial, we cleared through Detroit and were told to pick up any car we chose at the vast showrooms of the Cadillac Motor Car Division in downtown Los Angeles. Our selection was a Series 62 sedan, chosen because we feel this car to be the best buy of its line and therefore the car of the greatest popular appeal. The four-day shakedown we gave it covered nearly 1000 miles over our customary test course, including all shadings of metropolitan traffic, broad super-highways, narrow country roads, long stretches of washboard, twisting mountain highways, and the flat-out surface of a five-mile long top-speed strip on famous El Mirage dry lake.

FUEL CONSUMPTION: This was the most surprising feature of the entire Motor Trial. Its 331 cu. ins. of displacement makes the Cad engine one of the world's largest. In a luxury car, designed for definitely brilliant performance, one hardly expects to find a penny-pinching appetite for gas. But the Cadillac actually gives better gas mileage than many more utilitarian cars!

In moderately heavy traffic our highly accurate instruments showed figures as high as 21 mpg. At a steady 30 mph our best figure was 24.4 mpg and at a steady 45 we once hit 24.0 mpg. The top reading at 60 was an astonishing 18.1 mpg! This sort of economy from a big-engined car weighing over two tons is a classic example of the new American trend toward powerplants of high efficiency—a trend which was kicked off by Cadillac and Olds back in '49 and which the competition is forced to match.

ACCELERATION: A two-ton, plus, machine is usually lacking in distinction as a form of rapid transit. That the opposite is the case with Cadillac is another outstanding feature of the 160-bhp-engined cars. Our test machine packed the sporty weight:power ratio of 27.6:1 and this, plus a smooth, fast-shifting Hydra-Matic transmission gave us acceleration times which, averaged, rank fourth among the cars tested by MOTOR TREND Research this year. Having all this urge at the tip of one's toe gives the feeling of being in complete control of any traffic condition. With such power on instant tap one is inclined to drive more relaxedly, less hurriedly, even more courteously—after all, you are the boss of the road.

ENGINE: Cadillac anticipated the advantages of the V-type engine back in 1914 and has built no other type since. In 1930 the first ohv, V-type engine was introduced in the first V-16, followed in '31 by their first V-12, also with ohv. This experience, which continued through most of the Thirties, furnished the factory with an immense amount of practical experience with ohv-type engines. No other manufacturer had the benefit of such extended know-how and it's not surprising that Cad, accompanied by Olds, introduced America's first ohv V-8s.

Porting of the Cad engine is highly rational, aside from in-line valve arrangement, and intake manifold feed sequence has been carefully, intelligently worked out. Another direction in which this engine blazed a new trail was in bore:stroke ratios. Short-stroke engines had been played with decades before, but Cadillac startled America by following an already-established Continental trend and using, in a production engine, a stroke actually less than the diameter of the bore.

What this accomplishes is reduction of piston speed at any given rpm, making for reduced hp losses within the engine. Further effects are quicker revving, improved economy, lighter weight in relation to output, and more compact dimensions. The combined advantages of the short-stroke engine have sent competition scurrying to follow Cadillac's lead, but the purchaser of a '51 Cad can be confident that his engine is probably the best-developed and least "buggy" of any of the truly post-war powerplants.

The ohv Cad engine's reliability and punch have been convincingly demonstrated in the most demanding test of all, road racing. Cad-Allard cars have competed successfully all over the US with a remarkable record of success for the past two seasons. Such troubles as they've had have never—to our knowledge—been traceable to their trusty engines. One last word on this subject deals with the unusual silence of the engine, notable even when wound tight on the Clayton dynamometer. And starting from stone cold is always amazingly quick and easy.

TRANSMISSION: Cadillac's Hydra-Matic for '51 has been improved, many of the troubles which plagued owners of earlier models having been eliminated. The shift from first to second is very fast, slower from second to third, quick from third to fourth. Engine braking is fine in both LOW and DRIVE ranges and the changing of gears is perfectly silent. Second gear comes in at about 14 mph, third at 25, fourth at 60. Study of the acceleration times in the Table of Performance shows that gear ratios in LOW are so low as to hold no advantages for quick getaways. With the car's wt.:power ratio, getaway in DRIVE matches the dig of just about anything on the road.

BRAKES: These tend to be like a race car's clutch: all off or all on. They lock with the greatest of ease, dissipating the heavy car's dynamic inertia between tires and pavement, rather than between brake drums and linings.

Many cars today use what is known as Hotchkiss drive, the alternative arrangement being torque tube drive. As the rear wheels turn or, because of braking, do not turn, the rear axle tends to do a lot of turning, too. A torque tube is a steel tube around the driveshaft which is anchored at both ends and which absorbs the twisting effort (torque) of the rear axle. Hotchkiss drive has the advantage of lighter unsprung weight and lower cost but, unless steadied by torque arms from rear axle to frame, throws all the twisting load upon the rear springs. In the modern American car, these springs are soft and can be twisted a long way.

Cadillac uses Hotchkiss drive and the

MODEL OF EFFICIENCY. The Cad engine is notable for many of its features; among them are short rocker arms, very friction-free porting, good exhaust-valve cooling, excellent location of spark plug in efficient combustion chamber

CAVERNOUS ACCOMMODATION for luggage is provided. Rear-seat radio speaker is visible above spare tire. Switch on instrument panel permits any degree of balance between front and rear speakers, adds to listening enjoyment

EASE OF control has been carefully engineered into car's interior. Phyllis Avedon demonstrates convenient, feather-light seat-adjustment control

Cadillac Motor Trial

loads imposed upon the rear springs and universal joint are severe. When braking hard, the rear axle winds up on the springs, reaches the limit, snaps back to normal. This produces the breaking of traction shown below: the distance between full traction marks is about four ft. Cadillac brakes are not among the best.

SKIPPING OF rear wheels was a defect revealed in strenuous 45 mph braking tests. White lines are 3 ft. 10 ins. apart, indicate centers of full-traction marks with poor traction between

HANDLING QUALITIES: Cadillac's chassis has been much improved in '51. While the suspension layout remains its same, orthodox self—coil spring independent suspension in front, half-elliptics in the rear—it now bristles with shock absorbers and stabilizer bars. Still, the ride is not what it should be. The Caddie leaves nothing to be desired as a town conveyance, but on the open road it's another matter. At an indicated 70 mph, the rear end begins to skip from side to side in a very disturbing manner, becoming more pronounced with increased speed. Steering is very positive on corners up to a certain point—depending upon the sharpness of the curve—where control simply slips away from you. Steady 60 mph gas mileage checks were attempted on a gently-curving, six-lane highway. But real control wasn't there, and we dropped to 45.

Like most cars with the comfortable advantage of enormous cross-section tires, the Cadillac wheel must be tugged on heavily in the turns. If you touch the soft, or raised, shoulder of an asphalt road while moving at any speed at all, the front wheels give a mighty sidewise twist. Street car tracks are also a menace, flip the front wheels aside.

While the Cad doesn't seem to heel unusually in turns, passengers complain of being rolled about, this generally to the hair-raising accompaniment of tire shriek. Washboard roads—hardly the Caddie's design element—are hard for car and passengers to take. Cad's steering has an unusually full swing from lock to lock, therefore has a small turning circle and is deceptively, pleasantly easy to park and to handle in traffic.

BODY AND INTERIOR: A glaring defect of almost every car today—blinding dashboard reflections on windshield when the sun is high—has not been corrected in the Cad. Interior appointments of the test car satisfied our somewhat austere and very functional tastes. Body components are nicely fitted, but detail finish —edges of doors, for example—is poor by pre-war Cadillac standards. Speaking of doors, there are two ways of designing interior door locks: so that the inside door handle will or will not work against the locking pin placed in the window trim. We feel that a pin which locks inside *and* outside handles has marked safety value; but the test car was not so constructed.

The rear-view mirror is suspended ⅓ of the distance down the windshield, effectively blocking vision on turns and in intersections. Aside from this one danger spot, visibility for the driver of a '51 Cadillac is a close approach to perfection.

A center arm rest would help anchor the

STYLING IS combined with function in the case of Cad's tail-light-covered gas tank filler cap. Button reflector at base is push-release lock

front-seat passenger. While the rear-seat passenger rides in superb comfort, his level is low and his view forward is poor. Upholstery is of nice quality, nicely fitted, and the Nylon slip covers, available as extras, are finely tailored. The front seat is high, limits headroom but makes for fine visibility, and legroom fore and aft are excellently provided for. The Cad's body contours make the outside rear mirrors unusually useful, give a perfect view of conditions at the rear. Instruments are well-grouped and our only recommendation for instrument panel improvement is the trivial one of an ash tray handy to the driver, plus the already-mentioned relocation of the rear-view mirror.

GENERAL IMPRESSIONS: America's Dreamboat, badge of the successful man, is a truly remarkable car, exceedingly luxurious, well-suited to town driving or highway cruising. It has all the acceleration you'll ever need in a utility, as opposed to a sports, machine. Its dimensions and handling qualities are not intended to satisfy the automotive acrobat or the devotees of maximum control. The Cad has a lot in common with a dry lakes hot rod in that it's at its best on the straightaway. Its tires protest against low-speed cornering and control vanishes early when cornering at speed. Rear end wander suggests staying below 70 mph on the straightaway and cornering behavior suggests staying below 55 when the highway begins to wind. Opening the car up to top speed should be reserved for absolute emergencies.

Cadillac is not the ultimate automobile. It is outstanding for style, elegance, silence, economy, and a fine engine. Its greatest shortcoming in our eyes is that it is not more securely glued to the road. This is the point of view not of the sporting enthusiast, but of the safety-minded critic of design in terms of function—the job to be done. Cadillac is good, aims at being the best. Being one of US' costliest cars, it should stand at the top in design.

TREND TRIALS NO.: Our uniform evaluation of a car, *as a buy*, gives a figure of 41.6, remarkably good for a car in this price class, better than some cars in the next lower-priced class. Responsible for this low figure are Cadillac's low fuel consumption and very low depreciation rate. As an investment, this is a good deal.

TABLE OF PERFORMANCE

DYNAMOMETER TEST

1200 rpm (full load) 20.5 mph	58 road hp
2000 rpm (full load) 35.5 mph	82 road hp
3100 rpm (full load) 82.0 mph	(max.) 92 road hp

ACCELERATION TRIALS (SECONDS)

	Low	Drive
Standing start ¼ mile	:21.22	:21.36
0-30 mph	: 5.79	: 5.66
0-60 mph	:17.00	:16.62
10-60 mph	:18.00	:16.34
30-60 mph	---	:13.77

TOP SPEED (MPH)

Fastest one-way run	97.08
Average of four runs	95.44

FUEL CONSUMPTION (MPG)

At a steady 30 mph	21.9
At a steady 45 mph	20.8
At a steady 60 mph	16.4
Through light traffic	17.8
Through medium traffic	15.8
Through heavy traffic	13.2

BRAKE CHECK

Stopping distance at 30 mph	45 ft. 4 ins.
Stopping distance at 45 mph	101 ft. 6 ins.
Stopping distance at 60 mph	226 ft. 2 ins.

SPEEDOMETER TEST

At 30 mph indicated 33.5 mph	11.7% error
At 45 mph indicated 49 mph	10.2% error
At 60 mph indicated 64 mph	6.3% error

GENERAL SPECIFICATIONS

ENGINE

Type	pushrod ohv 90° V-8
Bore and stroke	3¹³⁄₁₆ x 3⅝ ins.
Stroke/Bore Ratio	0.95:1
Cubic Inch Displacement	331
Maximum Bhp	160 @ 3800 rpm
Bhp/Cu. In.	.483
Maximum Torque	312 ft.-lbs. @ 1800 rpm
Compression Ratio	7.5:1

DRIVE SYSTEM

Hydra-Matic four-speed transmission.

Ratios:	First—3.819	Second—2.634
	Third—1.450	Fourth—Direct
		Reverse—4.304

No clutch pedal. 12 quarts oil capacity.
Rear Axle: Semi-floating, Hotchkiss drive, hypoid bevel gears, ratio 3.36:1

DIMENSIONS

Wheelbase	126 ins.
Overall Length	215.5 ins.
Overall Height	60¹⁵⁄₁₆ ins.
Overall Width	80⅛ ins.
Tread	Front 59 ins., rear 63 ins.
Turns, Lock to Lock	4.5
Weight (test car)	4420 lbs.
Weight/Bhp Ratio	27.6:1
Weight/Road Hp Ratio	48.0:1
Weight Distribution (Front to Rear)	52.8/47.2

The Autocar ROAD TESTS

Sober black and elegant harmony of line make the Cadillac an exemplar of quality in the American style of product.

No. 1447 : CADILLAC SERIES 62 SALOON

DATA FOR THE DRIVER

PRICE (at factory), with saloon body, $3,096.83 = £1,106 at $2.80 = £1. Not available in Great Britain.
ENGINE: 46.5 h.p. (R.A.C. rating), eight cylinders, overhead valves 96.84 × 92.07 mm, 5,420 c.c. Brake Horse-power: 160 at 3,800 r.p.m.
Compression Ratio: 6.7 to 1. Max. Torque: 312 lb ft at 1,800 r.p.m.
24.4 m.p.h. per 1,000 r.p.m. on top gear.
WEIGHT 38 cwt 0 qr 22 lb (4,278 lb). Front wheels 52 per cent ; rear wheels 48 per cent. LB per C.C. : 0.79. B.H.P. per TON : 83.7.
TYRE SIZE : 8.20 × 15in on bolt-on steel disc wheels.
TANK CAPACITY : 16.7 English gallons. Approximate fuel consumption range, 14-16 m.p.g. (20.2-17.7 litres per 100 km).
TURNING CIRCLE : 45ft (L and R). Steering wheel movement from lock to lock : 5 turns. LIGHTING SET : 6-volt.
MAIN DIMENSIONS : Wheelbase, 10ft 6in. Track, 4ft 11in (front) 5ft 3in (rear). Overall length, 17ft 11½in ; width, 6ft 8½in ; height, 5ft 2 11/16 in. Minimum Ground Clearance : 7¼in.

ACCELERATION

Overall gear ratios	From steady m.p.h. of				
	10-30 sec	20-40 sec	30-50 sec	40-60 sec	50-70 sec
3.36 to 1	6.2	6.6	7.0	9.3	13.9
4.87 to 1	4.1*	5.6*	—	—	—
8.84 to 1	—	—	—	—	—
12.84 to 1	—	—	—	—	—

From rest through gears to :—

	sec.		sec.
30 m.p.h.	4.8*5.0	60 m.p.h.	17.1
50 m.p.h.	11.8	70 m.p.h.	25.2
		80 m.p.h.	37.7

SPEEDS ON GEARS :

(By Electric Speedometer)	M.p.h. (at change point)	K.p.h. (at change point)
1st	17	27
2nd	30	48
3rd	59	95
Top	90	145

* Using Low ; remainder on High.

Speedometer correction by Electric Speedometer :—

Car Speedometer	Electric Speedometer m.p.h.
10	9.0
20	18.5
30	27.0
40	38.0
50	47.0
60	54.0
70	63.0
80	71.0
90	81.0

WEATHER : Dry, no wind. Air temperature 70 deg F.
Acceleration figures are the means of several runs in opposite directions.
Described in " The Autocar " of April 6, 1951.

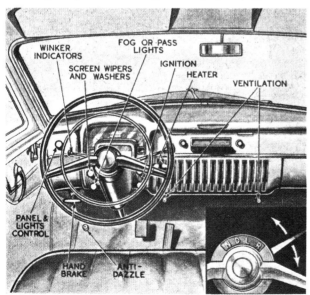

THE Cadillac division of General Motors introduced four new series of cars for 1951, providing a range of eight models. These include a convertible, a long wheelbase limousine, three two-door fixed head coupés and three four-door saloons; it is in this last category that the Series 62 model is placed. As it occupies a position in the expensive car class, it was interesting to test this car shortly (in Belgium, with the co-operation of General Motors Continental, Antwerp), after having had experience of other less expensive models produced by the same parent company.

Once inside the car it did not take very many minutes to realize that, in the Cadillac, General Motors have produced a car that has really " got something."

The 160 b.h.p. developed by the 5½-litre V eight overhead valve engine is transmited by means of an improved version of the well-known Hydramatic transmission, which automatically provides four forward gear ratios. The result is a car with an outstanding performance, and more especially when its size and weight are considered. A maximum speed of a genuine 90 m.p.h., plus the ability to accelerate from 10 to 30 m.p.h. in 4.1 sec is something that is not possible on some so-called sports cars, and, indeed, one run of just under a hundred miles was covered at an average speed of 52 m.p.h. without apparently hurrying, and at a fuel consumption of 14-16 m.p.g.

The improvements made to the Hydramatic drive enable the change from forward to reverse, or vice versa, to be made while the engine is still revving fast, and, apart from preventing accidental damage should the lever be moved by mistake, it is also claimed that this modification enables the car to perform more easily the American manœuvre known as " rocking." For all normal driving the hand control lever is placed in the D position and in this range the car will climb all main road hills quickly and with complete absence of fuss. Even after being baulked on a hill of around 1 in 10 it is not necessary to change down to the Low ratio, but if this is done an extremely brisk getaway will result. The change from one gear to another is particularly smooth, and unless one is looking out for a change point it is hard to detect.

In spite of the fact that there are five turns of the steering wheel from lock to lock, the car handles extremely well at speed, and possesses a certain " quality " feel. On the straight there is a feeling that it will steer itself, yet it obeys the slightest wish of the driver. So much is this so, in fact, that in a very short space of time one thinks of the car as almost a small one, as far as manœuvring is concerned. On corners there is a minimum of roll, and the car has a " solid " feel, although a certain amount of tyre squeal occurs on some

Although large, the Cadillac retains a well-proportioned layout. Width makes the car seem lower than most of its compatriots. Bumpers, both front and rear, are exceptionally massive. The radio aerial is automatically extended by pressing a control inside the car.

More than most American cars, the Cadillac has retained the "pursuit plane" suggestion at the rear. A false duct entry at the front of the rear wing is part of the same conception. The final effect suggests the luxury and high speed that the Cadillac possesses in good measure.

ROAD TEST . . . . continued

types of road surface; but, of course, the suspension is by no means hard. The slight degree of understeer that is apparent does not seem to be affected very much by the small amount of roll produced by normal cornering, and the quick self-centring action of the wheels also helps to produce a general feeling of manœuvrability.

The suspension is by coil springs and wishbones at the front, and long leaf springs at the rear, a combination that produces a very even ride with an absence of pitch and kick up at the rear end. Over all types of surface, including "colonial" sections and Belgian pavé, the car kept a very even keel, with the minimum amount of movement transmitted to the passengers. The noise level from inside the car is very low, and even over the bad surfaces there is only a slight amount of rumble.

With under 18 lb weight per sq in of brake lining area, the Cadillac can be stopped quite easily from normal speeds, with only a light pedal pressure. However, under the conditions imposed during performance testing, a considerable amount of fade was experienced; although the brakes quickly regained their normal working properties on being allowed to cool, the efficiency did not seem quite as high as before. The hand-operated parking brake, situated on the extreme left of the car, is fitted with a warning light which comes on when the brake is applied.

The driving seat is extremely comfortable and gives good support, but by comparison with other G.M. products that have been tried it appears to be noticeably higher, and consequently a much better view and sense of control are obtained. The steering wheel and pedals are very well positioned, and reduce fatigue to a minimum when the car is driven for long periods. The design of the steering wheel, with two sloping spokes, enables the driver to have an extremely good view of the instruments, which are grouped with the small controls above the enclosed steering column.

Below the large speedometer, and to the left of the column, are two controls; the upper one is a combined windscreen spray and control for the suction-operated wiper motor, and the lower converts the front flashing indicator lamps into pass lights, provided that the head lamps or side lamps are switched on. Below an electric cigarette lighter, to the right of the steering column, is a multi-position ignition switch which operates auxiliaries only, if turned to the left, and the ignition when turned to the right. A further right turn automatically starts the engine, provided that the control lever is in the neutral position. Warning lights are used to indicate dynamo charge and oil pressure, while two small gauges show water temperature and petrol level. Instrument lighting can be varied by means of a rheostat built into the main light switch.

Two small interior lamps are mounted in the facia just above the radio panel. These are automatically switched on when either of the front doors is opened, and may also be controlled from inside the car by means of a small switch built into the left-hand lamp. The glove locker is also illuminated automatically when the lid is opened, and can be locked by means of the ignition key.

The relatively high driving position partially offsets the disadvantage of a fairly high bonnet line, but it is not possible to see the right-hand front wing from the driving seat in a left-hand drive car. However, the general outward vision is extremely good, and there is the minimum of

Considerable bonnet space is well filled by the V-eight engine. The battery is accessible and an oil bath cleaner serves the downdraught carburettor. One of the impeller housings of the air-conditioning system can be seen to the right of the big air cleaner.

Luggage space is more than ample. The lid of the locker is automatically retained in the open position. As shown in the inset, the left-hand stop-light installation opens to reveal the fuel filler cap.

interference from the windscreen pillars. The large wrap-round rear window, in conjunction with a well-placed mirror, ensures good rear visibility. At night the mirror can be dipped by pressing a small catch, to prevent dazzle from following traffic.

On an expensive car one expects certain refinements as regards upholstery and interior trim generally, and in this respect the Cadillac comes up to expectations. It is neatly trimmed in grey cloth piped with leather. A fold-down arm rest is provided in the rear seat only, and this could with advantage be wider. A combined cigarette lighter and ash tray is built into the back of the front seat.

Interior air temperature control, although somewhat complicated, is very comprehensive, and the use of a thermostat reduces the control mechanism to a minimum of two levers, to operate the fans and water supply, plus two controls to operate the forward-facing air intake ducts. Apart from the scuttle mounted heater unit, there is another blower under the front seat, which conveys air to the rear passengers' feet, while a third extractor fan is fitted in the luggage compartment, with a communicating duct behind the rear seats. Adequate de-misting ducts are formed in the interior of the screen casing strip. The quarter lights

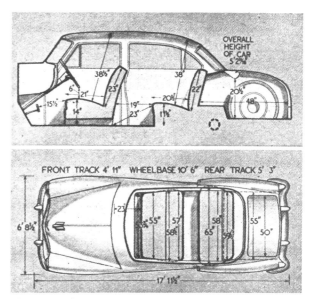

Measurements in these scale body diagrams are taken with the driving seat in the central position of fore and aft adjustment and with the seat cushions uncompressed.

in the front doors can be opened by means of winding handles which hold them against the outside air pressure when in the fully open position, when they act as very effective air scoops.

Even when housing the spare wheel and tools, the luggage locker retains very generous proportions, and is of a most convenient shape to accommodate a large number of suitcases. The lid, hinged at the top, is spring loaded, so that it will remain in the open position for loading.

The head lights, although having the appearance of being of small diameter, prove to be very powerful, and to give the good range essential for night driving at high speed. The note of the horns is also powerful, yet pleasant, and in keeping with the character of the car. Starting from cold was at all times instantaneous.

Judged by any standards of performance, comfort or manœuvrability, this car would fulfil the needs of a most critical driver, but perhaps one is impressed most of all by its extreme silence as regards both engine noise and wind noise. It is a most pleasing car to drive.

The windscreen, it will be seen, has a high degree of curvature. The upholstery, as this view of the front seat cushions shows, is luxurious.

The interior is capacious, and finished in soft pale grey cloth. Arm-rests are fitted to all four doors. Small handles provide a positive, simple opening for the front ventilation panels. The draughtproof ash tray, with roll-top cover, is interesting, as also is the conveniently placed seat adjusting control.

Road Testing the 50TH

Our tests reveal that the '52 Cadillac not only has luxury, but performance to match

An MT Research Report
by Walt Woron

THROUGH THE YEARS the name Cadillac has been synonymous with the word Class. Despite the fact that more than a million cars have been built since the founding of the Cadillac Automobile Company in 1902, the prestige of becoming a "man of distinction" in the circle of your society still goes with the purchase of a Cadillac.

Although it may be questioned how long Cadillac can hold their leadership on the basis of class alone, MOTOR TREND Research's road test of the 1952 Cadillac "62" four-door sedan indicates that the prestige factor should enable them to stay out front for a long time to come. A deluge of questions about the styling and luxury of driving and owning a Cadillac greeted us wherever we stopped on our three-day, 1000-mile-long test through cities, over mountains, and through backcountry. Not once were we asked about performance. And yet the 1952 Cadillac *has* performance, performance to match its class: bounding acceleration, phenomenal top speed, and handling ability greatly improved over last year's product.

Power Steering—A Boon to Driving Ease

After driving the '52 Cad (picked up from the Cadillac Motor Car Division of Los Angeles) around the block once, we were amazed at the difference between it and our '51 test car. At that time we complained of having to tug heavily at the wheel in order to get around corners; what they've done this year is to devise a unit that frees you of this effort. As long as the car-buying majority insists on a soft ride (creating the need for large tires, along with soft springs, etc.), power steering (although not standard equipment) provides the antidote.

Cad power steering—a combination of conventional steering gear and hydraulic booster—is fairly simple in operation. Here's the way it works: Whenever the engine is running, a pump creates hydraulic pressure that is used, through the actuation of suitable valves, to assist the driver's steering effort. You begin to turn the wheel to move away from the curb, and as soon as you exert a pressure of more than three pounds the booster goes into operation, and your effort goes down to practically nothing. As you straighten out and drive down the street, the valve closes and steering becomes normal. Out on a straight highway, you're driving with conventional steering. But as you enter a turn which makes you exert an appreciable effort on the wheel, the hydraulic assist again comes into operation. Coming out of a turn, the hydraulic pressure is automatically relieved and the steering wheel returns to normal.

The most important feature of this system, MOTOR TREND Research feels, is that it does not make the driver *completely* dependent on power assist. It still provides most of the "feel" of a conventional system. In the case of hydraulic failure during high-speed cornering, the change in effort would be hardly noticeable; on a slow, city turn, you would feel a definite change.

Unlike a car with conventional steering, at least unlike our '51 test Cad, the '52 Cad did not get whipped from one side to another, either on tar strips, on railroad tracks or going over chuck holes. "Wheel fight" is virtually eliminated. All the hard work involved in parking is no longer there; instead of loads as high as 50 pounds, maximum is eight pounds.

Disadvantages? (1) Until you get used to it you have the tendency to over-control, because you don't realize how easy it is to turn a corner. Without being accused of crying "Wolf" we would like to point

1902—First car built by Cadillac

1912—First with electric starting, lighting and ignition system

1915—First with the V-type, water-cooled, eight-cylinder engine

Speedometer dominates easy-to-read instrument panel, good safety feature

Six stop watches and an electric speedometer are used for acceleration runs

Fred Bodley and Bob Hoeppner, technical men, and Walt Woron, editor, talk it out at stop near Indio, Calif. Temperature hovered around 110 F. in shade

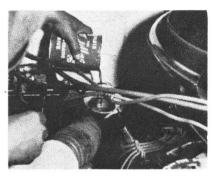
Filling Hydra-Matic unit in Cad requires a funnel and considerable ingenuity; however, filling is not usually necessary between the regular changes

ANNIVERSARY CADILLAC

1923—First to build the inherently balanced 90° V-type engine

1933—First to provide cars with the no-draft ventilation feature

1949—Cadillac builds its one-millionth car since company's founding

Luxury items on Cadillac include automatic radio selector (above, left), cigarette lighter in back of front seat for rear-seat passengers (right), defroster for rear windows, and radio speaker for the passengers in the rear seat (below)

PHOTOS BY ERIC RICKMAN

Performance of 190-horsepower engine was outstanding on test. Record run of 115.4 mph top speed was recorded, highest ever obtained on one of our test cars

CADILLAC TEST TABLE

PERFORMANCE

CLAYTON CHASSIS DYNAMOMETER TEST
(All tests are made under full load conditions)

RPM	MPH	ROAD HP
1200	29	80
2003	51	80
3000	74 (maximum)	100

Per cent of advertised hp delivered to driving wheels—52.6

ACCELERATION IN SECONDS
(Checked with fifth wheel and electric speedometer)

	LO-D3	D3
Standing start ¼ mile	18.4	18.4
0-30 mph (0-34.5 car speedometer)	4.0	4.1
0-60 mph (0-67 car speedometer)	13.2	13.5
10-60 mph through gears	12.4	12.4
30-60 mph in Third		9.4

TOP SPEED (MPH)
(Clocked speeds over surveyed ¼ mile)
Fastest one-way run 115.4
Average of four runs 109.6

FUEL CONSUMPTION IN MILES PER GALLON
(Checked with fuel flowmeter, fifth wheel and electric speedometer)

	D-3	D-4
Steady 30 mph	14.7	17.0
Steady 45 mph	15.7	17.7
Steady 60 mph	—	15.8
Approximate average in traffic	—	16.3

BRAKE STOPPING DISTANCE
(Checked with electrically actuated detonator)
Stopping distance at:
30 mph .... 47 ft. 3 in.
45 mph .... 114 ft. 3 in.
60 mph .... 204 ft. 5 in.

GENERAL SPECIFICATIONS

ENGINE
Type .... Overhead valve V-8
Bore and stroke .... 3 13/16 x 3 5/8 in.
Stroke/bore ratio 0.95:1
Compression ratio 7.50:1
Displacement .... 331 cu. in.
Advertised bhp .... 190 @ 4000 rpm
Piston travel @ max. bhp .. 2416 ft. per min.
Bhp per cu. in. 0.57
Maximum torque .... 322 lbs. ft. @ 2400 rpm
Maximum bmep .... 146.6 psi @ 2400 rpm

DRIVE SYSTEM

Transmission: HydraMatic, Dual Range
Gear Ratios: First, 3.82:1; Second, 2.63:1
Third, 1.45:1; Fourth, 1:1
Rear axle: Semi-Floating, Hypoid Drive
3.36 ratio with 3.07 to 1 optional

DIMENSIONS

Wheelbase	126 in.
Tread	Front—59, Rear—63 in.
Wheelbase/tread ratio	2:1
Overall width	80 1/10 in.
Overall length	215 ½ in.
Overall height	62 11/16 in.
Turning radius	22 ½ ft.
Turns, lock to lock	5 ½
Weight (test car)	4510 lbs.
Weight/bhp ratio	23.7:1
Weight/road hp ratio	45:1
Weight distribution (front to rear)	front 54%, rear 46%
Weight per sq. in. brake lining	20.6 lbs.

INTERIOR SAFETY CHECK CHART

QUESTION	YES	NO
1. Blind spot at left windshield post at a minimum?		X
2. Vision to right rear satisfactory?		X
3. Positive lock to prevent doors from being opened from inside?		X
4. Does adjustable front seat lock securely in place?	X	
5. Minimum of projections on dashboard face?		X
6. Is emergency brake an emergency brake and is it accessible to both driver and passenger?	X	
7. Are cigarette lighter and ash tray both located conveniently for driver?		X
8. Is rear vision mirror positioned so as not to cause blind spot for driver?	X	
TOTAL FOR CADILLAC	75%	

OPERATING COST PER MILE ANALYSIS

1. Cost of gasoline $166.66
2. Cost of insurance 168.40
3. First year's depreciation 258.00
4. Maintenance:
   a. Two new tires 39.90
   b. Brake reline 32.28
   c. Major tune-up 8.75
   d. Renew front fender .. 81.52
   e. Renew rear bumper ... 42.29
   f. Adjust automatic transmission, change lubricant ... 16.00
First year cost of operation per mile ... 8.1c

Cadillac Road Test

out that drivers using this system should become accustomed to its ease of steering effort and the fact that you *can* overcontrol. Going into a corner, you set the wheel, preparing for a certain amount of effort. When the hydraulic assist takes over, your own unexpended effort turns the wheel an additional amount, causing the car to go through a shorter radius than required (which can cause you to slide or spin). (2) It drains off some of the increased horsepower. (3) The steering gear box is fairly hard to service since it's located under the air vent duct, slightly below the engine left bank, although the pump is right on top.

The steering wheel, quite thick and easy to grip, is set in a good position as far as the seat is concerned. Driver comfort and safety have both been taken into account with the seat being adjustable to the extent that when it is moved forward (either by manual control or the hydraulic-electric system on deluxe versions) it also raises—a definite advantage to shorter persons. The full circle horn ring is recessed below the level of the wheel, and operates at the mere touch of the thumb from anywhere on its circumference.

In general the car handles well, sticks in corners, has little tendency to break loose, doesn't feel mushy, gives a fairly flat ride through corners taken at moderately high speeds. Some road shock is felt in the wheel but not enough to be bothersome. Tire squeal is there, as it will inevitably be with large (8.00 x 15) tires, inflated to their recommended pressures.

One thing that sold us on the way the Cadillac handled was its reaction to crossing a railroad track of the "hump" type, causing any car approaching it over 30 mph to be thrown into an unexpected leap through the air. We crossed it deliberately at twice this speed, becoming airborne for 15 to 18 feet, a good 12 to 18 inches off the ground, returning to earth nose first. You would think it might "pancake" there, but steering wheel jar was at a minimum, there was no swerve, no sway. It just held a straight course, except that after the rear end came down, it made two fairly severe bumps, then quickly settled down.

It Literally Flies—115.4 Top

Starting with a run of about two miles before entering our ¼-mile measured trap, the Cad picked up its speed phenomenally quickly, the needle passing the 110 peg on the speedometer long before the near end of the trap was reached. At the average top speed of 109.6 (the average, incidentally, of four runs, two each in opposite directions) there was only a trifle of "floating" (oscillation of the body on the springs, over a virtually level course). The car held a perfectly straight course on these runs—the fastest we have made

Cadillac Road Test

(by eight mph) with any American stock car MOTOR TREND Research has tested.

With the new "performance range" Hydra-Matic, the Cadillac can definitely take advantage of its increased power, utilize it with a greater versatility, though at the sacrifice of completely automatic driving. Like other General Motors cars, this transmission provides manual control over two gears (third and fourth) in the driving, "DR," range. For city traffic and mountainous driving you use third, which gives you less lugging, more engine braking, less economy. On the open road you use fourth, which is considerably more economical, giving you two to 2½ mpg more than third gear in 30 to 45 mph speed ranges. Up around 60 mph, of course, you are winding the engine too tightly in third gear for best fuel economy, so it's best to use fourth in the higher speed ranges.

For some reason, or reasons, unexplained at the time of this writing, the '52 Cadillac gave us considerably less fuel economy than our '51 test car. Weights were approximately the same (4420 vs. 4510), rear axle ratios were the same (each 3.36:1), testing conditions were the same. There are, of course, differences between seemingly identical cars. Another explanation could be that the '51 Cads were slightly overboard fuel economy-wise, with the carburetor power jets set too high for best acceleration performance.

The 12-inch ribbed brake drums in the '52 Cadillac are both stronger and larger, allow for more effective cooling

Unfortunately, the way the Hydra-Matic gear selector is set up, it's sometimes difficult to read what gear you are in. For us it wasn't hard, because in tests such as we make our ears are attuned to the sound of the engine. We can tell by the number of revs it is turning up what gear it is in. For the person who drives a car automatically, paying little attention to the car once it's rolling, a better selector dial would be desirable. There is only the smallest of tick marks to indicate the difference between third and fourth gears.

Accelerates Like Some Sports Cars

With a power/weight ratio (number of pounds that each horsepower has to push) of one to 23.7, the Cadillac was bound to have much better than average acceleration. As it worked out, running acceleration checks through various gears, using high alone, clocking to certain speeds and to distances, the '52 Cadillac turned in a most creditable performance—best of any stock car tested so far this year. Its "dragging" qualities were comparable to those of some sports cars. As an example, its speed at the end of the ¼-mile trap was 72 mph, a speed attained in 18.4 seconds, much better than average.

Pick-up was somewhat better using the LOW range of Hydra-Matic, then shifting to third gear of DRIVE, which kept the car in second gear for a longer period of time than is possible using DRIVE alone. The shift was made at around 42 mph, whereas in DRIVE the shift is automatically made at around 30 mph.

With a Cadillac you would expect to get a better ride than in any other car on the road—an expectation that is not realized. Although the front and rear seat rides are comfortable and you don't have to brace yourself for ordinary curves (you do for fast, sharp ones), the high spring rates, canted shock absorbers and anti-sway bars still seem insufficient to bring the ride up to Cadillac standards.

Rear end bottoming was not noticeable from the driver's seat, or from any other place within the car, but when we placed the car on a hoist to check the underside, we discovered a point of contact between the left rear leaf spring and the gas tank filler neck. This was probably inadvertent interference, however, and not bottoming.

Plush, Comfortable Interior

It is easy to get into and out of either front or rear seat of the '52 Cadillac. There are 35 and 28 inches, respectively, of space designed to give you plenty of maneuvering room. Once you're seated, you find you have all sorts of legroom. A diagonal drawn from the floorboard to the front of the *front* seat to the seatback measures 44 inches; from the floorboard to the front of the *rear* seat to the seatback measures 38½ inches. Headroom is ample, 34 inches both front and rear. When you're behind the wheel, there's plenty of freedom for your left leg; even if you're the middle passenger in the front seat, the transmission tunnel doesn't cut down your legroom excessively.

The plain instrument panel is free of knobs, incorporates a large glove compartment, but a dull finish would eliminate some of the glare from the painted top. The instrument cluster (placed behind a glass that picks up too many reflections) has an extremely legible speedometer, fuel and water temperature gauges that are fairly small and located somewhat low for easiest reading. Red lights are used to indicate low oil pressure and low generator charging rates.

Controls are all within easy reach, and though the ratchet-type emergency brake is located on the left side, it's simple to pull to the ON position. When it is on, a red warning light, located above the 50 to 60 mark on the speedometer, flashes off and on. The ignition key is also the starter switch, with a cut-out to prevent the engine from being started when the car is in gear.

No noticeable blind spots are evident from within the Cadillac: the triangular-shaped windshield post is slim and angled properly; the rear quarter panel is down to a bare minimum; the glare-proof, two-

These views show how exhaust is designed into integral part of the rear bumper, another Cadillac refinement

position, rear view mirror has several adjustments to reduce the blind spot normally created to the right front; but a lower hood line, or higher fender (as some of the manufacturers are using) would help distance-judgment in traffic.

All appointments are of usual Cadillac elegance, with the possible exception of the rear quarter windows. These have small pull-and-twist handles that are awkward to operate; it seems that a luxury car like the Cad should have window cranks.

Construction of the body, which has only superficial 1952 styling changes, is about average; here again, its finish did not seem up to the par of what you have grown to expect from Cadillacs. Hood and trunk lid are both easily raised; the well-braced, undercoated hood by an outside

CONTINUED ON PAGE 49

WILBUR SHAW REPORTS FROM THE DRIVER'S SEAT OF

America's Most Powerful Car

Pepped up by a 210-horsepower engine—that still runs soft and saves gas—the new Cadillac spurts ahead of its rivals.

TWELVE SECONDS after taking off abreast of the 1952 Cadillac the photographer was riding in, the 1953 Cadillac I was driving (arrow) was hitting 60 and leaving the other car well behind.

KICKING up its heels in celebration of its 51st birthday, Cadillac has nosed out its closest rival in the horsepower race among big mass-production automobiles.

Cadillac started the race, was left behind for a while and now once more is out in front. The 1953 Cadillac has a 210-horsepower engine. That's five horsepower more than the new Lincoln has (PSM, Jan. '53, p. 110), 30 more than the 1953 Chrysler produces.

Smart Engineering Pays a 20-Hp. Bonus

But, strange as it may seem to you, Cadillac isn't doing much boasting about that power. What its engineers really are proud of is that they have coaxed more fuel economy, efficiency and smoothness out of their spirited high-compression engine. The added zing—20 horsepower more than the 1952 Cadillac had—nice as it is to have available, is really a by-product, they say.

Still, if you want a race-horse start and acceleration like a plane's take-off, the '53 Cadillac has them. With a four-passenger load, it will spurt from a standing start to 60 miles an hour in 12.2 seconds and will hit 80 in 20.8 seconds. The 1952 car took 13.1 seconds to reach 60 from a standstill, 24.2 seconds to get up to the 80-mile-an-hour point.

The engineers preferred to talk to me about gas mileage, however—16.2 miles to the gallon in average city driving, 18.2 on the open road. That is 1½ to 2½ miles per gallon better than the 1952 Cadillac could do.

For an engine as powerful as this one and a car as big and heavy, those are impressive figures.

I must say, though, that I've often wondered why there's so much fuss about fuel economy in passenger cars. The difference between getting 15 miles to the gallon and 25 would cost the average driver less than $50 a year. You'd think the added comfort and pleasure of a bigger, more powerful car would more than offset its tendency to drink up more gasoline.

'53 Engine Takes Life Easier

To gain economy, Cadillac engine experts first lowered the rear-axle ratio from 3.36 to 3.07 to 1. This means that the engine doesn't have to do as much work per mile. The fewer r.p.m. required, the slower the pistons, valves and all moving parts need travel. In other words, less engine friction is created. And the less friction there is, the less horsepower is lost by that route. There's where your economy comes in.

A drop in r.p.m. naturally also brings a drop in engine noise and vibration.

But economy and quiet are all you would gain from the lowering of the rear-axle ratio if you didn't have some compensating gain in propelling force, or torque. You'd immediately notice that the car had become sluggish.

The easiest way to restore drive to the engine would have been to increase the piston displacement, but that's the most expensive way to do it in terms of fuel cost.

Cadillac engineers retained the economy they had gained by lowering the rear-axle ratio and at the same time increased the torque produced by their engine, in these ways:

• Changing the shape of the combustion chamber to promote more even burning of the mixture of gasoline and air.
• Lowering the spark plugs, for better flame propagation.
• Reducing the quench, or "squish," area in the cylinder.
• Changing the valve timing and in-

now. Will 1953's most powerful car seem equally charming on a mantle in 2003?

They've Done Quite a Bit to This Car

The car that Cadillac put out in 1903 is a model-makers' favorite, sold in kit form

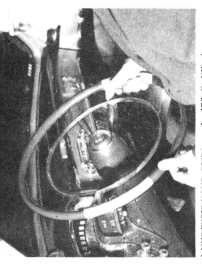

I LIKE THESE HAND GRIPS on the '53 Cadillac's steering wheel. They are of greenish roughened plastic. The grips on the El Dorado deluxe convertible are of leather.

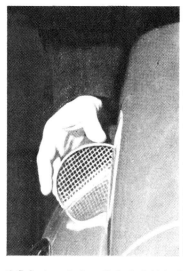

THE MASSIVE BUMPER-GRILLE is attached in one piece on the assembly line. It is entirely separate from the front of the hood, to avoid crumpling sheet metal in slight collisions.

THIS AIR SCOOP on the rear fender has a twin on the other side of the car. They are the only outward signs that the 1953 Cadillac to which they are attached is air-conditioned.

don't cost the buyer anything extra, to chrome wire wheels, which do.

The sound level of the new Cadillac is, I'm sure, lower than that of any other car in America. It is now at a new low, partly because the engine is quieter and because there are resonators and mufflers on the twin exhausts, but largely because of added insulation.

Insulation Added

There's a glass-fiber blanket under the hood, for instance, enclosed in a sheath of black plastic so that it is hard to distinguish from the metal. There is insulation between the ceiling fabric and the roof, too, for half the distance to the rear window. They tried insulating the entire ceiling but an unnerving boom resulted. Half-insulation turned out to be best.

A safety feature worth mentioning is the new locking arrangement on the doors. With small children in mind, Cadillac body designers fixed it so that once the door is locked, you can't open it from inside by turning the handle. You have to pull up the locking plunger first.

Shifting Is Smooth as Silk

Automatic transmission and a 12-volt electrical system are now standard equipment on practically all Cadillacs. In keeping with a smoother engine, the Hydra-Matic transmission has been further refined. The shift points have been modified to conform better to throttle openings. As a result, gears shift so easily that there's no engine fuss and barely noticeable difference in "feel."

A rear-shelf speaker for the radio, located under the package shelf, is optional for all Cadillacs.

And in the eight-passenger limousine there is a duplicate set of radio controls in the rear seat that override those in front. If the chauffeur has tuned in bebop and the boss doesn't like it, a flick of the rear dial can force the poor guy at the wheel to listen to Beethoven. END

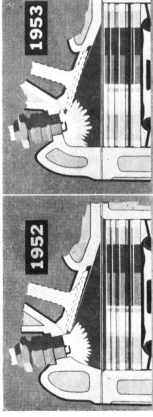

SEAT OF POWER is the engine combustion chamber. These comparative drawings of the 1952 and 1953 Cadillac combustion chambers show how the contours have been altered and the spark plugs lowered to speed up progressive burning of the fuel-air mixture.

creasing the lift of the valves to enable the engine to breathe deeper.

● Improving the distributor to give a faster response to changes in engine speed.

● Altering the carburetion to provide generally leaner mixtures, though rich enough to avoid ping.

Luxury Is the Keynote

You expect quality features in a Cadillac, and in the 1953 lines they are evident everywhere, from the firm, heavy click of the doors to the push-button radio aerial and window lifts.

Air conditioning, capable of lowering interior temperatures from above 100° to 75° in a few minutes, is available at extra cost. For winter driving there are heaters for the passengers in back as well as those in front.

Power steering is obtainable, too, of course, and it has been improved in the 1953 cars. Cadillac still hangs back from full power steering, however, with the excuse that it is unsafe. I don't agree with that attitude, and I am sure that Cadillac, perhaps under pressure from its buyers, will eventually come around to my point of view.

The company offers the biggest tires available for passenger cars—8.20 by 15 super balloons—to all clients who choose the whitewall variety. This gives the cars bigger footprints to go with 12-inch brakes all around. The tires are mounted on any of five kinds of wheel, ranging from the standard ones, which

FACTS ON '53 CADILLAC

Model: Series 62 4-door sedan.
Engine: V-8 overhead valve; 210 hp. at 4,150 r.p.m.; compression ratio, 8.25:1; piston displacement, 331 cu. in.; piston travel (in feet per car mile at 20 m.p.h.) 1,328; bore and stroke, 3.81" by 3.63"; torque, 330 lb.-ft. at 2,700 r.p.m.
Weight: 4,372 lb.; per hp, 20.82 lb.
Transmission: Hydra-Matic; rear-axle ratio, 3.07:1.
Steering ratio: 25.47:1; radius of turning circle, 21.6'.
Effective brake-lining area: 258.5 sq. in.
Springs: front, coil; rear, semi-elliptic.
Outside dimensions: height, 62.7"; overall length with bumpers and guards, 215.8"; width, 80.1"; wheelbase, 126"; overhang, front 34.9", rear 54.9"; tread, front 59.12", rear 63.10".
Inside dimensions: seat-cushion width, front 63.7", rear 64.3"; leg room, front 43.9", rear 43.6"; headroom, front 35.8", rear 35.6"; seat height, front 14.6", rear 12.5"; vertical distance, steering wheel to seat cushion, with seat in rear position, 5.1"; front-seat adjustment, horizontal 4", vertical, 6".
Tire size: 8.00 by 15 super balloon (black sidewall), 8.20 by 15 super balloon optional (white sidewall).

Testing the CADILLAC SERIES 62

By JULIAN P. LEGGETT

Cadillac taking a fast turn on a rough dirt track. Stability of this car was good.

With fire hose nozzles on this time, pressure is stepped up to 137½ pounds and water streams are aimed at points around windows, doors, hood and luggage compartment where leaks might occur. After 1½ hours of this water penetration test, not over 6 ounces of water got in around window vents and door seam, and none got in trunk—Cadillac has a tight body!

How wet can it get? Here the Cadillac Series 62 Sedan is being deluged by hoses during 1½ hour test to determine body tightness and seal against moisture.

SINCE there are mighty few bathtubs around in which you could dunk a Cadillac, our crew of engineers from Motor Vehicle Research rigged up another way of determining the tightness of the body construction on the new Cadillac they tested for SCIENCE AND MECHANICS. For an hour and a half, they played water from fire hoses against and over the car body, paying particular attention to closed doors and windows, windshield, back window and hood and luggage compartment areas. Over 18,000 gallons of water were poured on the car from all angles, using fire hoses that delivered 90 pounds pressure with nozzles removed for the first hour, and 137½ pounds pressure with nozzles on for the last 15 minutes.

During this entire test, an observer stationed inside the car with an inspector's magnifying glass checked every point where leakage might conceivably occur, and, after the tests, a complete inspection for leakage was made of the entire car. Despite this deluge, not more than one glassful of water entered the car, and the only leakage points that showed up under this extreme test were minute amounts through the front window vents and around the center door jamb between the front and rear door. The luggage compartment was absolutely free of any water. And there was no evidence of damage to the car's finish from the hosing under high pressure. This car, the engineers decided, had an exceptionally tight, well-sealed body.

Road performance of this car kept pace with the quality of the body construction. Its top true speed of 105.75 mph on one radar-timed run places it among America's fastest stock cars. The speedometer hit bottom at 110 and bounced, but the radar and 5th wheel recorded the true speed. At that rate of travel, the 190 hp engine was turning up 4,480 rpm.

For all its 4,175 pounds dry weight, this Cadillac showed itself to be remarkably frisky on acceleration. It stepped from 10 to 50 mph in 7.62 seconds and from 20 to 60 in 9.96 seconds in the two fastest runs. Zero to 60 took longer, 10.89 seconds, but that's still mighty sharp performance. On these acceleration runs, the car carried 360 pounds of passengers.

Braking efficiency tests also produced some top-notch performance, such as the emergency stop from 30 mph. in 27 feet, for an efficiency of 90%. All of the panic stops resulted in efficiencies of 75% or better, with the car coming to a halt straight, with wheels locked, no slewing or side thrust, and a normal weight shift.

And, after the initial series of 18 normal and panic stops, an additional series of 14 panic braking stops from speeds ranging from 20 to 60 mph revealed no primary fade and exceptionally fine brakes for this heavyweight vehicle.

Our readers have often asked just what power demands various automatic devices make on an automobile's engine. Since this Cadillac was equipped with both power steering and Hydramatic transmission, MVR's engineers set out to find what power the engine had to deliver to these automatic units to operate them. With the car at a standstill and engine idling at 600 rmp, the steering wheel was turned, with the booster's aid, ¼ turn. The rpm reading dropped to 585. Turning the wheel all the way to lock position reduced the rpm to 525. On the Hydramatic test, with the engine idling at 520 rpm the gear selector was moved from N (neutral position) to LO (low range) but without setting the car in motion.

On this fast jump test, note that this Cadillac's heavy front end barely leaves the ground.

Cadillac makes straight-line panic stop from 50 mph. Brakes on this car were excellent.

The rpm reading promptly dropped to 460. That meant it required that much effort to turn the hydraulic coupling. Turning the steering wheel hard left to lock during this same transmission test further reduced the rpm to 400. The total power loss, 120 rpm, becomes quite apparent—again proving that you can't get something for nothing. For the convenience and comfort of power steering and automatic gear shifting, you give up some engine power. This is true, of course, of all cars so equipped and doesn't apply solely to Cadillacs.

That this car has plenty of power left after the loss to steering and transmission was forcefully demonstrated in two ways. First, MVR's engineers tried a tow, attaching the Cadillac to a tractor-and-loaded-trailer with a total weight of 31 tons or 62,000 pounds. A pull gage in the tow chain showed the Cadillac exerted a 2,700-pound

Another *Science at the Wheel* Report

Science at the Wheel — Cadillac "62" Performance

START OF TESTS: March 11, 1952

MAKE OF CAR: 1952 Cadillac Series 62 4-door sedan

WEATHER CONDITIONS (prevailing at time of recorded road tests): Temperature: 68-73°F. Humidity: 20-58%. Wind velocity: 3-7 mph. Wind direction: W-NW to SE. Barometer: 29.30-30.1

ROAD CONDITIONS (for gas mileage, acceleration and brake efficiency tests): Asphalt-covered crushed rock, clean and dry

MILEAGE AT START OF TESTS: 1,461.3

MILES COVERED IN TESTS: 2,600

GAS USED: Premium (slight ping under load in preliminary run with Regular) **OIL USED:** SAE #10

TEST DATA

GASOLINE MILEAGE (checked with fuel velocity meter, gas volume meter, 5th wheel and Mile-O-Meter vacuum gage. Passenger weight 370 lbs., test equipment weight 97 lbs. Average of two steady runs made in Drive or Hi-Drive range north and south on 2% grade at each speed. Tire pressure 24 lbs. cold, 5th wheel pressure 24 lbs. cold. Speedometer correction not applied to miles-per-gallon readings)

MPH Speedometer	True Speed	Miles Per Gallon	RPM
20	20.5	21	890
30	30.5	20.75	1250
40	40.5	18.75	1680
50	48.85	18.5	2010
60	57.85	17	2380
70	68.25	15.25	2700
80	75.85	12.5	3010
90	86.25	13	3420

FUEL ECONOMY ACCELERATION TEST (both tests made in Hi Drive range): Full throttle from 0-50 mph speedometer, then holding 50 for 1 mile (1 min. 16 4/5 sec.), consumed .075 gal. at an approx. rate of 13.33 mpg. Slow acceleration from 0-50 mph speedometer, then holding 50 for 1 mile (1 min. 25 1/5 sec.), consumed .06 gal. at an approx. rate of 16.66 mpg.

ACCELERATION (checked with dampened pendulum meter and timed electrically. Times subject to speedometer correction. Carried weight 370 lbs. front. Figures are average of two successive runs at speeds specified):

MPH Speedometer	Gear Range	Average Time (Seconds)	MPH Speedometer	Gear Range	Average Time (Seconds)
0–20	LO only	2.15	0–60	LO and shift at 30 mph	10.89
0–30	LO only	3.71			
0–40	LO only	5.29	10–50	Hi Drive	7.62
0–50	LO and shift at 30 mph	7.85	20–60	Hi Drive	9.96

ACCELERATION FACTOR (roughly speaking, a measure of potential pickup performance. Full throttle in gears indicated):

MPH Speedometer	Accelerometer Reading	Pull in Lbs. per ton	MPH per second	Feet per sec per sec.
20 (LO)	34%	630	7.48	11.66
20 (Drive 1)	34%	630	7.48	11.66
30 (LO)	32%	606	7.04	10.58
30 (Drive 1)	32%	606	7.04	10.58
40 (Drive 1)	27%	530	5.94	9.18
50 (Drive 1)	21%	411	4.6	6.8
60 (Drive 1)	13%	259	2.9	4.2
60 (Hi Drive)	13%	259	2.9	4.2
70 (Hi Drive)	12%	239	2.65	3.95

TOP SPEED AND SPEEDOMETER CORRECTION (average of north and south runs in miles per hour with passenger weight of 360 lbs. and indicated peak rpm of 4480 on each run. Tire pressure 24 lbs. cold, 5th wheel pressure 21 lbs. cold, wind 17 mph with gusts to 24, wind direction W-NW. Speedometer bottomed at 110 mph and bounced):

MPH Speedometer	5th Wheel Check	Radar Timer Check	MPH Speedometer	5th Wheel Check	Radar Timer Check
110 Top Speed	104.5	105.2	50	48.85	48.85
90	86.25	86.25	40	40.5	.....
80	75.85	75.85	30	30.5	.....
70	68.25	68.25	20	20.5	.....
60	57.85	57.85			

ODOMETER CORRECTION (checked with Veedor Root counter and calibrated new "6th wheel," with error checkout of ½" in 5,000 ft. Hairline magnifier used. Indicated speed during tests 9 mph): Car's odometer—5,450 feet; true distance by 6th wheel—5,280; error 170 ft. Two-mile checkout, error 347 ft. short of indicated distance. 10-mile checkout, error 1,604 feet short of indicated distance

HILL CLIMBING (checked with pendulum performance meter. All tests at full throttle with 360 lbs. passenger weight, 51 lbs. instrument weight):

MPH Speedometer	Gear Range	Grade in %	MPH Speedometer	Gear Range	Grade in %
20	LO	34	50	Drive (1)	21
30	LO	32	20	Hi Drive	23
40	LO	27	30	Hi Drive	25
20	Drive (1)	34	40	Hi Drive	22
30	Drive (1)	32	50	Hi Drive	17
40	Drive (1)	27	60	Hi Drive	13

BRAKE EFFICIENCY (checked with decelerometer and Sioux pressure cylinder. Tire pressure 24 lbs. cold. Weight in car, 360 lbs. passengers, 87 lbs. instruments. Time between normal stops 4½ mins. average, between panic stops 3 mins. average. Temperature 72°F, barometer 30.1, humidity 58%. Pavement dry. Normal stops all straight, no slewing; panic stops straight with all wheels locked, weight shift normal):

NORMAL STOPS

Speedometer MPH From	Pedal Pressure in lbs.	Efficiency in %	Approx. Time in secs.	Stopping Distance in ft.
20	40	86	1.26	25.8
20	36	84	1.37	29.2
30	32	62	2.11	40.8
30	35	54	2.24	54.1
40	34	59	3.1	87.1
50	32	59	3.24	129.7
60	45	78	4.03	191.6

PANIC STOPS

Speedometer MPH From	Pedal Pressure in lbs.	Efficiency in %	Approx. Time in secs.	Stopping Distance in ft.
20	48	75	1.01	15.4
20	41	83	.99	13.4
30	72	83	1.79	33.11
30	54	90	1.64	27.0
40	64	78	2.24	73.1
50	56	84	2.73	113.1
60	68	80	3.93	142.6

REAR WHEEL HORSEPOWER (checked on dynamometer. Temperature in laboratory 70°F, under hood 90°F, barometer 30.05, air-fuel ratio 13.6-1, rear tire pressure 24 lbs. cold):

At an indicated 2,000 rpm, with 2½-3" vacuum and gear selector at Hi Drive, developed horsepower at rear wheels was 79.653

CAR FRICTION or HOLD-BACK (tractive resistance in lbs. per ton, checked on dynamometer):

Miles Per Hour (speedometer)	10	20	30	40	50	60	70
Declutched	29	31	32	36	55	73	94
Drive (clutched, ignition off)	68	71	73	75	98	120	149

SPECIFICATIONS

ENGINE: 8 cylinder V-type, hydraulic overhead valves. Bore 3.8125, stroke 3.625, maximum brake horsepower rated 190 at 4,000 rpm; compression ratio 7.5 to 1; maximum torque 322 at 2400 rpm; piston displacement 331 cu. in.; fuel specified, premium or high test.

TRANSMISSION: Hydramatic automatic—LO and split drive ranges; rear axle ratio 3.36 to 1.

STEERING: power booster type (power required to start operation); turning circle 45 ft.; lock to lock 5¾ turns sprung; 5 unsprung.

EXTERIOR: wheelbase 126"; overall length 215.5"; overall width 80.1"; overall height 62.68"; weight 4175 dry (before fueling for road), road clearance 7.3", gas tank capacity 20 gals.

INTERIOR: head room, front seat, 35.81"; rear seat, 35.56"; leg room, front seat, 43.94"; rear seat, 42.13"; hip room, front seat, 63.56"; rear seat, 64.25"; shoulder room, front, 58.1"; rear seat, 56.50".

VISIBILITY: windshield area (1 piece) 963 sq. in. approx.; rear window (3 piece), 793 sq. in. approx. Driver's eye to road over left front fender (5' 8" driver, seat in extreme rear) 21' 3.75"; driver's eye to road over hood center 36' 7.5"; driver's eye to road over right front fender 29' 5".

EQUIPMENT: Battery 6-volt, 17-plate, 115 amps, located under hood. Tires 8.00x15", recommended pressure 24 lbs. cold. Luggage capacity 14 cu. ft. with spare tire in place. 10-gallon pumping time 1 min. 37.40 sec. with 2 gallons in tank at start; no surge or spillage. Filler tube neck in rear tail lamp housing (if gas overflowed it would run down fender to exhaust pipe which might produce fire hazard). Powerful backup lights. Springing, front independent coil, rear semi-elliptic leaf.

MOTOR VEHICLE RESEARCH herewith certifies that these are the true and accurate findings in tests conducted on the automobile named under the conditions specified.

A. J. White,
Director,
Motor Vehicle Research

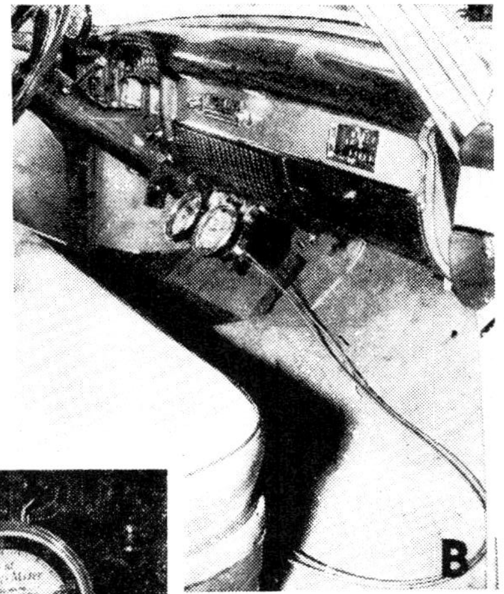

(A) Fifth wheel (right) double-checks car speed and sixth wheel (left) is an entirely new innovation that records actual traveled distance as a check on the car's odometer. Cables from these wheels run to meters shown in photo B inset. (B) Interior showing meters and glove compartment low on dash.

Drivers' Observations

ROADABILITY: This car came equipped with power steering and steering wheel response was excellent, yet retained considerable "road feel" because of effort required in General Motors' system before power mechanism takes over. Front end seems quite heavy—almost logy—at low speeds on rough roads, but this disappears on good roads or as rate of travel increases, evidently a result of intentional design to prevent loss of steering stability when air stream tends to lift front end at upper speed range. Cornering (ability to take curves) very good and side thrust minimum though tires howl in cornering at high speed. Some wander noticeable in 7 mph crosswind.

RIDING COMFORT: Weight and design result in excellent ride on pavement; MVR test on railroad crossties abandoned due to low clearance (7.3"); this car obviously intended for boulevard and open highway, not for rough country roads. Exceptional comfort in rear seat with no extreme side thrust on curves and almost complete absence of noise.

HARMONIC BALANCE POINT (best cruising speed as determined by "feel" of car to driver): 73 mph.

INSTRUMENTS AND CONTROLS: Dials easy to read, although by day the dash picks up pronounced reflection and glare when sun is directly ahead; by night, white letters show up sharply on black background; speedometer figures are easily discernible at a glance. Gear selector quadrant becomes difficult to read while wheel is being turned because horn assembly hides quadrant; light for quadrant is controlled by rheostat on headlamp switch. Word "Brake" lights up on panel in red if hand brake is on; ignition key causes bull's eye to light up on panel if battery is not charging, while another lights if oil pressure drops too low. No ammeter or oil pressure gage on panel. All doors lock from outside without using key (don't leave it inside!). Green direction signals are large and operate with distinct click. Accelerator pedal seems too close to brake for fast foot action and brake pedal could be larger. Windshield wiper, heater and ventilator controls are well-positioned, easy to work. Front seat moves backward or forward automatically at touch of button. Radio antenna has positive vacuum operation. Automatic control raises all four windows in 7.11 seconds, lowers them in 6.05 seconds and works well.

SPECIAL COMMENTS: Service men will find this car easy to work on, fenders are low and mechanic has little bending to do in reaching engine parts. Tests of Hydramatic transmission from standstill to 30 mph indicate low slippage factor, decreasing as speed increases. Hood has no dash release but opens by working primary and secondary catches though the latter was difficult to work on the car tested. With hood open, card for owner's name is visible on frame, giving permanent record. Rear trunk lid required considerable force in closing and trunk compartment matting didn't seem up to Cadillac standards. Twin exhaust pipes extend to extreme outer edge of rear bumper and give appearance of being integral with body. Car received equipped with relatively large fog lights but not undercoated. Car has sufficient power and torque to start wheels in all gear ranges. Place shift lever in Reverse when parking to prevent pushing or rolling. One of flexible hoses between air scoops and car's interior was found disconnected and poorly installed. Air cleaner atop 4-barrel carburetor is one of largest in use and should do a good job of keeping dirt out of the engine. Arm rests are too close to door latches, limiting useful area. Parking brake is one of best tested, giving 33-34% braking efficiency. Glove compartment is set too low on dash, making it difficult to inspect or use, and material in compartment spills easily on opening. Interior is well-finished.

pull to get the load moving on a paved highway. Then the gage was removed and the car took this load in LO range up to 41 *mph* for a distance of 5½ miles on a 1% upgrade, moving along smoothly with little effort. The exceptional potency of this 190 *hp* V-8 power plant was also demonstrated in the regular hill-climbing tests. With 360 pounds of passenger weight, the car took a 34% grade in LO at 20 *mph*, a 27% hill in Drive (1) at 40 *mph* and a 13% hill in Hi Drive at 60 *mph*. That's good climbability!

The Hydramatic transmission has a new performance range in the 1952 version. Suppose we call it Drive (1). On hilly, winding roads, this 3-gear ratio range allows a steady, powerful pull in third, as well as a reserve acceleration surge when needed. It's also handy for downgrade driving for the 3-gear range automatically holds third gear, allowing a coasting speed on the average descent of approximately 25 *mph* without applying the

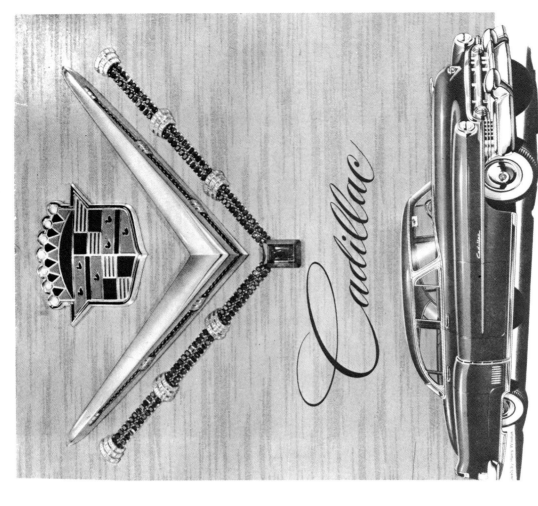

For a Lifetime ...if You Prefer!

It is reassuring, when you buy a Cadillac, to know that you yourself will make the decision as to how long you wish to keep it and drive it. The car will be at your service throughout your pleasure... Give it reasonable care and reasonable usage, and there is no practical limit to a Cadillac's utility. Authenticated records show various Cadillacs well into their *second* five hundred thousand miles of service.... Of course, the original owner seldom has any requirement for such exceptional mileage. Being progressive, he wishes to change his cars sufficiently often to keep reasonable pace with Cadillac's advancement in design and appearance... But the benefits, all the same, from this matchless capacity for service. It means that, month after month and year after year, his Cadillac stays at the peak of its performance—with the minimum of care and attention. ... The great Cadillacs for 1951, now gracing America's streets and highways, are built in the finest traditions of Cadillac quality. If you have not inspected them, you ought to do so at your dealer's—today.

CADILLAC MOTOR CAR DIVISION ★ GENERAL MOTORS CORPORATION

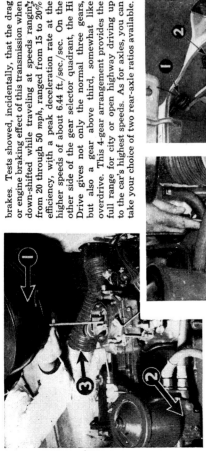

In the photograph above, note the huge air cleaner (1) which should keep this Cadillac 190 hp power plant clean. The power steering unit (2) worked well under test. But the connection of the air intake duct at (3) was quite loose on this car. Inset, screwdriver points to hose found lying on exhaust manifold when car was delivered—hose would have burned through in time after continuous running.

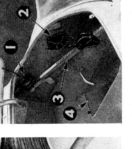

Areas cleaned by windshield wipers showed large blind spots in either corner, a common failing with many modern cars.

brakes. Tests showed, incidentally, that the drag or engine braking effect of this transmission when down-shifted while traveling at speeds ranging from 20 through 50 mph, ranged from 15 to 20% efficiency, with a peak deceleration rate at the higher speeds of about 6.44 ft./sec./sec. On the other side of the gear selector quadrant, the Hi Drive gives not only the normal three gears, but also a gear above third, somewhat like overdrive. This 4-gear arrangement provides the full range for city or open highway driving up to the car's highest speeds. As for axles, you can take your choice of two rear-axle ratios available.

Left above, note blower (1) in luggage compartment that serves as a defroster for rear window. Also note positioning of jack parts which are held well out of the way (rear tire has been temporarily removed).

The 3.36-to-1 ratio will give you the most sparkling acceleration; the 3.07-to-1 axle ratio will give you the greatest overall economy. While the manufacturer recommends premium fuel for this high compression engine (the compression ratio is 7.5-to-1) MVR's engineer's tried out regular gasoline and only got a slight ping when the engine was under load. Right here it should be mentioned that Cadillac, like some other General Motors cars, is equipped with a 4-barrel carburetor. Half of the carburetor works at lower speeds, therefore tends to cut fuel consumption below the rate required when the other half also goes into action upon the driver's demand for more power. Intake capacity of this carburetor is almost doubled in comparison with the carburetor used previously, yet economy has been improved, MVR's experts determined in the rigorous tests.

Ceiling price on the Cadillac as established by the Office of Price Stabilization is $3,636.48 for the Series 62, including Hydramatic transmission. This figure is at the Detroit factory and includes federal excise taxes, factory handling charges and dealer delivery-and-handling charges. It does not include transportation charges, state and local taxes, or optional equipment such as the power steering ($198.43).

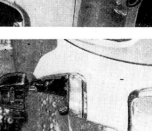

Left, gas tank filler is located inside this rear lamp housing and exhaust pipes (right) are built into each rear bumper.

Here is a frank appraisal of why Cadillac gets the 1952 Motor Trend Engineering Achievement Award. How does your car rate?

By Walt Woron

CADILLAC—CAR OF THE YEAR

"CADILLAC—CAR OF THE YEAR!" That's what it says, and MOTOR TREND Research is ready to back up that statement—ready to back it up with facts and figures. For although many cars come close to the '52 Cadillac, *no* other American production stock car can lay claim to the honor of being *the* car of 1952. *Why* is Cadillac the car of 1952? Sure, it has style, prestige, and creates a pride of ownership surpassed by only the princeliest of products, but this isn't what we are talking about. We claim that Cadillac is the car of the year on the basis of performance, handling, safety, economy. How do we determine that? Draw up a chair and we'll go into a detailed explanation.

First of all, most of the figures used in determining the 1952 MOTOR TREND Engineering Achievement Award were gathered during the road tests of the 20 listed cars. These tests were conducted for publication in MOTOR TREND during 1952. Other figures were added later, but *all* of them, with the one exception of the evaluation on handling, are based on cold, hard, engineering test data.

The staff of MOTOR TREND Research does not claim to be engineers. Practical engineers, yes; theoretical, no. With critical eyes, the guidance of our readers, the use of engineering instruments, and the help of engineering specialists, we are able to come up with figures in which we have the utmost confidence. With these figures in chart form, we are then able to give you an *overall* rating of the 20 cars tested.

We have used a system that places less emphasis on power to determine the 1952 Award winner. The method used in 1951 may have favored more powerful cars. This year's method does not: In first place is a heavy car, in second a light car, third a medium car, fourth a light car, fifth a medium car.

This year's categories are four basic ones that go into a car's engineering qualities: Performance, Handling, Safety, and Economy and Maintenance. The first includes those factors that determine the *overall* efficiency of the engine, by itself, in relation to the transmission, and in relation to the entire car. Handling includes roadability: how the car reacts to movements of the steering wheel under many assorted conditions. Safety includes interior safety as well as brake efficiency. Economy and Maintenance are indicated by fuel consumption, cost of operation, and how much it costs to repair and maintain.

Each of the main categories was assigned a value of 25 per cent, with a possible total of 100. Since Performance has eight sub-items, Handling only one, Safety three, and Economy and Maintenance four, factors were needed that would result in a total of only 25 per cent for each category. After all the figures were determined, the cars were given positions from first to twentieth in each column. Twenty points were given for first place, 19 for second, 18 for third, etc. The total points each car received under all sub-items in each category were then added. A theoretical total of 160 points was therefore possible for a car that placed first in each of the eight columns under performance. To reduce this to 25 per cent (the total value assigned to each category) the conversion factor of .156, or $^{25}/_{160}$, was used. Each car's total for the eight columns under performance was multiplied by this figure. The same method, but with different reduction factors, was then used for each of the other categories (.417 for Safety, .312 for Economy and Maintenance; no factor was necessary for Handling, which has no sub-items).

How Did Cadillac Rate?

In automobiles, like anything else, a compromise is the rule, rather than the exception. It's therefore not at all surprising that the Cadillac 62 won the 1952 MOTOR TREND Engineering Achievement Award. Cadillac has built a better automobile, on a comparative basis, than the 19 other cars rated. It's a compromise automobile, one that's good in all factors. This enabled it to total enough points to

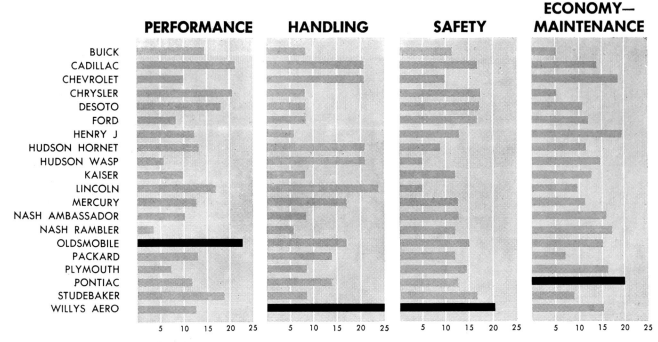

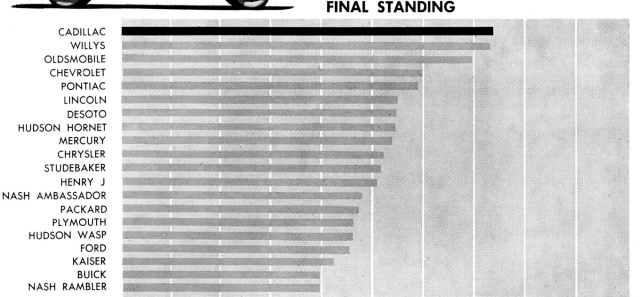

CADILLAC—CAR OF THE YEAR

outdistance any other car that was tested.

In Performance, the Cadillac came in second because of its good acceleration, high top speed, low number of pounds car weight for each ft.-lb. of torque and high maximum bmep. These latter factors, plus the relative number of pounds each horsepower has to push, result in the acceleration qualities evident at low, medium, and high speeds.

In Handling, the Cadillac 62 with power steering has been placed in a tie for third by the MT Research staff. The steering wheel is well-positioned, overall handling characteristics are good, the car sticks in corners, has little tendency to break loose, does not feel mushy, and maintains a steady course with little wind wander.

In Safety, the Cadillac 62 had the least number of pounds loading on each square inch of brake lining (making it tops in this sub-item), and was sixth in the sub-item, interior safety.

The Cadillac is fairly economical to run and has a high trade-in value (tie for third in cost per mile), is efficient (fourth) in the strictly engineering analysis of fuel economy (ton mpg), and is the most economical in its price class when it comes to repairs, parts, and labor.

So much for the winning car and how it won. A study of the chart will show *why* Cadillac wound up in each position as it did. Now, let's take a closer look at the four main categories and the various sub-items under each of them.

PERFORMANCE DATA CHART

Line No.	Car Make and Model	PERFORMANCE								Handling	SAFETY			ECONOMY & MAINTENANCE				Line No.
		Average ¼ Mile Acceleration in Seconds	Average High Speed Acceleration in Seconds	Average Top Speed	Per cent of BHP at Wheels	Pounds Per RHP	Pounds Per Lb.-Ft. of Maximum Torque	RHP Per Cu. In.	Maximum BMEP in PSI	(By Position)	Average Braking Distance in Feet	Weight Per Sq. In. of Brake Lining	Interior Safety Check in Per cent	Average Fuel Consumption in MPG	Average Fuel Consumption in Ton MPG	Cost Per Mile	Maintenance and Repair Costs	
1	Buick Roadmaster...	20.2	15.9	100.1	50.0	53.2	16.2	.265	131.8	11T	135'3"	20.7	86	13.9	31.5	13.3	175.07	1
2	Cadillac 62........	18.4	10.9	109.6	52.6	45.1	14.0	.302	146.6	3T	122'0"	18.7	86	16.7	37.7	6.7	183.00	2
3	Chevrolet-Standard..	20.8	19.8	80.9	67.4	52.7	18.5	.286	122.5	3T	121'3"	20.6	43	19.1	31.1	5.3	98.65	3
4	Chrysler Saratoga V-8	19.5	11.3	106.0	54.0	44.4	13.9	.294	142.0	11T	115'3"	21.5	100	15.0	32.5	11.9	192.77	4
5	De Soto V-8.......	20.4	13.8	98.1	55.0	46.5	16.3	.317	136.5	11T	125'2"	20.3	100	17.3	35.4	11.3	177.76	5
6	Ford V-8	21.4	22.0	86.7	58.2	55.1	18.0	.268	123.5	11T	94'0"	20.4	72	17.0	30.0	7.0	139.71	6
7	Henry J-Corsair 6...	20.8	19.5	83.9	63.1	50.0	18.9	.313	124.6	19T	128'0"	19.1	72	23.3	30.1	5.4	113.17	7
8	Hudson Hornet.....	20.2	13.9	99.2	50.7	53.9	15.4	.238	125.8	3T	119'5"	25.0	72	17.3	34.4	11.4	146.03	8
9	Hudson Wasp.......	20.9	18.0	97.8	47.5	62.9	19.0	.231	115.0	3T	130'6"	23.9	72	18.9	36.0	10.5	146.03	9
10	Kaiser............	19.7	19.2	90.8	50.4	60.8	18.5	.256	126.7	11T	129'6"	20.0	72	17.8	31.2	11.4	120.18	10
11	Lincoln...........	21.6	13.1	98.3	59.2	48.7	16.3	.299	134.9	2	132'7"	23.5	72	17.4	40.4	14.9	250.79	11
12	Mercury...	20.1	19.3	91.7	57.6	51.0	17.4	.282	124.5	7T	119'8"	23.1	86	18.3	33.6	8.0	194.79	12
13	Nash Ambassador...	20.6	15.2	95.2	50.0	62.8	17.1	.238	131.4	11T	121'0"	22.1	86	22.2	41.8	11.9	146.21	13
14	Nash Rambler......	22.5	19.6	81.3	51.2	63.0	19.2	.243	120.6	19T	116'10"	27.6	86	22.6	30.0	7.3	119.25	14
15	Oldsmobile Super 88.	19.0	12.2	104.3	60.0	42.7	14.5	.316	140.5	7T	121'8"	21.5	100	18.9	38.7	8.7	148.48	15
16	Packard 300.......	20.7	15.9	96.3	57.3	50.9	16.2	.263	124.5	9T	129'6"	21.0	86	15.2	33.3	11.7	186.52	16
17	Plymouth..........	22.9	22.8	85.6	61.9	55.8	19.1	.275	121.2	11T	106'6"	21.1	72	19.6	32.7	7.6	135.02	17
18	Pontiac 8.........	21.4	13.9	92.9	57.2	54.2	16.7	.261	127.5	9T	111'3"	22.1	72	19.7	37.3	6.7	126.84	18
19	Stude. Comm. V-8..	20.5	13.7	87.6	74.1	37.0	17.3	.382	127.5	11T	113'4"	20.1	72	16.2	26.7	8.4	143.13	19
20	Willys Aero.	20.8	17.2	81.5	60.0	50.2	20.1	.335	126.4	1	113'10"	20.4	100	21.5	29.2	7.5	121.56	20

Performance

The first column under Performance is *Average Acceleration over ¼-mile* in seconds of elapsed time. This indicates the effectiveness of the power/weight ratio, which provides the car with the pickup required for traffic driving. If the car is too heavy, or if it is underpowered, it will naturally have slow acceleration. MT Research tries all possible combinations of shifting before finally recording the figures, so we are certain to wind up with the best obtainable times (for the particular car and test conditions).

Average High Speed Acceleration is the average of acceleration from 10-60 and 30-60 mph. These tests are conducted by cruising at the indicated low speeds, then stomping the throttle (letting the car down-shift if that is the operation of the transmission) and accelerating until the upper speed is reached. Acceleration at these speeds is important when you have to slow down behind another car on a grade, then wish to pass and need the added push.

Average Top Speed speaks for itself. The figures (derived from two-way runs, two each in opposite directions) give an indication of possible cruising speeds.

Per Cent of Brake Horsepower delivered to the rear wheels is the ratio of bhp *advertised* (by the manufacturer) to road hp (the latter determined with a Clayton chassis dynamometer). Road hp is the bhp *minus* losses through the transmission, driveshaft, rear axle, and rear wheels. A percentage of 50-60 is about average; some cars may be on the low side if *advertised* bhp is higher than *actual* bhp.

Pounds per Road Horsepower is another factor in the performance of the vehicle, and not the engine. The engine will deliver a certain bhp at each rpm, finally tapering off after it reaches maximum bhp. Required road hp for the vehicle to maintain level road speed is somewhere below these values. Where the two curves cross on a graph is the theoretical top speed. The difference between the two factors at any given speed is available for a change of speed, dependent on the weight of the car and the torque. This, then, explains the reason for the next column.

Pounds per lb.-ft. of Maximum Torque. While high torque (for which we depend on the manufacturer's figure) is a highly desired engine characteristic, we tie it in with performance potential by equalizing it with the weight of the car. One car may have considerably more torque than another, but the ratio of torque to the weight it has to push may be higher, resulting in less available acceleration. Torque is also important because although two cars may have the same maximum bhp, one may have more torque throughout the entire rpm range, which will be reflected in more available acceleration.

Road Horsepower per Cubic Inch is a rating that involves engineering "finesse" in the development of power rather than brute strength through size. Since we measure power at the rear wheels, this figure also includes the mechanical efficiency of the drive train.

Maximum Bmep (brake mean effective pressure) is another way of expressing engine torque per cubic inch at the maximum torque speed range. This figure, along with maximum brake horsepower per cubic inch, is a comparative measure of how efficiently an engine develops power per unit of displacement over a fairly wide operating speed.

Top car in the Performance category is the Oldsmobile Super 88, equipped with the Super (dual-range) Hydra-Matic transmission. Its overall engine efficiency (top maximum bmep, high torque per lb., high road hp per cu. in.), its engine-to-rear axle and engine-to-car relationship (tie for fifth in per cent of brake hp delivered to rear wheels, third in pounds per road hp), results in outstanding acceleration and top speed.

Handling

Handling is one category that is based on selective personal opinion; however, it is a consensus of the MT Research staff, all members of which drive all the cars, using unbiased judgement in looking at handling characteristics. These opinions are based on the roadability of the car, rather than the ease of handling.

We take into account the car's versatility at all speed ranges, keeping in mind what the car owner will be doing with his car in traffic, on dirt roads, on smooth asphalt highways stretching beyond the horizon, and on roads that curve over and around mountains. Also, what the car will do when it hits a soft shoulder, how it acts on streetcar tracks, how it reacts to ruts in the road, how mushy the front end is in a tight corner, how much the body leans, how easy it is to correct after going through a corner, how much corrective action it needs to hold it in a straight line, and how much it is affected by crosswinds.

Best car for all-around handling qualities, according to the opinion of MT Research, is the new Aero Willys. The steering wheel is positioned properly to give the driver excellent control, the car maneuvers gracefully in traffic, takes very little corrective action on a straightaway, is barely bothered by powerful crosswinds, does not break loose on sharp turns (except on dirt, where it goes into a safe, controlled slide), does not get whipped aside on streetcar tracks or by shoulders, and has an overall cornering ability on a par with many sports cars (despite the fact that the steering ratio is slow by comparison).

Safety

Safety, as we see it, based on items other than personal opinion, should include braking, how safe the interior of the car is, and how good the vision is. Other items are also important, such as handling ability and acceleration at high speed, but these two factors show up elsewhere in our evaluation.

Average Braking Distance is the overall average of stopping distances required at speeds of 30, 45, and 60 mph. These are obtained for all cars on the same road surface, checked with an electric speedometer, an electrically-actuated brake detonator, and a steel tape. Tires are as provided as standard equipment.

Weight Per Square Inch of Brake Lining is the weight of the car in pounds, divided by the number of square inches of brake lining for all four wheels. This indicates the energy that each square inch of lining has to dissipate during a stop, and possibly indicates the durability of the lining (more square inches means less heat per unit of surface for a given energy absorption).

Interior Safety Check includes items that affect the safety of driver and passengers alike: blind spots in vision, positive locks to prevent rear doors from coming open while driving, a secure locking device on the front seat track, projections on the dashboard, convenient location of lighter and ashtray for the driver.

The ratio of noes to yeses determines this percentage. with the safest cars getting the highest score.

The Aero Willys also rates tops in this category, on the basis of its No. 1 position in weight per sq. in. of brake lining. Actual stopping distance is not outstanding (13th overall) but during our test of this car the brakes were subjected to a destructive beating. Fade did not occur, possibly due to weight loading and the fact that the drums have deep cooling fins. In interior safety, the Willys ties for sixth.

Economy and Maintenance

Average Mpg is the overall average of fuel consumption readings taken at steady, level road speeds of 30, 45, and 60 mph, and during a drive through a 13-mile course laid out through traffic. Type of fuel used (regular or premium) depends on the manufacturer's recommendation.

Average Ton Mpg is an engineering figure based on how much weight a certain car can haul at what fuel consumption. It is obtained by multiplying the weight of the car in tons by the actual fuel consumption.

Its usefulness is in comparing the overall thermal efficiency of the vehicle in converting fuel energy into useful work, and to what extent the transmission and gearing take advantage of the engine's inherent fuel economy.

Cost Per Mile is determined on the basis of four items: cost of fuel operation for one year, cost of insurance coverage, first year's depreciation, and that maintenance which, on an average, may be required on any car (not necessarily every car). To determine fuel cost, it is assumed that the car will travel the national average of 10,000 miles. This figure is divided by the overall mpg average obtained on our road test, multiplied by the cost per gallon of fuel used (regular or premium) as recommended by the manufacturer. Insurance cost is for the following coverage: comprehensive, $50 deductible, public liability of $10,000-$20,000, and $5,000 property damage. Maintenance includes: a wheel alignment, a brake reline, two major tune-ups, an adjustment and change of lubricant of the automatic transmission (if the car is so equipped).

Maintenance and Repair do not necessarily mean that all the items are necessary for a full year's maintenance, but indicate the *relative* cost of maintaining and repairing one car, as compared to another. Cost of parts and labor are taken from *Motor's Flat Rate Manual,* and include: distributor, battery, fuel pump, fan belt, a valve grind, one front fender, one tire, and one bumper.

The most economical car to operate, on the above basis, is the Pontiac Eight, with Dual Range Hydra-Matic. Although it does not excel in any one of the four sub-items under Economy and Mainte-

nance, it falls into the upper range in all four. In fuel economy it is fifth in both miles per gallon and ton mpg, in cost per mile of operation it ties for third, and in maintenance and repairs it is sixth.

A Few Final Words

Well, there you have it. If you can't figure out why your car did not wind up in first place in overall standings, or why it didn't take first in performance (or one of the other categories), take another look at the basic numerical chart. Rate your own car, compare it to the others, see why it finished where it did. You may not agree with our method of selecting the winner, but it's hard to deny the proof of figures obtained during the critical tests we conduct.

On the basis of such searching analysis, conducted over the period of a year in which we road tested 20 different makes, all four-door sedans (except where no such model is manufactured), all equipped with that model's most popular transmission, we are proud to present the Cadillac Motor Car Company with the 1952 MOTOR TREND Engineering Achievement Award.

—*Walt Woron*

Sectioned *Cadillac*

Above: Rear quarter window is too long to roll down into the sectioned body. Here it is slid out of position and subsequently stored in trunk.

Below: Wide appearance of 1952 Cadillac is shown in this head-on view. Section was removed from lower edge of hood eliminating the usual "V".

Seldom Customized, The Cadillac Makes A Good Car For Transformation

By Spencer Murray
Photos by Ralph Poole

"UNUSUAL" is the word for this car. At first glance it appears to be just what it is, a 1952 Cadillac Coupe deVille. A closer look proves, however, that something is missing from, or added to, it.

When Ed Wilder of Los Angeles decided to alter his 1952 Cadillac convertible, he made up his mind that it should be altered radically but still retain the stock Cadillac appearance. Chopping the top, channeling the body, altering the grill, or making any similar changes would detract from the Cadillac quality. The only remaining solution was sectioning.

Many of our readers have written to us asking why Fords seem to be about the only cars that people section. Here is the answer.

Wanting nothing but top quality body work, Ed took his Cadillac to Jay Everett, also of Los Angeles. He told Jay that he didn't want to detract from the stock Cadillac appearance so they put their heads together and finally came up with a workable solution. They decided to section the car *above* the fender line. This necessitated rebuilding the hood and drastically altering the deck lid but, undaunted, Jay set to work.

Two parallel lines, four inches apart, were scribed on the car just below the belt molding (the chrome strip that encircles the car just be-

Drawing attention wherever it is driven, Coupe de Ville looks stock at first glance.

neath the windows). Carefully following the lines, Jay made the two cuts and the upper part of the body was allowed to drop four inches.

Realigning the top to the bottom was a little more work than Jay had originally planned on. The major body sections such as the cowl, the quarter panels, the doors, and inner body panels went together comparatively easily, but the hood and deck lid presented major problems.

The deck lid was removed from the car and a mark was made about four inches in from the outer edge, all the way around. Cutting on this line, the outer lip of the deck lid and the metal immediately surrounding it was separated from the remaining inner portion. The outer section was discarded and a new, wider section of metal was welded to the inner part. By first reworking the deck lid to fit the new body contours, then shaping up the new outer edge and rounding the lower corners, the lid was completed.

The hood also presented its problems. A four inch section was removed from the vertical sides of the hood and from the leading bottom edge. Like the deck lid, a new outer edge had to be built so that the hood would line up with the fenders. At this point it was noticed that, although the sectioning job gave the car a new, wider, appearance, it was still not as wide appearing as Ed wanted it.

The front fenders were each moved out from the body three quarters of an inch. This made it necessary to add still another outer edge to the hood to conform with this increase in width. The remaining portions of the car also had to be widened; the doors, the quarter panels, the rear fenders, the bumpers and the grill.

When the fenders were replaced on the body, it was found that the top edges of the fenders were actually higher than the belt molding, so a panel had to be fitted to the body to conform with this. If the body had not been widened this would have been, probably, an almost insurmountable problem, but the width increase of three quarters of an inch on each side gave Jay some room to work. The result may be seen in the accompanying photographs. This area, above the front edges of the rear fenders, is actually concave, so much so, in fact, that a drain hole had to be made to let the water run off that would otherwise accumulate from rain or from washing the car. Next, the seams between the body and the fenders were filled in.

Always full of ideas, Ed decided now that he wanted a Coupe deVille instead of a convertible. An order was placed at a Cadillac agency and soon a deVille top, complete with windows and hardware, arrived.

The top was installed with no little difficulty, but it was discovered that the deVille quarter windows would not roll down in the conventional manner. It seems that the windows were longer than the body was thick so an alternate method was worked out. The quarter windows are now completely removable from the car. By rolling down the door windows, the quarter windows are slid out of position and stored in the trunk.

With the exterior of the car pretty well along by now, work was directed

Instrument grouping has been slanted in at the top to reduce glare. Hardware is brass plated.

to the interior. The cowl had been sectioned below the level of the instrument panel, so the panel had dropped with the upper part of the body. The results were somewhat astounding; the lower edge of the panel came so close to the floor that the driver was unable to get his feet under it. It was eventually found, however, that a 1950 Cadillac instrument panel was not so deep as the later one, so the earlier one was fitted to the car.

The seats also had to be rebuilt to fit the body and still retain plenty of head room. The seat cushions were dropped closer to the floor and the seat backs were, also, cut down. The result is perfectly proportioned seats, just a little lower in all respects than stock seats.

The only exterior trim that was removed was the trunk hardware and the Cadillac signs on each front fender. The hood "V" was eliminated in the sectioning process.

All metal work being completed, the car was given an outstanding black lacquer job. This is an unusual color to paint so radically customized an automobile and many shops frown on customers who want their cars this color because it has a marked tendency to show up any rough metal work.

The final touch was to lower the entire car three inches in the rear and two and a half inches in front. The result is a beautifully proportioned automobile that is, very unusual.

The cost for a job like this, if anyone has a Coupe deVille that they want sectioned, will run close to $3,000.

Cadillac Road Test
CONTINUED FROM PAGE 37

latch, and the trunk lid by a key and over-center springs that eliminate the effort of lifting.

A Long Line of V-8s

It's inevitable that the Cadillac V-8 for 1952 would have more horsepower, greater efficiency, and easier accessibility for servicing—it has behind it 37 years of engine building, starting with the pioneering of the water-cooled V-8 of 1914—an engine smaller (314 cubic inches) than today's, developing only 60 hp. The present Cad engine, basically the same as the overhead job introduced in 1949, has 30 additional horsepower—developed at a rate higher by 200 rpm than previously—gained through a four-barrel carburetor and a general opening up of the intake and exhaust systems. The carburetor uses two barrels for part-throttle driving, calling on the other two for maximum power requirement conditions. The intake mani-

Coupe De Ville—$3978 FOB Detroit

Limousine—$5300 FOB Detroit

Four-Door Sedan—$3648 FOB Detroit

fold has been enlarged, as have the exhaust valves and exhaust ports. The exhaust system uses independent exhaust pipes (not headers) for each bank of the engine, one large and one small muffler for each pipe, ending through the outer ends of the rear bumper (giving added road clearance over steep driveways and dips, which often cause flattening of the tail pipes). The smaller mufflers, known as resonators, are for removing noise frequencies which cannot be removed by the regular mufflers. Cadillac is striving for a completely silent exhaust system.

Placement of the various components of the engine were made apparently with an eye to ease of service; the oil filler neck and both fuel filters are out in the open; the distributor is in a good location; all spark plugs (except no. 1 and 4 on the right bank) are simple to remove; valve covers are easily detached; the only thing in the way of servicing the distributor is the removal of the large carburetor air cleaner.

Better Brakes This Year

The only changes, but welcomed, to the '52 chassis (or running gear) are the larger

Convertible—$4128 FOB Detroit

front (12-inch) ribbed brake drums that are both stronger and allow more effective cooling. With the increased horsepower, providing more acceleration and top speed, better brakes are called for. At no time during the normal performance of our test (except at the tail end of our full-on brake stops) did the Cad brakes fade. Recovery was very rapid. Compared to last year's test car, brake stopping distances remained about the same at 30 mph, increased at 45 and were greatly reduced (by 22 feet) at 60 mph (see Test Table).

Another Stride Forward

With the introduction of its Golden Anniversary Cadillac, the Cadillac Motor Car Company has taken another stride forward in producing pioneering innovations: the multi-cylinder engine; the first to equip cars with electric starting, lights and ignition; the first to build a water-cooled V-8 engine. Even though the 1952 Cadillac doesn't have the distinction of introducing another new automotively world-shaking development, the combination of power steering, 190 horsepower engine, luxuriousness of interior and fantastically low depreciation make it a car to be desired.

CADILLAC ACCESSORIES	
Wheel Disks	$ 28.40
Windshield Washer	11.36
Oil Filter	11.34
Fog Lamps	36.91
License Frames	4.28
Outside Mirror	6.24
Vanity Mirror	1.85
E-Z-Eye Glass	45.52
Heater and Blower	113.66
Radio Push Button & R. Speaker	112.47
Radio Sig. Seeking & R. Speaker	129.22
Power Steering	198.43
Autronic Eye Beam Control	53.36
White Sidewall Tires 62 and 60	33.76
Automatic Window Regulators	138.64
Trim Rings	10.69

luxury, performance, even economy—the cadillac has them—but above all, it is the car with prestige

An MT Research Report
By Walt Woron and Pete Molson

Photos by Jack Campbell

BOX SCORE:	POORER THAN AVERAGE	AVERAGE	BETTER THAN AVERAGE
ACCELERATION Standing ¼ mile		■■■	
30-60 mph		■■■	
BODY WORK		■■■	
BRAKES Stopping distance avg. @ 30, 45, 60 mph		■■■	
EASE OF HANDLING		■■■	
FUEL ECONOMY Averages @ 30, 45, 60 mph			■■■
INTERIOR		■■■	
RIDE		■■■	
ROADABILITY		■■■	
TOP SPEED		■■■	

This box score is based on the average of all '52 cars tested except for the ratings on Interior and Ride, which refer to the average of other cars in the same price class (see February '53 MT).

IN A LITTLE OVER A FIFTH of a minute, a '53 Cadillac will hit 60 mph from a standing start. In not too much longer, it will top 115. Much more impressive to us at MOTOR TREND, however, is the fact that the fuel economy of the '53 Cad is *30 per cent* better than that of the '52 Cad. For this Cadillac should take a bow. They are increasing engine efficiency in a place where it hits you and us—the pocketbook. Let's hope we see similar increases with other '53 models.

America's Glamour Queen

Cadillac is the car that most Americans —if their purses were unlimited—would choose above all others. It has so entrenched itself on the domestic scene that it has become to many people a symbol rather than a tangible automobile with direct competitors, at least pricewise, among four other well-known and highly respected U.S. cars. The most important factor in Cadillac's desirability is very probably the elusive one of prestige.

People Like Its Looks

In appearance, General Motors' top-drawer offering has grown a little less distinctive since it became virtually undisputed King of the Mountain in 1941. The ever-larger decorative Vs, the chrome wheel discs of 1947, and the fins of 1949 were quickly taken over by other makes, though GM wisely held back whenever possible before using them on its lesser cars. On the other hand, Buick—not only on the Roadmaster but also on the medium-priced Super—has used the same body shell as the Cadillac for many years. The current body was introduced simultaneously on the two cars three years ago and has continued without visible change except for a heightened trunk lid.

CADILLAC-

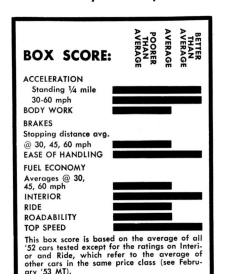

Here sit the country's most envied drivers. Power steering put wheel grips out of their usual position with easy half turn

Cigarette lighter is located conveniently for rear seat passengers. Rope cord has concealed mountings in padded recess

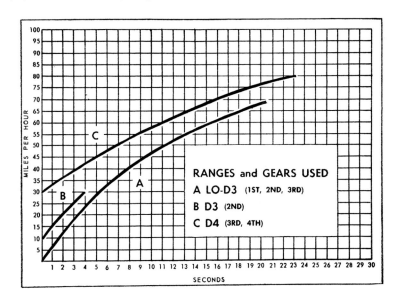

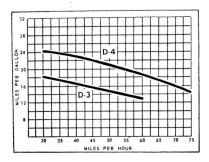

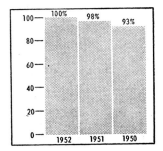

ACCELERATION, FUEL CONSUMPTION & DEPRECIATION CHARTS

This is not to say that it is not satisfactory; in many respects it is extremely so. Not the least of these would seem to be appearance, if the popularity of both makes is an indication. Few Americans will wholeheartedly support something whose looks they don't like. Cadillac represents the heights of the solid GM school of design, whose main stock-in-trade consists of considerable length, width, and weight, even on the Chevrolet. Its second time-proved tactic lies in making all of these dimensions appear greater than they actually are.

Whether the appealing work of the Italian designers will eventually influence all American automobiles remains to be seen. It offers the advantage of better vision and of lower cost through the elimination of chrome. But it is a good bet that General Motors, at least, will not make radical changes in the looks of its standard products for some time to come.

Other Makers Please Copy?

For 1953, the Cadillac grille is even more massive than before. Two raised and

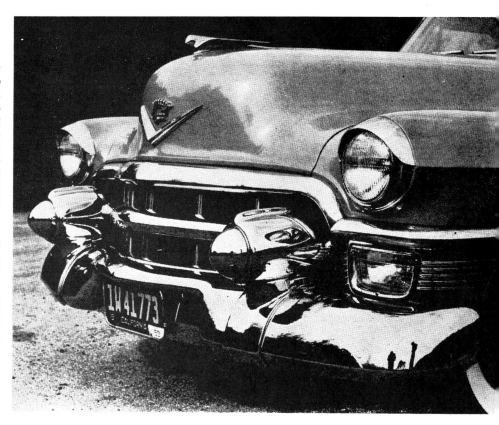

AMERICA'S FAVORITE LUXURY CAR

enlarged bumper guards dominate it. Other cars may shortly adopt two new styling touches: extended chrome "eyelids" on the headlights, and the extremely handsome, optional chrome wheel discs with concave centers. Except for these changes and the squared-off rear deck, the casual observer will find the new car practically indistinguishable from 1950 and later models. From the standpoint of continuing owner satisfaction with a luxury car, this policy is wisdom itself.

From Inside

Let's take a look at the surroundings in which the typical owner of a '53 Cadillac controls his car. We say "controls," for driving, in one sense, is no longer necessary here. In minor respects, such as keeping aware of exact engine oil pressure, it is not even possible. Being typical, our owner has a Series 62 four-door sedan, the model used for testing by MT Research.

Doors, both front and rear, are wide. Getting in and out through them is easy. Their interior panels, like the rest of the interior, are finished in conservative good taste. Armrests are now an integral part of the panel; as a result they are much longer, and more comfortable for a variety of human statures. They incorporate a door pull, whose shape and metal finish make it resemble an ashtray. Fabrics and trim used on the doors, as elsewhere in the car, are excellent, on a par with other 1953 luxury cars.

The seats follow GM practice in being deep, comfortable, and of medium height. The MT Research car was equipped with optional power seat adjustment and window lifts (the combination costs an additional $138). Travel of the seat is the same as with the standard hand control: It rises as it moves forward; the seat back, rather sharply canted to the rear, does not change its angle.

Instruments, grouped directly in front of the driver, are surmounted by a large and legible speedometer. Fuel and temperature gauges use a white needle on a chrome ground and are not easy to read. Warning lights are provided for low oil pressure, battery discharge, and parking brake position. Replacement of the conventional oil pressure gauge and ammeter with light signals is hard to justify on an expensive car. Lights are an excellent adjunct to dials, but their information is too limited to make them a satisfactory substitute. The Hydra-Matic transmission range indicator has moved to the panel, where it can be scanned with the other instruments. As the staff observed last year, the two DRIVE range "notches" are too close together on the dial.

In many respects the Cadillac's beautifully finished dash does not reflect the best in present-day arrangement. The heater and ventilation controls, though solid and pleasant to operate, are unlighted. Two vent knobs, evidently not considered a part of the panel's design, are awkwardly located under the radio speaker. Twin map lights are a good feature.

Cadillac's wheels are always a center of interest, and for good reason. These unusual concave discs are optional extras

Cadillac's powerhouse lies in this seemingly crowded compartment, but access for service is not bad. Note 12-volt battery

CADILLAC

New Safety Ratings

This month MOTOR TREND is making a number of changes in its Safety Check, and it is interesting to see how Cadillac stands on the new points, and what improvement has been made over last year. The Cadillac mirror, unlike others, is adjustable up and down, and may be called the industry's safest in terms of effectively eliminating the blind spot. It is free of sharp edges. Again this year, the dash panel glares irritatingly at the driver. At the left side of the dash, where the driver's knees can slide forward quickly in a crash stop of even medium intensity, the hand brake and sharp ignition key protrude at too low a point for safety.

Location of the glove compartment has now joined that of the lighter and ashtray as a safety item. With front seats increasing in width, right-hand compartments have moved farther and farther away from the driver. The "reasonable man" of legal terminology cannot be expected to stop his car whenever he needs his sunglasses, and reaching across a front seat as wide as the Cadillac's is not at all safe while driving.

On the passenger's side, the dash is commendably free of dangerous projections with the exception of the radio knobs; however, even one projection is a potential hazard. If you order a Cadillac without a radio, the right side of its dash will be as safe as that of any American stock car. It does not deserve a completely clean bill of health in this regard, for—in common with all other U.S. cars—it lacks a crash pad with high shock-absorbing ability. (Those on the Kaiser and Chrysler, though a step *toward* safety, have little function in a serious crash, but offer protection—especially to children—in ordinary quick stops.)

Safety for rear seat passengers is also a part of the new check list. The back of the front seat should be padded but solid; this the Cadillac's is, but its ashtray and cigarette lighter project from the seat back. Its rear doors cannot be opened, from inside or out, when the pushbutton

The test Cadillac took fast corners, like this one, without discomfort for passengers

---

1953 CADILLAC TEST TABLE

PERFORMANCE
ACCELERATION IN SECONDS
(Checked with fifth wheel and electric speedometer)

Standing start ¼ mile	18.4
0-30 mph (0-32, car speedometer reading)	4.0
0-60 mph (0-63, car speedometer reading)	12.8
30-40 mph (DRIVE range)	2.9
40-50 mph (DRIVE range)	3.2
50-60 mph (DRIVE range)	3.3
60-70 mph (DRIVE range)	3.8

TOP SPEED (MPH)
(Clocked speeds over surveyed ¼ mile)

Fastest one-way run	116.9
Slowest one-way run	113.9
Average of four runs	115.4

FUEL CONSUMPTION IN MILES PER GALLON
(Checked with fuel flowmeter, fifth wheel, and electric speedometer)

	D-3	D-4
Steady 30 mph	18.2	24.2
Steady 45 mph	15.6	22.1
Steady 60 mph	13.4	18.6
Steady 75 mph	—	14.5

BRAKE STOPPING DISTANCE
(Checked with electrically actuated detonator)

Stopping distance at:
30 mph	44.9
45 mph	113.9
60 mph	195.9

GENERAL SPECIFICATIONS
ENGINE

Type	Overhead valve V-8
Bore and stroke	$3\frac{13}{16} \times 3\frac{5}{8}$
Stroke/bore ratio	0.95:1
Compression ratio	8.25:1
Displacement	331 cu. in.
Advertised bhp	210 at 4150 rpm
Piston travel @ max. bhp	2507 ft. per min.
Bhp per cu. in.	.63
Maximum torque	330 lbs.-ft. at 2700 rpm
Maximum bmep	150.14 psi

DRIVE SYSTEM

Transmission: Dual Range Hydra-Matic
Ratios: Reverse 4.30, 1st 3.82, 2nd 2.63, 3rd 1.45, 4th 1:1
Rear Axle: Semi-floating hypoid drive
Ratio: 3.07:1 on series 60 & 62; 3.77:1 on series 75

DIMENSIONS

Wheelbase	126 in.
Tread	Front—59 in., rear—63 in.
Wheelbase/tread ratio	2:1
Overall width	80⅛
Overall length	215¹³⁄₁₆
Overall height	62¹¹⁄₁₆
Turning diameter	45 ft.
Turns lock to lock	5
Weight (test car)	4660
Weight/bhp ratio	22.1
Weight distribution	Front—53.2%, rear—46.8%
Weight per sq. in. brake lining	18.0

PRICES
(All prices are factory delivered prices and include retail price at main factory, provisions for federal taxes, and delivery and handling charges.)

Series 62:
Club Coupe	$3571.33
Four-door Sedan	3666.26
Coupe de Ville	3994.57
Convertible Coupe	4143.72
El Dorado Convertible	7750.00

Series 60:
Fleetwood Sedan	4304.88

Series 75:
Eight-passenger Sedan	5407.54
Eight-passenger Imperial Sedan	5620.93

ACCESSORIES

Power steering	$176.98
Tinted glass	45.52
Radio (Signal seeking, pre-selector)	131.92
Radio (Signal seeking, pre-selector, remote control)	214.45
Autronic Eye	53.36
Heater	119.00
Wire wheels (chrome)	325.00
White wall tires (5)	47.77
Air conditioning	619.55

SAFETY CHECK

	YES	NO
DRIVER SAFETY:		
1. Blind spot at left windshield post at a minimum?		X
2. Blind spot at rear vision mirror at a minimum?	X	
3. Vision to right rear satisfactory?	X	
4. Windshield free from objectionable reflections at night?	X	
5. Dash free from annoying reflections?		X
6. Left side of dash free of low projections?		X
7. Cigarette lighter, ash tray, and glove compartment convenient for driver?		X
DRIVER AND PASSENGER:		
8. Front seat apparently locked securely at all adjustment points?	X	
9. Metal strip eliminated between front quarter window and main door window?		X
FRONT PASSENGER:		
10. Mirror free of sharp corners?	X	
11. Right side of dash free of projections?		X
12. Adequate shock-absorbing crash pad?		X
REAR SEAT PASSENGERS		
13. Back of front seat free of sharp edges and projections?		X
14. Rear interior door handles inoperative when locked?	X	
15 Adequate partition to keep trunk contents out of passenger compartment on impact?		X

(MOTOR TREND constantly improves its test procedures. Because of this, we are dropping percentage ratings on the Safety Check Chart to avoid seemingly inaccurate comparisons between cars from month to month.)

OPERATING COST PER MILE ANALYSIS
(In this portion of the test table, MOTOR TREND includes those items that can be figured with reasonable accuracy on a comparative basis. The costs given here are not intended as an absolute guide to the cost of operating a particular make of car, or a particular car within that make. Depreciation is not included.)

1. Cost of gasoline	$149.85
2. Cost of insurance	146.60
3. Maintenance	
a. Wheel alignment	6.00
b. ½ brake reline	13.50
c. Major tune-up (one)	16.50
d. Automatic transmission (adjust, change lubricant)	16.00
First year of operation per mile	3.5¢

MAINTENANCE AND REPAIR COST ANALYSIS
(These are prices for parts and labor required in various repairs and replacements. Your car may require all of them in a short time, or it may require none. However, a comparison of prices for these sample operations in various makes is often of pertinent interest to prospective owners.)

Part	Cost	Labor
1. Distributor	$19.03	$ 2.10
2. Battery	25.80	1.75
3. Fuel pump	17.50	1.75
4. Fan belt	3.34	1.05
5. Valve grind	9.72	33.25
6. One front fender	60.17	12.25
7. Two tires	61.72	
8. One bumper	53.49	1.40
TOTALS	$250.77	$53.55

CADILLAC—America's Favorite Luxury Car

locks are down, which should prevent children from inadvertently opening them.

In sudden stops, momentum can hurl heavy objects from a car's trunk through the rear seat back if it is not securely braced. In the Cad, there are brackets.

MOTOR TREND will continue to include in its analyses all items that it considers of relative importance and that could easily be incorporated into all cars, regardless of whether only one car—or, as in the case of an adequate crash pad, none—is satisfactorily equipped.

A Test Drive

Guiding the Cadillac is an almost effortless undertaking when it is equipped with power steering. The wheel position is a high one, in typical GM fashion, and the ratio is high too (25.47:1), requiring five turns from lock to lock. Last year, MOTOR TREND mentioned that the hydraulic booster might cut in too suddenly, causing the driver to overshoot his mark. On further familiarity with the various systems, such a possibility seems unlikely. At any rate, we were utterly at ease in the Cadillac. We did note a small amount of play in the wheel. Many makers claim that their variety of power steering gives a true feel of the road, but seldom has the testing staff noted so little loss of "road sense" as on this car. There is little sensation that the system is a hydraulically assisted one. Rather, it suggests exceptionally easy conventional steering.

Non-slip plastic grips on the wheel are located at the "8:20" position. One driver of average height found that the armrest struck his elbow at this position. In any event, many drivers prefer a "10:20" or even "10:10" position, and grips above the crossbar as well as below it would give them more freedom.

Unlike last year's test car, this one was whipped aside (though not at all badly) by soft shoulders on the highway. Streetcar tracks gave it some trouble, and so did ruts. Very little steering vibration was noted. At high speeds on straight roads, the car held its direction well, requiring no correction.

Parking, which requires so little physical exertion, would be simpler if the fenders were visible. Because of the high hood, the right front one is hidden, and even the right rear tail fin, which could be a useful guide, cannot be seen from the driver's seat. Aside from this, vision is excellent in all directions. Directly ahead of him, the driver has a view of the road close to the car.

Hydra-Matic transmission is standard. Smoothness has increased to the point where this more efficient drive can now be compared (at least, as it operates on the Cadillac) with the torque converters. Unless one is watching for the shift points, they frequently pass unnoticed.

Brake lining area is up from 241.5 to 258.5 square inches; stopping distances showed a slight improvement. Pedal pressure, though not unduly high, is noticeably greater than on the Chevrolet, for example. Cadillac is the only car in its field on which power brakes are not available. Left-foot operation of the brake pedal is rather difficult, the pedal being close to the throttle and a little small.

Riding comfort is fine. Some vibration is transmitted to the body on washboard roads. Sidesway does not disturb the passengers. After a very bad dip taken fast, we noticed some "walking" (the wheels left the road for brief intervals). Aside from this, there were no complaints.

More Performance, More Fuel Economy

Acceleration and top speed, of course, are remarkable, topping the 1952 figures by varying margins. Highest top speed recorded was 116.9 mph, about 1.5 mph faster than last year, but the average of four runs was 115.4 or nearly six mph faster.

Credit for the increase is divided. Horsepower is up 10 per cent. Last year's optional rear axle ratio of 3.07 (3.36 was then standard) is now regular equipment, and there is a new 12-volt electric system.

In the engine itself, a new combustion chamber has increased the compression ratio to 8.25:1. Flame travel is shortened and turbulence is increased. Longer aluminum alloy pistons are slipper type, permitting them to nest between crankshaft counterweights. Valves now open wider. The 1952 dual exhaust system continues in use.

Already an economical car to drive, this large V-8 shows increased gasoline mileage in nearly every department. Most startling were comparisons with the '52 model in fourth gear (D-4 range). These yielded increases of 7.2 and 4.4 mpg at 30 and 45 mph, respectively. Engine changes (see above) are responsible. Improvement here, too, must be credited to the higher rear axle ratio and, in lesser degree, to the 12-volt system. Mobilgas Special fuel was used, the car, of course, requiring premium gasoline.

Some Trifles—Pro and Con

In small items of finish and detail, a mixed impression is presented. A rain seal at the forward outside edge of the doors prevents unexpected showers when leaving the car in the wet. Metal pads on lower surfaces throughout the car will effectively halt much evidence of wear. Door jambs, though they compare favorably with those of most other cars, are not finished with the care one expects to find. Variations in the fit of door panels are clearly visible. The new wheel discs fit the valve stems too closely for convenient tire checks.

For neatness under the hood, the fiber blanket is trimly bound in plastic, making it easy to keep clean. Considering the large number of standard and optional engine accessories that have to share the compartment, accessibility is good except for the power steering gearbox, which is under the left-hand exhaust manifold and the heater duct, as it was last year.

Accessories

As far as publicity goes, GM's leading accessory this year is unquestionably its air conditioner. This is, of course, made by Frigidaire, and on the Cadillac it costs a little over $600. Operation is simple for the driver. For particularly hot climates, cool air flows from continuous ducts above the doors; for temperate zones, it comes from the parcel shelf behind the rear seat and above the evaporator itself. The evaporator and blowers take up surprisingly little space in the trunk. Separate controls are provided for the two sides of the car, so that the sunny side can be cooled more than the other. Since the air-conditioner operates with the windows closed, freedom from wind noise, with its consequent lessening of fatigue, is a pleasant feature. Wind noise is of average intensity in the Cadillac with windows open.

The "Autronic Eye" on our test car appeared identical with the one on the Pontiac. (MOTOR TREND is planning an accessory trial for the photo-electric unit.)

Undercoating and an oil filter still are extra on this car, costing, respectively, $45 and $11. The MT Research staff feels that both these items should be standard equipment on this luxury car.

Summary

The Cadillac could be better, like any other car we ever heard of. It has few truly unusual features; compared to the American classics of yesterday, it isn't even very big. But it will give you comfort and luxury with its thickly padded seats, high-grade materials from floor to ceiling, and room for everyone. You can sell it for a high percentage of what you paid for it.

It is very easy to handle, economical to run and a top-notch performer. No doubt this combination, along with reputation, will sell many '53 Cadillacs.

—*Walt Woron and Pete Molson*

"This little gem comes complete with radio."

Cadillac's El Camino

THIS is a two-passenger hardtop coupe, bearing a Spanish name which means "the highway," and features what its designers term "aircraft styling and "supersonic" tail fins on the rear fenders. The car has a 115-inch wheelbase and the Cadillac V-8 engine is similar to the 1954 production type which has a power output of 230. Overall length of the body is 200.6 inches, while height is 51.5 inches. Highly streamlined, the silver-grey El Camino has a brushed aluminum roof top coated with clear lacquer, tinted glass panoramic windshield, twin tail lights with side slots for a warning effect, and a keel below the tail lamps for extra protection when backing. The tail lights are mounted in cylinders of bumper material. Below the trunk is a spare tire compartment with a concealed, hinged door. Horizontal flutes sweep along the sides to provide both fresh air intake, by means of a compressor, and a hot air exhaust from the engine compartment. Four hooded headlights have been incorporated into the front end—an outer pair for normal city driving and an inner pair for long range, pencil-beam use. The latter set are put out of action automatically by an Autronic eye when in traffic. Below the headlights are a gull-type front bumper, sharp and slim, with two "bombs" projecting forward. On the hood is a recessed V crest, flush with the surface. Inside, the car has a cluster of instruments around the steering wheel. Between the two leather-covered seats is a tunnel housing the Hydra-Matic gearshift selector lever. This lever is of the "aircraft stick" type with a locking button on top that is pressed when the lever is to be moved into reverse position. Behind the gear lever is a radio and vanity compartment. Heater and air conditioning controls are forward of the gear lever.

Cadillac's Park Avenue

WHAT Cadillac stylists have in mind in the four-door sedan field is pointed up in the Park Avenue model. Constructed of fiberglass, design is more restrained than the sport models—yet it is undeniably futuristic. Exterior is dark blue trimmed with bright chrome and topped with a hand-brushed aluminum roof.

Cadillac's La Espada

A FIBERGLASS experimental convertible finished in Apollo gold and trimmed with chrome and aluminum is the La Espada. High luster black leather and brushed aluminum is the interior theme. Wheelbase is 115 inches, with overall length running to 200.6. Engine, of course, is the 1954 Cadillac V-8 of 230 hp.

Camino

Espada

Park Avenue

By Jim Lodge
AN MT RESEARCH ROAD TEST REPORT

Advertising copywriters extoll the virtues of a comfortable, smooth ride so often that we hesitate to add our bit. But one car that has these qualities in full measure is . . .

'54 Cadillac

THE NEXT BEST THING to driving a new Cadillac is to ride in one—which is what we did when we first received the test car from the division's Los Angeles zone office. You're impressed immediately by the car's extreme silence; the next characteristic may not even occur to you, because of the inborn smoothness of the car—it's the unusual lack of body movement, be it sidesway or up-and-down motion, as you roll along.

The almost hi-fi output of the rear seat speaker might have you completely relaxed with soothing music, slouched down in the seat with your feet stretched out in front of you (there's unlimited legroom in the rear compartment); but you really don't have to slump unless you *are* relaxing, for headroom is outstandingly plentiful. The seats are wonderfully comfortable, and their five-and-a-half-foot width gives your passengers plenty of room to move about.

That's the passenger's point of view; the driver's boils down to this: Driving-ease accessories make it physically easy to drive, but they don't make it any shorter or narrower when you want to park it.

Maybe you'll say, "If that's road testing, someone's got it pretty easy!" That *is* road testing (and it *is* pretty easy), but it's only

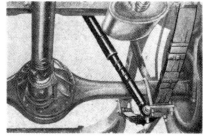
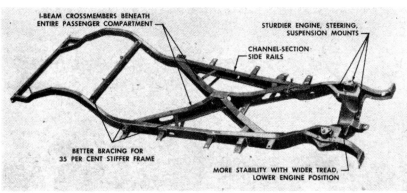

A quiet, comfortable, and controlled ride, keynote of '54 Cadillac design, is the result of blending together a redesigned frame and new shock absorbers with strategically placed soundproofing (shown in phantom photo at top left). "Living room" legroom combines with generous headroom and comfortable seats to provide a restful ride for passengers

TEST CAR AT A GLANCE

(In acceleration and fuel economy, the car is rated against the average of '53 cars in its own class. All other items are rated against the average of all '53 cars)

REAR WHEEL HORSEPOWER

(Determined on Clayton chassis dynamometer; all tests are made under full load, which is similar to climbing a hill at full throttle. Observed hp figures not corrected to standard atmospheric conditions)

48 road hp @ 1200 rpm and 32 mph
83 road hp @ 2000 rpm and 54 mph
97 road hp @ 2500 rpm and 68 mph
122 road hp (max) at 2850 rpm and 77 mph

SPEEDOMETER ERROR

Car speedometer read 30 @ true 30 mph, 45 @ true 45 mph, 60 @ true 60 mph

ACCELERATION

(In seconds; checked with fifth wheel and electric speedometer)
Standing start 1/4-mile (reached 77 mph) 18.4, 0-30, 3.7; 0-60, 11.3; 10-30 (D4), 3.4; 30-50 (D4), 5.7; 50-80 (D4), 12.7

RATING: EXCELLENT

TOP SPEED

(In miles per hour; clocked over surveyed 1/2-mile)
Fastest run 116.2, Slowest 110.2, Average 113.0

FUEL CONSUMPTION

(In miles per gallon; checked with fuel flowmeter, fifth wheel, and electric speedometer. Mobilgas Special used)
22.3 @ steady 30 mph, 22.0 @ steady 45, 18.9 @ steady 60, 16.2 @ steady 75, 13.9 in simulated traffic over measured course, 16.9 overall tank average for 2058 miles

RATING: EXCELLENT

STOPPING DISTANCE

(To the nearest foot; checked with electrically actuated detonator)
46 @ 30 mph, 98 @ 45 mph, 171 @ 60 mph

RATING: EXCELLENT

---

part of it. We just wanted to start off with the things that make a Cadillac a much-desired car—roominess, a quiet, smooth ride, and comfort.

The following day, however, in 100° desert heat, the aloof machine brought its tail fins down out of the blue, dropped all formality, and became "the Caddy," or more familiarly, the "Cad"; these are the terms that pop up when conversation shifts (automatically, of course) to performance.

The '54 Cadillac has even more horsepower (upped from 210 to 230) this year; the increase comes largely from a general cleanup in intake manifolding, and slightly increased valve lift, with a resulting change in valve timing. The '54 test car delivered 122 horsepower (at 2850 rpm) at the rear wheels; the '53 test car (210 bhp) produced 120 at 2800 rpm.

But the overhead-valve V8 carries no increase in displacement, torque, or compression ratio, some of the determining factors in acceleration. You may have noticed our typo in the April '54 Buyers Guide, where Cadillac's power/weight ratio should have read 19.0 instead of 14.0; the '53 Cadillac's ratio was only slightly higher at 20.2. The '54 test car, 160 pounds heavier than the '53, had the same rear axle ratio (3.07 to 1—one of the highest-geared differentials in the industry); the cars had similar power-robbing equipment. Adding up all these factors, a pre-test estimate indicated a stalemate between the two cars.

And it wasn't too far off. Compare results in these standings, with the '54 faster in all acceleration runs: Quarter-mile times, one-tenth of a second average difference; 0-60, 1.5 seconds difference; the two cars were separated by only four-tenths of a second at 50-80 mph. Top speed runs show the '53 test car out in front by a slight margin. The '54 Cadillac is the first test car to turn less than 12 seconds in *all* 0-60 runs; one run, timed at 10.9 seconds, is another "first" among all stock cars MT has tested.

Given "proving ground" treatment, the "62" sedan set a tough pace for others in its class. Being noted for a soft ride, the heavy (MT's test car weighed 4820 pounds) Cadillac is expected by many to act not unlike a tugboat in a Gold Cup regatta. Its roadability rates good, although it doesn't instill utmost confidence in the driver (largely because of the uncertain sensation of power steering, partly because of general bulkiness); but for all its gentlemanly behavior under normal conditions, it takes dips, bumps, sand traps, or what-have-you with little discomfort to its passengers and with little loss of its own dignity. In severe dips, the test car came close to scraping its jutting bumpers, but recovery was rapid. The '54 Cadillac's redesigned frame includes a wider front track, giving less mushiness to the front end and an edge over the '53 model in stability. There's no wind-wander, even at maximum speeds. It's not easy to break loose the rear wheels, even considering the '54's lower center of gravity (which does away with much of the heel-over common to past Cadillacs without making the car hard-riding or too prone to broadsliding); large, and very quiet, 8.20 x 15 tires (standard black tires are 8.00 x 15) bite into the road for added traction, and offer surprisingly little resistance to streetcar tracks—power steering takes all the fight out of the low-pressure tires' desire to stick in the grooves.

Choppy road surfaces were soaked up efficiently in the Cadillac's suspension, although some road noise broke through the car's "sound barrier." At speeds above 50, wind noise was quite high. There was some wheel bounce, but no steering wheel shock, the latter due largely to the Cadillac's unusually well-braced steering wheel column.

How is handling under these conditions? With its improved power steering system, the Cadillac is hard to criticize on a basis of actual handling ease. The easy-turning steering system continues

Continued on next page

MT Research feels the neat-appearing but hard-to-read instrument panel deserves the attention paid to other details

Tail fins are a little higher, longer this year, but unmistakably Cadillac. Exhaust ports have jet-like appearance

'54 Cadillac Road Test

its eerie lack of the "feel" that's so important to control at high speeds, but the '54 model has been given a new steering ratio of 21.5 to 1; our test car required only 3¾ turns lock to lock at the steering wheel. (The '53 had an overall ratio of 25.4 to 1 and called for five turns lock to lock.) This quick-turn-and-power-steering combination *can* get the unwary driver into trouble in an emergency maneuver at high speed, but it's a real boon to driving ease under normal conditions.

In keeping with the trend that started with the very first '54 test car, braking ability is improved over the Cadillac's '53 counterpart. Off by a foot from the 30-mph mark set by the '53, the new car came back to provide a 16-foot margin of safety over the '53 at 45 mph, and a 25-foot improvement at 60. Cadillac's new brake lining, grooved to dissipate heat more quickly, is said to provide greater lining life as well as give surer stopping power; although we experienced severe fade under extreme usage, in normal driving the brakes felt good and never approached fade conditions, indicating that when properly conditioned, or broken-in, the new brakes will probably give good service.

An interesting sidelight is the Cadillac's gas pedal-brake pedal setup: The brake pedal is fairly high, higher than most booster systems; this allows good leverage for positive application, even with the engine shut off. The accelerator pedal, too, is high off the floorboard; this gives an overall effect of having a low-set brake pedal requiring only a simple pivot on the heel from the gas pedal to the brake.

Economy remains at the high par set by last year's test Cadillac. Turning in slightly lower averages at 30 and 45 mph, the '54 test car bettered the '53's record at higher speeds by an equally slight margin. The '54 sedan turned in a remarkable "tank" average of 16.9 mpg. (A large part of this high average is the result of many miles of driving at steady highway speeds; traffic conditions normally comprise the bulk of the mileage put on our test cars.)

Instrumentation is not up to Cadillac's reputation. The speedometer position is good, and the unit is readable in the daytime; at night, however, it's impossible to make out the graduations on the bright metal dial. (In its favor is the fact that it was the most accurate speedometer checked to date.) Fuel and temperature gauges are in an unhandy position, low and toward the outer edges of the panel, where they're usually hidden by the steering wheel crossbar; their dials are small and somewhat hard to read. Warning lights substitute for oil pressure and ammeter gauges.

The Cadillac's Hydra-Matic quadrant is on the face of the instrument panel, where it's operated through mechanical linkage from the shift lever. Highlights prance about the face of the panel during the day, but there are no reflections in the windshield either day or night because of a hood over the instruments and a plastic covering across the top of the dashboard (it's not a "crash pad," simply an anti-glare measure).

Everywhere we took our test car, people scrutinized the interior and body; many of the onlookers were quick to point out flaws common to any mass-produced automobile—an uneven gap at a body panel, or a thread out of place in the upholstery—things that would normally go unnoticed in a less-expensive car. Our own inspection disclosed few other faults. Our displeasures? The quality of the plastic dashboard covering was below the standard of other appointments; ditto the glove compartment, in both size and finish; door checks were unable to hold the doors open when the car was on a slight grade. Hard-to-reach glove compartment and ash tray, hard-to-read gauges (including the clock), and hard-to-keep-clean upholstery detract from the car's "livability."

Brightwork is of good quality, the interior appears to be assembled with care, the upholstery and floor-covering befit the car's price, and quality of workmanship throughout the interior rates high in MT's books.

Throughout the test, drivers and passengers were annoyed by gasoline fumes filling the car when the driver's windwing was opened. (A Cadillac representative tells us this is common only to some early '54s.) It's explained this way: An improperly sealed gas filler neck allows fumes to escape; with a front wing open, the vacuum created within the car draws the fumes forward from the gas tank area. The result? An unbearable, dangerous condition—but fortunately one that will be rectified immediately and without cost by your dealer. (Later model Cadillac filler necks have been resealed to prevent fume seepage.)

Bodywork is good; uneven gaps around doors and average-sized (for its class) trunk were few. File marks, a bugaboo to many of the cars tested this year, were not overly rough; metal trim was secure, and chromed brightwork seemed well above the quality common to post-Korea materials seen on some '53 and early '54 cars. There were no ripples in side panels or the top of the car, and paint was smooth and free of orange peel.

The big V8 rates about average in accessibility for its size. Valves, of course, are readily serviceable; getting at the plugs, distributor, generator, fuel pump, and other components offers problems that are typical of modern ohv V8s. Removing the huge oil-bath air cleaner is a must for easy engine servicing.

The engine ran smoothly throughout the test; it refused to heat up even under load in desert heat. We half-expected the high-compression (8:25 to 1) V8 to be octane-critical, but it didn't "ping" under any test condition. Accessories are easy to get at, but some, like the windshield washer, are becoming more and more complicated. On most cars nothing more than a solvent bottle and a vacuum line, the unit as installed on the Cadillac approached Rube Goldberg proportions with its solenoid, wires, and hoses. (It all starts with the featherlight touch of a button on the dashboard; you have cleaner on the windshield and the wipers automatically hard at work for about a dozen sweeps—then everything stops. But it's almost too much fun to complain about.)

MT can't rate the '54 Cadillac test sedan a true all-purpose family car; children with dusty shoes would feel as ill-at-ease in the hushed interior of a Series 62 sedan as they would in the hyper-spaciousness of a Cadillac limousine—in short, you just don't wipe the family pet's pawmarks off the seat-backs of the Cadillac 62.

But for sheer comfort, and high-quality surroundings with acceleration and cruising speeds you'll never fully utilize, the Cadillac earns its reputation as our top-selling high-price-class car.

—*Jim Lodge*

PRICES

(Including retail price at main factory, federal tax, and delivery and handling charges, but not freight) SERIES 62, hardtop $3838, four-door sedan $3933, coupe de ville $4261, convert'ble $4404, Eldorado $5738. SERIES 60, four-door sedan $4683.

ACCESSORIES, automatic transmission standard, power steering standard, power brakes $48, radio $120, heater $129, air-conditioning $620, power-operated windows and seat $124, chrome wire wheels $325, whitewalls (exchange) $49.

GENERAL SPECIFICATIONS

ENGINE: Ohv V8. Bore 3$\frac{13}{16}$ in. Stroke 3⅝ in. Stroke/bore ratio 0.951. Compression ratio 8.25 to 1. Displacement 331 cu. in. Advertised bhp 230 @ 4400 rpm. Bhp per cu. in. 0.69. Piston travel @ max. bhp 2653 ft. per min. Max bmep 150.3 psi.
DRIVE SYSTEM: STANDARD transmission is Dual-Range Hydra-Matic, four-speed planetary gearbox with fluid coupling. Ratios: 1st 3.82, 2nd 2.63, 3rd 1.45, 4th 1.0, reverse 4.03.
REAR AXLE RATIOS: 3.07 standard, 3.36 optional (standard with air-conditioning).
DIMENSIONS: Wheelbase 129 in. Tread 60 in. front, 63 in. rear. Wheelbase/tread ratio 2.09. Overall width 80 in. Overall length 216½ in. Overall height 62 in. Turning diameter 45 ft. Turns lock to lock 4. Test car weight 4820 lbs. Test car weight/bhp ratio 20.9 to 1. Weight distribution 51% front, 49% rear. Tire size 8.00 x 15.

ESTIMATED COST PER MILE

(A complete explanation of our method for figuring estimated cost per mile is given in this issue on page 26)

OPERATING COSTS:
Gasoline	$178.00
Oil	13.95
Lubrication	8.25
Oil filter	1.80
Wheel alignment and ba ancing	12.00
Brake relining and adjustment	20.60
Major tune-up	8.80
WHAT IT COSTS PER MILE TO RUN	2.4¢

OWNERSHIP COSTS:
Sales tax and license fees	$107.20
Insurance	172.40
Estimated depreciation	1.00
WHAT IT COSTS PER MILE TO OWN	2.8¢
TOTAL PER MILE COSTS IF YOU PAY CASH	5.2¢
Finance charges	159.00
TOTAL PER MILE COSTS IF YOU FINANCE	6.8¢

PARTS AND LABOR COST

(These are prices for parts and labor required in various repairs and replacements. Your car may require all of them in a short time, or it may require none. However, a comparison of prices for these sample operations in various makes is often of interest to prospective owners. First price is for parts, second for labor.)
Distributor $27.85, $2.40; battery $29.95; fuel pump $17.50, $2.20; valve grind $2.16, $38.00; one front fender $73.50, $24.40; bumper $65.50, $2.40; two tires $82.68. Total parts $299.14, labor $69.40.

Murphy's Law
1953 Cadillac Coupe De Ville

Words: Peter 'PC' Callen Photos: Allan Walton

The eleventh century AD may seem like an odd point for a Cadillac story to commence but PC discovers that the Cadillac family's coat of arms, still in use today, really does have its origins that far back in time. He also finds it somewhat ironic that the man who founded the city of Detroit, hub of American auto-mania, was a 'Cadillac' himself – none other than Royal French Army officer Antoine de la Mothe Cadillac

Love them or loathe them, depending on whether you find them pleasurably stylish or garishly ostentatious, there can be no denying the impact Cadillacs have had on the automobile world during the final century of the previous millennium.

The goal of company founder William H Murphy (one of Henry Ford's initial backers) was to provide a motor car with outstanding qualities to the more 'well-heeled' of the world but a vehicle not outrageously priced, either. GM simply labelled the Cadillac 'the most moderately priced, strictly high-grade motor car in the world'.

The craftsman's creed

To make such a statement you must have something fairly substantial in the back shed and Murphy certainly had that in one Henry Leland, a highly skilled gunsmith-cum-toolmaker, to provide the engines for the first Cadillacs. These rolled into the light of day in October of 1902, and made a splash at the New York Automobile Show the following January.

Simple and robust, they carried with them the famous Cadillac motto, 'craftsmanship a creed, accuracy a law' – an ethos that continues to this day.

Not so long ago I was privy to a viewing of an amazing publication (from the pen of a fellow Kiwi) detailing the history of Cadillac and amongst the paraphernalia was a holographic 'cutaway' picture of the latest model. On one angle you could see the car in all its painted glory and on another angle you could see the inner workings in startling detail. One interesting sales point was the claim that the wipers would stay in contact with the windscreen at speeds of up to 100 miles per hour! If things like that will not induce you to buy, they will certainly intrigue you.

Correct proportions

Richard Glasson's 1953 Cadillac Coupe De Ville does have tail fins, but as this vehicle was produced early in the decade of 'tail-fin-mania' they aren't up to the giddy heights of the 1959 edition. Imported in 1984, the vehicle was in need of a restoration but was in solid, rust-free condition.

Richard has since replaced all the glass, which gives a clear view and adds that 'new car sparkle'. If I find the '53 a little easier on the eye than some models, that isn't to take anything away from the others. To me the proportions for '53 seem 'just right' and this car doesn't look as if it is too long to have only two doors.

Naturally, there is an abundance of chrome but it sits well with the Cadillac Bordeaux Metallic paint job. Kerry Brocas of Classic Car Painters in Pukekohe, applied this lovely coat, contrasted tastefully by the metallic silver roof.

The vehicle, sold new in California, was fitted with every power-assisted option offered for the 1953 Cadillac Coupe De Villes but most are not, as one might imagine, operated by *electric* motors. Most are hydraulically activated from a central pump. The power seats, windows and aerial are all hydraulically operated – the original plumber's nightmare, no doubt.

More conventional are the fog lights, 'Signal Seeker' radio, air conditioning and power steering.

A dash-mounted automatic headlight dipper labelled the 'Autronic Eye' is a clever device but, wouldn't you know it, this piece of equipment doesn't comply with the New Zealand Warrant of Fitness regulations and Richard has had to augment the system with a foot-operated dip switch.

Smooth and aromatic

The sumptuous, aromatic leather interior is so comfortable it's hard to believe the vehicle is nearly half a century old. The engine runs as smoothly as anything from this side of 1990 and propels the heavyweight quite capably. Power was up for '53 over the '52 models, due in no small part to the increase in the compression ratio from 7.50:1 to 8.25:1. In fact there was so much listed as "New" in the 1953 sales brochure one could be excused for thinking that Cadillac had reinvented the wheel! New high lift camshaft, new longer pistons, new high lift valve mechanism, new combustion smoothness,

Coup De Ville's interior features a vertitable battery of power operated equipment

V8 is a 'smooth-runner' and well up to the task of powering Cadillac's heavyweight cruiser

new higher compression ratio, new economy and the best of all was the new twelve-volt electrical system!

There were many more 'new' items but I think by now you get the picture. The Cadillac sales machine was never backward in coming forward but many feel that a large percentage of the hype is justified. Sales figures speak for themselves.

Transmission is the four-speed 'Hydramatic' and this was performing poorly when Richard, who described himself thoughtfully as a 'trader', bought the car in 1992. The actual purchase of the vehicle is a story in itself but to put it briefly, the deal was done in the early hours in Tauranga shortly after the then owner had offered the car for sale at the Pukekohe swap meet of that year. Added to the uncooperative transmission, there was some panel damage in one rear quarter (thanks to a wayward glass truck) that Richard has since had professionally repaired. It's a lovely job and a credit to the craftsman responsible.

Worshipping from afar

Riding on the more modern radial tyres with wide whitewalls (rotated by those beautiful Cadillac wire wheels) the coupe drives superbly. There is some 'wandering' of the steering wheel, characteristic of American vehicles of this era, and the large diameter of the steering wheel itself accen-

The Cadillac really shows of its subdued style in side profile – the fins are there but haven't yet assumed their famous '59 proportions

tuates this. However, after a short period – and a small adjustment in driving style – any initial apprehension is easily overcome. Top speed is listed in the specifications

Cadillac's Earldom

Going back to 1916 we find that Cadillac became a division of William Durant's General Motors Corporation and Henry Leland, with his son Wilfred, kept up the high standards that were by now the talk of the automotive world. Standards high enough to have received the Dewar Trophy not once, but twice by 1912! That's an astonishing achievement and, to my knowledge, one unequalled by any manufacturer.

Then, in September of 1914, the V8 was announced and every year since 1914 Cadillac has produced V8 engines, with or without global conflict. The Cadillac V8s soon became renowned for their power and found their way into all manner of race cars in later years.

In 1927, the decision was made to hire a rather tall and reportedly intimidating chap named Harley Earl, who, in the fifties especially, was to stand automobile styling on its head. Earl, a snappy dresser, was placed in charge of GM's 'Art and Colour Section'. This was a new term in the still relatively young automobile world but after a decade Earl changed the tag to the 'Style Section'. Within this unit he would produce rough sketches and line drawings, then move into the realm of the clay model. These would then be presented to management as realistic, full-size and three-dimensional 'approval test-beds'. The section was so successful that staff grew from an initial 50 to an incredible 1,100 with Earl at the helm.

It was plain to see that 'Mister Earl', as was his preferred title, was pushing the 'longer and lower' barrow at every opportunity. Styling concepts came thick and fast and in 1950 Earl produced a concept car, carrying the monika 'LeSabre'. (The name was adopted by Buick at the end of that same decade). One strange device fitted to the concept LeSabre was the amazing rain detector that, when contacted by errant precipitation, actuated the convertible roof! It was things like that, plus the jet fighter-inspired styling, that made it a hit on the automobile show circuits.

The tail fin was, by 1950, already an Earl trademark. The first inkling of such an unnecessary, but oh-so-attractive, addition to the sheet metal of a Cadillac appeared on the 1948 model. Not very tall, it was there nonetheless and was to grow and grow, and grow, as the fifties produced some of the most outrageous vehicles ever to grace the planet.

More than half a century has passed since the public first caught sight of tail fins, and they still manage to turn heads.

When he was happy with the basic design, Earl would then set about emblazoning the mock-ups with bright metal trimmings. Adjustments to belt lines and the like could be minuscule yet vital and the big man wouldn't rest until things were 'just so'. One report states that after a communication breakdown between stylists, two bright metal proposals ended up on the one clay model. When Earl caught sight of it he congratulated his staff with the cry "Fellas, you got it!" Obviously, to Earl anyway, if one piece of bright trim was good then two must be better.

Yes, with all of this and two-tone paint Harley Earl was definitely onto something and by the time he retired in 1959 he had either directly or indirectly influenced the design of no less than 60-million automobiles. Today his peers recall the Earl era and the tail fin craze with a hint of awe. On an old videotape I viewed, one man made the statement that "At the time, it was the right thing to do". With benefit of hindsight, who could argue?

Harley Earl died in April of 1969 but he left behind many true styling legacies, one being this 1953 Cadillac Coupe De Ville.

Specifications

Engine	V8, cast-iron block
Capacity	331 cubic inches
Bore/Stroke	3.81ins X 3.63ins
Max power	210 @ 4100rpm, torque 330ft.lbs @ 2700rpm
Valves	OHV
Compression ratio	8.25:1
Carburettor	1 4V Carter
Transmission	four-speed Hydramatic auto
Final drive	3.07:1
Brakes	drum/drum
Front Suspension	coil spring/independent
Rear Suspension	live axle, semi-elliptic leaf springs
Steering	Worm and sector
Chassis	Channel section side rails, I-section X-member
Wheels/tyres	8.00 x 15
Dimensions:	
Wheelbase	126ins
Length	18ft 6ins
Width	80ins
Track	F 59ins, R 63ins
Performance:	
Max speed	118mph
Economy	N/A
Price	US$4,938 (1953)

as 118mph but I think it would take a brave person to attempt that sort of pace in a car designed more for comfort and looks than for its handling capabilities. It isn't often you have to run a slalom on Van Nuys Boulevard, now is it?

Gliding through the back roads of the tiny hamlet of Drury it wasn't hard to envisage the DeVille Stateside in the mid-fifties. The car could so very easily be the property of an obese landowner, cruising his acreage, or perhaps the fashion accessory of an LA-based, up and coming young movie starlet.

The DeVille is just the vehicle for a backwoods preacher man to have parked behind a tiny church packed with predominantly black worshippers all fanning themselves furiously in a vain attempt to ward off the heat of a Louisiana summer Sunday. In such a scenario it would come as no surprise to hear that the dollar content of the collection plates was poured directly into the fuel filler after the service had ended.

I can see why this is Richard's favourite car, the car he claims he is taking with him when he goes. It is totally reliable and just such a good all-rounder for a large car.

In fact, it doesn't even feel that large. Because of its 'user friendly' disposition, the driving is easy and size is soon forgotten. You just get so wrapped up in the getting there you find yourself wanting to make detours to pass all the places you know your friends will be gathered at; it's compulsory Cadillac etiquette.

This is the kind of car you just love to be seen in and in 2001, ninety-nine years after Murphy chose the Cadillac name for his product, the company still strives to provide that which is touted as 'America's finest'.

Tail-light double as gas-cap

HELLO NORMA

Comparisons between legendary film star Marilyn Monroe and early '50s Cadillac convertibles seem natural somehow - maybe because they both possess the same star quality!

America in 1954. Eisenhower was in the White House and despite communist scares and growing problems in Vietnam, the accent was on glamour. One of the year's highlights was the marriage of film star Marilyn Monroe to New York Yankees baseball hero Joe DiMaggio and the first nationally televised beauty contest, the Miss America pageant, was broadcast.

Staying with the glamour theme, it comes as no surprise to learn that's exactly what Cadillac were using in their advertising campaigns. Luxury, status, high fashion, sex appeal - all these and more could be yours for the price of a brand new Cadillac.

Almost four decades later, it is often difficult for us to fully understand and appreciate exactly what it meant if you were a Cadillac owner back then. Not for nothing was the slogan 'Standard of the World' employed - a Cadillac was still very much a hand-built car (although with annual output hovering around the 100,000 mark this wouldn't last much longer) and a symbol of success on wheels. Being behind the wheel of a Cadillac bestowed the accolade of being somebody who had acheived both fame and fortune. At over 4,400 dollars, a 1954 Cadillac convertible like the one shown here, was over twice the price of a Chevy Bel Air ragtop.

This emphasis on glamour and status meant that Cadillacs were in much demand for wedding cars, indeed the company even promoted this in their adverts offering 'a special car for that memorable day'. It will come as little surprise to learn, therefore, that at least one enterprising couple on this side of the Atlantic has taken the message to heart and are now offering a fleet of mid '50s Cadillacs for hire.

Carl Browse and his wife Marilyn are the people behind Classic Cadillac Wedding Hire of Stanford-le-Hope in Essex (Tel: 0268 552562) and of their impressive line up we chose to concentrate on the 1954 Series 62 convertible known as 'Norma Jean'.

She (well, you could hardly call something as voluptuous as this 'it' now could you?) was found in California by Dream Cars and the Browses believe they are the fourth owners. All the bodywork is original although it has been resprayed in Ivory (the proper Cadillac colour) having first been green then black, and apart from the front bumper being rechromed all the brightwork is original too. Some interior retrimming was required and a new top was added to maintain the prestige image.

The 331 cu.in. (5.42 litre) V8 engine and Hydra-matic transmission are also the ones installed by the factory, but naturally enough given the passage of time, with normal servicing some minor parts replacement is to be expected. As the Caddy is a working vehicle, the engine bay hasn't yet been fully detailed, Carl preferring to remove the engine and do the job properly when such time allows.

For 1954, the actual engine specification wasn't that much changed from previous years, but even so the horsepower output increased from 210 to 230 over the '53 powerplant. Subsequently, with the compression ratio raised from 8.25:1 in 1954, to 9:1 in '55 and 9.75:1 in '56 the ratings got even more impressive - 250 bhp in '55 and 285 bhp in '56. The 1956 engine did, however, also benefit from a larger 4.00 inch diameter bore that increased the capacity to 365 cu.in. (5.98 litre).

Cadillac engines were regarded by hot rodders of the day as top performers and despite weighing in at a hefty 4,500 pounds plus these sedate carriages could still reach 115 mph and go from a standing start to 80 mph in 24 seconds. These days, getting the bride to the church on time doesn't involve any such antics, Carl only using chauffeurs who appreciate the rarity of the vehicles and who drive sympathetically. Not that driving this 38 year old flip-top is a chore as it is equipped with 'power everything'.

Before starting the wedding car business three years ago, 45 year old Carl had a high stress job in banking and finance in the City but he says "This is good fun, and a lovely way to earn a living". Friday, Saturday and Sunday are the busy days and Monday to Thursday is spent working on the cars, keeping them in pristine condition. The choice of Cadillacs from 1954 to '56 for hiring out was deliberate as Carl prefers the more restrained styling of these years, "In our market we are competing against older Rolls Royces and similar cars, and the mid-fifties designs have a 'presidential' feel about them. You can easily imagine Ike riding in the back of the convertible".

Purists will often declare that following on from the classic shape

JEAN

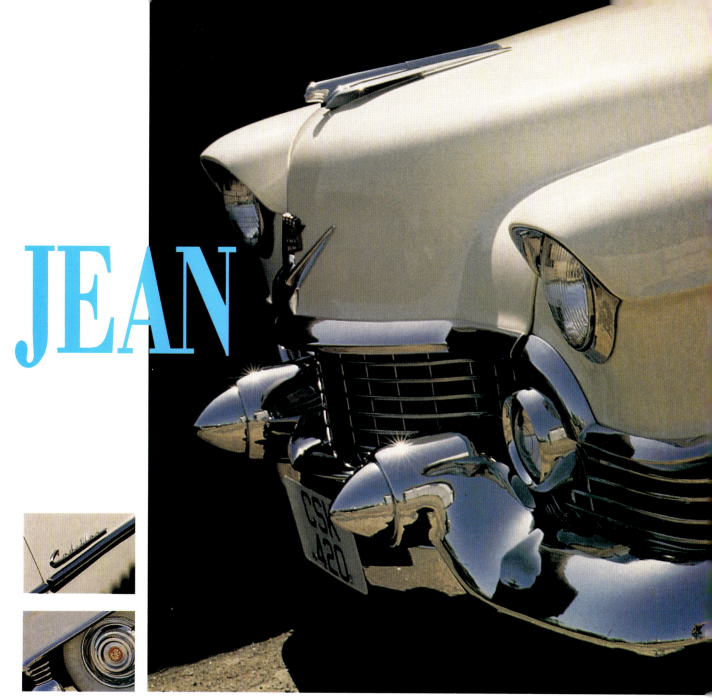

Photography: Garry Stuart

SPECIFICATION
1954 CADILLAC
Series 62 Convertible Coupe

Engine	V8, OHV
Capacity	331 cu.in.
Bore	3.81 inches
Stroke	3.62 inches
Compression ratio	8.25:1
BHP	230 at 4400 rpm
0-80 mph	24 secs
Top speed	115 mph
Trans	Hydra-matic
Wheelbase	129 inches
Overall length	223.4 inches
Weight	4598 lbs
Factory price 1954	$4404
Production total	6,310

HELLO NORMA JEAN

produced in 1948 by the team of Harley Earl, Bill Mitchell, Frank Hershey and Art Ross, Cadillac design gradually went downhill as more chrome and glitter were added each year. While the changes are today self evident and might seem quite drastic when comparing models over the six years to '54, buyers then would probably not have considered them to be out of place.

With the need to make each year's model look different from its predecessor, most manufacturers worked on a three year cycle with the first being a totally new design which was followed by two facelifts. 1954 Cadillacs, while retaining much of the overall look of the earlier cars were actually a new generation that had grown longer, lower, wider and heavier. The Sixty-Two Series wheelbase had increased by three inches when compared to '53 and proportions enlarged elsewhere to keep in line.

Most noticeable across all Cadillac models in '54 was the use of the curved windscreen which had only been seen on the top of the line Eldorado the previous year. This feature was to become a standard fitment throughout the US auto industry and will forever be regarded as one of the essences of Fifties design.

A lover of American cars from way back, Carl finds that while obviously most of the brides and grooms to be share his enthusiasm, sometimes the parents need a bit of persuading. "Once they actually see the cars though, there's usually no problem."

On one occasion, after the ceremony, the happy couple talked about nothing but American cars on the way from the church to the reception and Carl happened to mention that he had to sell a 1973 Cadillac to buy his house and get the business started. The bride said, "You mean like that one next to us?" Carl looked and it was the very car! The groom then suggested that they followed it so that Carl could ask if the owner was interested in selling! When reminded that they were en route to the reception he replied, "Don't worry about that, it doesn't matter if we're a bit late" Apparently the bride was not at all impressed with her new husband's suggestion and the atmosphere grew rather chilly, so much so that Carl wondered if he didn't ought to deliver them straight to the divorce court instead!

The Monroe/DiMaggio match quickly ended in such circumstances but it seems that this 'Norma Jean' will be enduring the rice and confetti for many years to come, and long may she continue to do so.

Tony Beadle

Our thanks to The National Motorboat Museum, Pitsea, Essex for the location

Cadillac 62 SEDAN

by ROBERT JOHNSON

PERFORMANCE
TOP SPEED
- Average of two-way runs............................114.8 mph
- Fastest one-way run...................................117.1 mph

ACCELERATION
- 0-30 mph... 3.6 sec.
- 0-60 mph...11.4 sec.
- Standing ¼ mile..18.5 sec.

FUEL CONSUMPTION
Checked by filling the tank, and then refilling to the same point: 17.4 average mpg for combined city and country driving.

SPEEDOMETER CORRECTIONS
- Indicated 30 mph...29.99 mph actual
- Indicated 45 mph...44.97 mph actual
- Indicated 60 mph...59.85 mph actual

DIMENSIONS
- Wheelbase ....129 inches
- Width ....80 inches
- Length ....216 inches
- Height ....62 inches

PRICES
- Series 62 (car tested) 4-dr. sedan..............$3,932.70
- Series 62 Club Coupe................................. 3,837.77
- Series 62 Coupe de Ville............................. 4,261.01
- Series 62 Convertible.................................. 4,404.31

Prices include factory retail, federal tax, and delivery and handling, but not freight.

THE CADILLAC Motor Car Division of General Motors has retooled for 1954. The new Eldorado special convertible plus 7 body styles comprising the 62, 60, and 75 series—has been extensively re-engineered. And in doing so, primary consideration was given to increased comfort, safety, and ease of handling.

We road tested the Series 62 Sedan. The test car had many extras, including air conditioning, power brakes, and Autronic Eye. This Cadillac had close to 3000 miles on it, for which we were grateful—putting a *brand new* automobile through its paces is not only rough on the engine but results in unjust performance figures.

The sedan was driven extensively both in town and on the highway, taken up and down Los Angeles' famous Fargo Street hill (32 percent grade) and tested on rough and winding mountain roads for maneuverability.

Let's take these locations one at a time, discuss the Cadillac's performance and handling characteristics under the varying conditions offered:

IN TOWN

Hydra-Matic Dual Range is standard. Stop-and-go driving is fun when you *don't* have to select the gears; the Hydra-Matic in the test car was surprisingly quiet and smooth, with a barely noticeable momentum surge characteristic of automatic transmissions. An acceleration graph from zero to 40 mph shows this clearly, with gear "peaks" hardly breaking an

otherwise clean curve. It is impressive on paper—and in the car.

The GM panoramic windshield offers greater visibility, lends an up-to-date, functional look to the '54 models. However, the windshield in the test car had a certain amount of distortion in its curved outer corners, which was distracting.

Power steering is standard equipment. Approximately 3 lbs. of manual pressure on the wheel is the extent of required driver effort; the rest of the job is done for you. This mechanism has been re-engineered too, is now a simpler, more compact unit with a better steering ratio, offering better road "feel" and ease of handling.

Despite the 3 inch longer wheelbase on the '54, the test car parks easily; the power steering is a blessing here, of course, as is the fact that all four fenders are visible from the driver's seat.

ON THE HIGHWAY

Cadillac is proud of their comfortable, quiet, vibrationless ride. They have a right to be. Generous use of insulating materials, including fiberglass mat, in body panels, top, hood, and deck, make the interior virtually soundproof. Engine noise, even at high speeds, is little more than a whisper; a 35 percent stiffer frame for '54 helps to eliminate chassis and body torsion, a major source of eventual annoying rattles.

While the seats in the test car were not as soft as they could be, a ride in the Cadillac on the highway *is* soft, and without an unnerving undulation often associated with soft springing. The ratio of length of the leaf springs fore and aft of the rear axle on all '54 Cadillacs has been changed, minimizing axle "wind-up" and propeller shaft shake.

ON FARGO STREET HILL

This steep pitch is a breath-taker in any automobile! Under no other circumstances are you more aware of the need for extra power and good brakes. It was necessary to shift into low in the sedan but in this gear the Cadillac went up the grade like going home. Bear in mind that the 230 hp V8 engine was handicapped by approximately 400 lbs. of optional equipment.

Coming down the hill, we deliberately tromped on the brakes; the extra-light rear end (in this attitude) showed no tendency to move over, and the brakes were as effective here as on the flat. Cadillac has, incidentally, a design change in the '54 brake lining; a new lining material increases brake life and a groove cut through the center of the primary lining *(see "car Brakes Rate a Break!," page 30)* makes for more even heat distribution, elimination of hot areas. Cadillac's power brakes (optional equipment) are noteworthy, compared to other types, due to their smooth action. A vicious characteristic with some is their *over*-light touch, requiring too soft, delicately applied pressure to avoid jarring stops. The Cadillac power brake is smooth, has the solid feel of a standard brake—without giving the driver's leg muscles a workout.

ON MOUNTAIN ROADS

A lower center of gravity (the engine has been dropped 2 inches), plus improved suspension, gives the Cadillac better all-around roadability. The compromise between a truly comfortable ride and great handling qualities is always a difficult one, but without sacrificing the comfort associated with Cadillac, their engineers have done much to improve roadability. We drove the sedan hard and fast around corners—the body *does* heel over, but not abruptly or severely; the car tracks well—an under-steer tendency is not alarming.

RESALE VALUE

The primary purpose behind automobile purchase is transportation suitable for the individual need; however, the smart buyer considers later resale value. Without a doubt Cadillac resale value is excellent, particularly with the 1948 and later models (since introduction of the tail light "fins"). This fact is an indirect compliment to the Cadillac Motor Car Division; Cadillac prestige is a symbol of fine styling and engineering. •

Spotlight on Detroit

FULL DETAILS: '55 CADILLAC

THE PARADE OF NEW CARS

YOUR 1955 CADILLAC should be of even higher quality than those of the past because even though more cars will be built, the time required to build each car will be greater. This, of course, means the addition of another workshift over on Clark St. The standard models have actually been restyled rather extensively, even though it is not too noticeable in pictures or on the road. Side chrome has been changed so that it now forms a true character line (accentuates a line actually formed in the sheet metal), and the Florentine-curve rear window treatment of last year's coupes has been extended to include sedans. Grilles have a wider mesh, and the parking lights have been squared off and moved outward. Trunk ledges are all graced by a series of vertical chrome strips which purportedly create the illusion of lowering Cadillac's prominent bustle back.

BIGGEST STYLE CHANGE is in the Eldorado, this year a $6000-plus convertible that has a rear end straight from the La Espada and El Camino show cars. It looks good enough to make us wonder why it is not available throughout the line, but perhaps they are saving this for 1956. The Eldorado is powered by a 270-horsepower, 331-cubic-inch V8 that mounts twin, four-barreled carburetors and has a 9 to 1 compression ratio. This engine is available as an option on other models, which normally have a single-carburetor, 250-horsepower version. The Eldorado's revolutionary and attractive aluminum-spoke wheels are also an option throughout the line. Standard equipment on all models includes power steering, windshield washer, and a smoothed-out, dual-range Hydra-Matic.

CADILLAC'S ENGINEERING PHILOSOPHY is premised on the statistic that over 90 per cent of their customers want the utmost luxury in a car that is the least possible work to drive. Agility is a secondary consideration, a fact which makes it the more amazing that Cadillac was our top performing road test car in 1954. Chief Engineer Fred Arnold has his problems because he would like "to do the most things for the most people." For example, shocks on the current model could be tightened up and "export" springs used for better cornering, but the "boulevard" ride would suffer. He would like to give you both, and does wherever a compromise is not necessary.

CADILLAC'S STYLING PHILOSOPHY is premised on what the public wants, not what they ought to want. Time and again, the so-called experts (ourselves included) hand out the concours ribbons to competition; in fact, others seem to have won everything lately but sales leadership in the high-price bracket. While sales leadership doesn't put one above criticism, it helps. It also causes people, especially those who don't own Cadillacs, to gripe about little things.

VANCLEEFF AND ARPELS' JEWELRY, as well as Harry Winston's, has become familiar to millions of common folk through the medium of Cadillac advertising. Honey-rich copy drives home one theme: you haven't arrived until you've bought your first Cadillac. While a few sensitive souls have undoubtedly been driven to Lincolns and Packards in defense against this clever sophism, it works beautifully on most people. Surprisingly enough, the default of others gave Cadillac its current hold on the prestige market. Back in the late Thirties, both Lincoln and Packard put their chips on middle-priced cars. They sold a lot of them, but in the process lost much of their prestige; the road back has been slow and painful.

A LITTLE KNOWN FACT is that General Motors nearly dropped Cadillac back in 1933 when the division was losing millions on its ponderous V-12s and 16s. Non-philanthropic GM gave it one last chance when the late and great Nicholas Dreystadt was moved up from service to production and then to general manager. He soon boiled the line down from four engines on eight different wheelbases to a standardized, modern V8 that actually excelled the multi-cylinder jobs in power and smoothness. A peculiar paradox during this hectic period was the LaSalle. Theoretically, it

Cadillac again shows two convertibles, the workaday version (above) and the Eldorado, with its new wheels and rear end

Note how deftly Cadillac stylists have refrained from outdating earlier models, but have given freshness to the '55

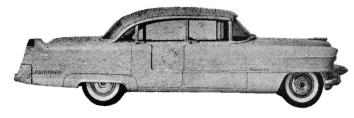

The Fleetwood Sixty Special has its usual long tail, but a new narrow center post, first sign of the four-door hardtop car

should have backfired on Cadillac the way the Zephyr did on Lincoln. However, this didn't happen because for some reason, the public never associated LaSalle with Cadillac, and secondly, LaSalle by 1940 was basically a Cadillac with a different nameplate. It became the Series 61 in 1941, and sold faster than Dreystadt could make them. Cadillac went into the war years with a top quality, relatively low-priced ($1345) car that still commands a premium on the used car market. This car is given credit for their enviable position today.

FRED ARNOLD'S CHIEF WORRY is the old saw that complacency is the downfall of the leader. He tries to keep one jump ahead of competition and this applies particularly to certain other GM divisions whose initials begin with "O" and "B." Cadillac saves a lot of money by sharing a body with Buick and in the process, gives you better value. Even more could be saved if the relatively low-production Cadillac (this year's goal is 150,000) used an engine or frame in common with another GM division. Right now, horsepower-leader Cadillac (270 in the Eldorado) is hard at work on a brand-new V8 which might be ready for production in 1956.

A PERFECT CADILLAC IS RARE, and so is a lemon. Regardless of how high the delivered price, truly fine workmanship is a problem on any assembly line. Twenty-five years ago, one craftsman *(Continued on page 128)*

Chrome on the attractive coupe de ville's sides is also done with restraint. The horizontal bar accentuates an indentation in the metal itself this year

Most popular car in the line will be the Series 62 sedan, this year with the Florentine curve rear roof line that GM pioneered on its '54 hardtops

With everyone else going rear-end happy, Cadillac shows surprising restraint in this back view of the new Sixty Special

Here is the 270-hp Eldorado engine, a souped-up version of that on the lesser Cadillacs. But you can have it on them, too

Better than the Best!

Cadillac say their new Eldorado will make people forget the Rolls-Royce. Larry Foley points out that's a tall order.

PROTOTYPE of Cadillac Eldorado Brougham was shown at 1955 Motorama. Blonde does not go with the car.

TWO leading United States car-makers have at last got round to considering the needs of their most-neglected customer — the multi-millionaire.

They believe it is high time he got a car worthy of his bankroll—an American equivalent of the Rolls-Royce.

So does he.

For years now this poor fellow has been the saddest thing on the highways. No one could tell how rich he was merely by looking at his car—which puts him at a disadvantage in the U.S., where you size a man up by the car he drives.

Now, the only obvious car for the extra-rich man here (known as the "Big Rich") is a Cadillac (or, possibly, a Lincoln or Packard).

Imported high-priced super-sports jobs don't rate among the Big Rich generally—only among their young sporting offspring as playthings.

No Longer Exclusive

To the driver of an Essex or an Overland the latest-model Cadillac may seem the last word in swank. But the truth is that the Cadillac has become so common on the U.S. highways that the man at the wheel is no longer necessarily a man of distinction (i.e., wealth).

Many quite ordinary people drive Cadillacs. They may be poor, but they want to look rich. So—a Cadillac. No one else need know that they are taking three years to pay it off. The postwar multi-millionaire cult has made the Cadillac another pebble on the beach. The manufacturers have simply ignored him. All they have done is gone on making bigger, better and dearer Cadillacs. The Big Rich have been reduced to buying strings of Cadillacs, which is not really satisfactory because they can only drive one at a time.

I know of one family in New Jersey, where the eggs come from, which owned seven Cadillacs—one for each member. Their way of showing their contempt for the commonplace Cadillac as a symbol of wealth was to use Cadillacs as farm-waggons, for transporting pig-food, poultry feed and crates of eggs.

About the only solace left the Cadillac man to whom money is no object is to be first with the new year's model. He who gets his delivered first by the town dealer is obviously top dog in local society.

But this is a short-lived triumph, lasting from late October to December, by which time anybody who is anybody should be burling around in the new model. Anybody who drives last year's model is a nobody. Down in Miami, where the sun goes in winter, it's not enough to own any old Cadillac. The girls sneer: "Yeah? What model?" If it's last year's, you're out, son. If it's not air-conditioned (or not a convertible), son, you're still out."

Relief in Sight

Well, that's all going to be changed. By the end of this year there will be a new class of car-owner. Two new cars, intended specifically for the Big Rich, are on the way:

- The Lincoln Continental Mark II, being made by the Ford people.
- The Eldorado Brougham, by Cadillac (General Motors).

Of the two firms, the more vociferous so far have been Cadillac. By comparison, Ford have been restrained. Ford are promoting the coming Continental with quiet, dignified advertisements which contrast sharply with the Power! Zoom! Glamor! school of modern motor ads: it favors a poetic picture of a four-pointed star against a star-filled sky, captioned "Rebirth of a proud tradition . . . the Continental Mark II," with blurb recalling that the old Lincoln Continental, created in 1940 and scrapped in 1948, was "considered one of the most distinctive and most admired cars in America."

But, says the blurb, the new Continental, "a daring and dramatically modern car," will "embody elegance and dignity" and "will surpass even the beloved Lincoln Continental . . . for we are determined to make he new Continental as fine a motor car as the world has ever known."

Ford will present this snazzy new job "with deep pride."

Move Over, R.R.

Cadillac have been much more characteristically American in their advance promotion of the Eldorado Brougham.

The Cadillac people announced, simply, that they were going into competition with Rolls-Royce of England.

Their new luxury car, they said, "will make people forget about the Rolls-Royce."

Rolls-Royce of England, who might perhaps have been amused by such presumption, appeared not to hear. Judging by the description of the Eldorado Brougham, R.R. have nothing to fear from the proposed transatlantic competition. With its racy, low-slung lines (overall height only 4ft. 6in.), four headlights, "quad" exhaust pipes, "projectile-shaped" rear bumpers and massive, flashy chrome-plating, the Eldorado Brougham is hardly likely to appeal to the gentry for whom Rolls-Royce of England have always catered—apparently to their mutual satisfaction, since R.R. have been going strong for 51 years and still need no more resounding form of advertising than their traditional plain, modest little insertions in such journals as **The Times**: "The best car in the world."

Nobody has ever gainsaid this claim—so you will either admire or smile at Cadillac for their brash prediction that their Eldorado Brougham will depose the Rolls.

The true test of a car's value in the eyes of the world is the legends which form around it. On that score Cadillac lags far behind Rolls. It is not true, for instance, that a Rolls-Royce engine is sealed at the factory and is never accessible except to a qualified Rolls mechanic dressed in morning clothes and cravat and presenting credentials signed by the Archbishop of Canterbury. Nor is it true that the buyer of a Rolls signs a life contract never to sell it except back to an authorised dealer, and is liable to prosecution if he sells it to a mere person whom the Rolls people would consider unworthy.

But a product that gathers such folklore about it must have something. It remains to be seen whether Cadillac, with their new super-duper car, can match that something. I doubt it. For one thing, the Eldorado Brougham won't even have a decent price-tag.

The best they will be able to do, it seems, will be something around 10,000 dollars. Why, that won't even beat their American rivals, Ford, who are expected to charge around 12,000 dollars for the Continental Mark II.

With such low prices, both will be far behind the Rolls, which costs 14,000 dollars—before the real work is put into it, like upholstery to match the linings of milady's furs, or hot and cold running water, or jewelled vanity-cases (3000 dollars alone), or gold-plated dashboards with diamond-studded clocks by Cartier, or twin folding-mirrors by Mappin and Webb of London, or concealed bars, or silver-plated bonnets, or costly fur lap-robes, or petit-point upholstery (all featured variously in the Rolls-Royces of well-known contemporary Britons, Indian rajahs, and Americans).

One comfort for the prospective buyers of these two new models: mass-production will not threaten the exclusiveness of their cars. Production of both will be limited—to 1000 a year for the Eldorado Brougham, and to about eight a day for the Continental.

As for the Continental, it will be hand-made, to order. Chances are no two Continentals will be exactly alike. Buyers will get a wide choice of fabric, trim, color and gadgets. They may even be invited to watch the final assembly of their car.

Both are being produced in great secrecy, and neither maker has yet come out with pictures and details. However, it is assumed that the Continental will retain some of the lines of the old Lincoln Continental; and the Eldorado when unveiled is expected to be less surprising, because its prototype was featured, and got wide publicity, as a "dream car" at this year's Motorama, the annual road-show of General Motors.

The dream car was in fact called the "Eldorado Brougham," but the production model will be a modified version of the Motorama exhibit.

One of the modifications will be the slinky blonde in a white evening gown who appeared to be part of the Motorama model. Discreet inquiries at Cadillac headquarters indicated that the blonde will not go with the production model.

That's too bad. I thought the blonde was one feature on which the Cadillac boys really had poor old Rolls-Royce licked.

Florentine curve rear-window styling is one of the characteristics of the Cadillac Series 62 four-door sedan. Nineteen solid body colors and two special upper body colors are available for many combinations.

Auto Review

The 1955 Cadillac

The distinctive front end was inspired by the success of Cadillac's Park Avenue experimental sedan which was displayed at General Motors' Motorama.

ADVANCED styling and major engineering refinements are featured in the 1955 Cadillacs. With Cadillac quality taken for granted, GM engineers and designers have kept pace with modern automotive development and taste by a sleek overall appearance and by offering a wide variety of color combinations.

This fine car is immediately identified by a distinctive front end, blending a finely etched cellular grille design with strength through the massive line of bumper, grille guards and rounded lowness of hood.

With the compression ratio increased to 9:1, the 1955 V-8 engine is rated at 250 horsepower at 4,600 rpms. This is the power plant for all standard models except the Eldorado convertible, a special sports type model which is powered by a 270 hp. V-8 engine. The Eldorado engine has dual, four-barrel carburetors, with new air cleaners, intake manifold and throttle controls.

The 250-hp. power plant also introduces a newly designed carburetor to insure engine smoothness while idling. Other new features are a redesigned, more rigid crankshaft; narrower connecting rod bearings made possible through the use of improved bearing material, and a new water pump which increases water circulation at lower speed by 20 per cent, thus providing more even engine operating temperature.

Adding new grace to the rear of the 1955 Series 60 Special Fleetwood Sedan is the curve treatment of the back window pillar. The vertical mounted chrome trim molding is also a distinguishing new feature.

The 1955 Eldorado is a special sports-type production convertible, styled to meet the growing demand for a 'different' car. The Eldorado boasts a 270-horsepower V-8 engine and a wheelbase of 129 inches.

Auto Review

Conservative luxury is stressed in the Cadillac Series 60 Special Fleetwood Sedan. The center door pillars have been reduced by more than half, giving a wider range of vision with no loss of structural support.

Fifth wheel is checked prior to gasoline mileage tests. Cad is surprisingly economical, can travel all day on single fill.

ROAD TEST

Cadillac
FLEETWOOD 60 SPECIAL

This car has the reputation... does it have the stuff to back it up? Here's a good look at all its features

Photos by Dean Moon

Cellular grille was derived from Park Avenue experimental shown in GM's '54 Motorama. Bullets are fixed to frame.

Cadillac probably is fastest volume production car on the road, with accelerating ability exceeded only by its top speed. When taken over 60 miles of hilly dirt road, as shown here, passenger and trunk compartments remained free of dust.

CADILLAC is regarded by millions of Americans as the ultimate in automobiles. Much of this reputation seems to be derived from the fact that ownership of a Cadillac has a certain amount of social significance. So it is interesting to determine if such extraordinary opinions are supported by the quality of construction, performance and design.

For road testing purposes, a Fleetwood Series 60 Special four-door sedan, with 76 miles on the odometer, was obtained. No customary break-in period was required, however, since Cadillac advises its owners that new models may be driven without limitations on maximum speed.

During an eight-day test, the Cadillac was driven over 1400 miles of California and Nevada, which provided a wide variety of city and open road conditions. Runs for top speed were made in the Mojave desert, while balance of the performance figures were secured near sea level.

The car does not have a clear monopoly on any important feature. Each separate item can be found on one rival make of car or another. But it is the *only* car that combines the maximum number of desirable features in a single package. In brief, Cadillac has just about the best of everything that is available on a modern car, plus a few items that come as extras.

The performance picture can be read at a glance in the accompanying tabulation. It reveals that Cadillac is the fastest volume production car on the road, at an actual 116 mph under the clocks. This high speed run was made with a strong sidewind, yet the driver found the car held to the road with perfect control.

This enormous performance potential has been achieved in Cadillac without sacrificing economy. Over-the-road fuel consumption figures are genuinely remarkable, considering the horsepower output, car weight and loading of powered accessories.

Refinements in Cadillac's engine compartment for 1955, which contribute to the overall performance increase, include boosting the compression ratio from 8.5 to 9-to-1. Valve rocker arms have been redesigned for better breathing on both intake and exhaust. The crankshaft has been strengthened, connecting rod bearings are now narrower, and the water pump is a new unit which gives 20 per cent better circulation at lower speeds, for more even engine operating temperatures. Horsepower is rated at 250 at 4400 rpm, against 230 in 1954, while torque is 345 ft.-lbs. at 2800 rpm, in contrast to 332 on last year's car.

Servicing ease on engine and accessories rates high on Cadillac. The fuel pump is above and in front of the block, with the sediment bowl visible and conveniently located. The generator also is favorably positioned. Spark plugs are above the exhaust manifold. All units involving liquids—oil filter, windshield washer, radiator cap, dip stick, power steering tank, and brake master cylinder —are handy to a wrench from the same side of the car. The voltage regulator has been removed from heat of the engine compartment for simpler adjustments and is immediately behind the grille. These are but a few examples how careful design has provided for efficient mechanical care.

On the roadability side, the reactions of various drivers of the test car were almost identical: the car has a "solid" feel. Road and engine noises are virtually absent, the result of good quality control and ample quantities of insulation in the body and under the hood (where the glass fiber is vinyl covered!). Handling, despite the Cadillac's size, was easy (power steering is standard equipment) and parking seemed to be no more of a problem than with any average car. All four fenders are visible from the driver's seat. The steering wheel itself has superior feel, with gripping areas cleverly designed for firm control. Riding in the Cadillac is exceedingly comfortable, even over long distances, without being excessively soft.

It was noted during the highway travel that drivers would sometimes run the car up to 50 and 60 mph with the selector lever in third gear of the dual-range transmission. While this is further evidence

(Continued on page 128)

MOTOR LIFE ROAD TEST

CAR TESTED: CADILLAC FLEETWOOD 60 SPECIAL

TEST CONDITIONS
Altitude	210 feet
Temperature	53 degrees
Wind	4 mph
Gasoline	MOBILGAS PREMIUM

ACCELERATION AND TOP SPEED
MPH	Seconds
0-30	3.6
0-45	7.5
0-60	11.2
30-50	5.3
40-60	5.9
Standing ¼ mile	19 seconds
Fastest one-way run	116 mph
Top speed avg. 4 runs	114.1 mph

BRAKING DISTANCE
MPH	Stopping distance
30	40.2 feet
45	88.7 feet
60	159 feet

FUEL CONSUMPTION
MPH	Average
30	21.7 mpg
45	20.5 mpg
60	16.5 mpg

SPEEDOMETER CORRECTIONS
Car speedometer	Actual speeds
20	19
30	27.5
40	37
50	46.5
60	55
70	64
80	72
90	80.5
100	—

REMARKS: ALL SPEEDS ACTUAL. PAVEMENT— DRY ASPHALT.

Although Cadillac is a big, heavy car, its brakes brought it to a quick stop in a straight line. Distinguishing feature of Fleetwood style is Florentine curve on rear window styling, which is shared with Series 62 coupe and Coupe de Ville '55 models.

Attention to detail can be found everywhere. For example, rubber molding catches water runoff when door is open.

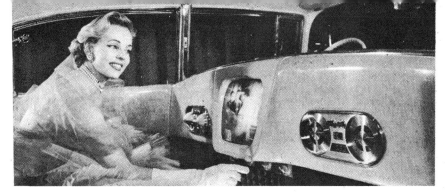

The 1955 Cadillac Series 60 Special Sedan offers such luxury features as 14-inch TV set, telephone, tape recorders, Korina gold wood paneling and mouton carpet.

Cadillac Specials

CADILLAC, never surpassed in the "show car" field, has come up with another one—the Eldorado St. Moritz, a little number that features a white pearlescent body with a smartly-styled interior finish of white ermine trimmed in pearlescent white English grain leather and floor carpeting of white mouton fur. Sounds cozy, in St. Moritz or Miami.

On a more practical plane, Cadillac also has introduced the Eldorado Brougham with an overall height of 54.4 inches and without a center door pillar. Fenders and characteristic tail lines are complimented by a tinted brushed aluminum roof. Dual headlight assemblies, Cadillac says, provide the most efficient road lighting yet devised. The outer lamps are flat beam city lights and inner lamps are highly penetrating highway lights. Both sets are controlled by an Autronic Eye mounted at top of windshield.

Using new methods of construction, Cadillac has reduced all outside dimensions without sacrificing passenger comfort. All seats are individual and are tailored to fit the body. Wheelbase is 124 inches, overall length is 209.6 inches and width is 77.5 inches. A highly iridescent exterior color—Chameleon Green—has been developed expressly for the Brougham and the interior is trimmed in matching paint, leather and imported French silk.

A third model, the Westchester, is a specially styled Series 60 Special sedan featuring television, a tape recorder and a telephone in the rear seat. This job also employs a novel interior treatment—Korina gold wood paneling, upholstery of black cloth interwoven with gold thread and a black mouton fur carpet. ☆

Cadillac's 270-horsepower Eldorado, the "St. Moritz," offers the latest word in luxurious upholstery—white ermine fur and white English grain leather.

THE ELDORADO BROUGHAM—

A NEW CADILLAC FOR 1956

The class of super-luxury cars, neglected since the 1930's, is on the way back, and this one is sure to be a style-setter in advanced features

TWIN HEADLIGHTS at the front end of each fender have five-inch lenses. Outer lamps are flat-beam city lights; inner lamps are for highway use. An Autronic Eye will switch from one to the other as conditions on the road require.

INTERIOR includes padded instrument panel with recessed controls. Driver's seat pivots outward for easy entry and exit, while center of both front and rear seats contains storage compartment. Note absence of small ventilator windows, considered unnecessary in car having air conditioner and heater as integral unit.

QUAD EXHAUST is what Cadillac is calling the system that has dual pipes issuing from rear fenders on each side of the car. This could be said to balance dual-dual headlights in front, but benefits in engine efficiency are unknown.

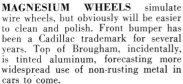

MAGNESIUM WHEELS simulate wire wheels, but obviously will be easier to clean and polish. Front bumper has been a Cadillac trademark for several years. Top of Brougham, incidentally, is tinted aluminum, forecasting more widespread use of non-rusting metal in cars to come.

REAR DOORS open into the wind (above), a characteristic of four-door hardtops. But Cadillac engineers say they have developed an adequate safety device to forestall mishaps. Note triangular section that forms upper rear of door. Only chromed strip on side of body (right) is vertical trim, another Cadillac trademark in recent years, which may point the way to more restraint in exterior treatments for the future. Significant item: the Brougham's wheelbase is 124 inches, five less than the current Cadillac 62 series. Are scaled-down cars coming from other U.S. auto manufacturers?

CADDIE COUPE

The Cadillac's contours are smooth and graceful. Twin exhausts protrude through the rear fender trim. The bulges behind the rear window are part of the air-conditioning intakes.

THIS month we've let our head go and put what we think is a lush combination on our cover. The car is a late 1954 model Cadillac Coupe de Ville; the girl is Sydney model Eve Newton; the background, for those of you who don't live in N.S.W., is the Sydney Harbour Bridge.

The Cadillac, which is identical with the latest 1955 model except for a slight power increase in the engine, belongs to an American business man who lives in Sydney. He is Mr. J. T. Rethers. He told us a few things about the car.

Everything is power assisted. There is power steering; there are power brakes; the windows and front seat are power lifted and adjusted. The Cadillac also has Hydramatic transmission.

The car is not as bulky as one would expect—it's around the size of the present Ford Customline.

It is a two-door saloon, and would seat five people very comfortably and six reasonably.

Important features are a real air-conditioning system (which dehumidifies and cools the interior air) and complete appointments for all passengers.

There are individual ashtrays and cigar lighters all around; the rear passengers can control the volume of their radio speaker or turn it out; the radio tunes automatically to the next station when a button is pressed.

Mr. Rethers bought the Cadillac in the U.S.A. and drove it for some time there before bringing it to Australia. He reports that its normal-cruising petrol consumption is 18 m.p.g.

The Cadillac's vital statistics are: ENGINE: V-8 ohv, comp. ratio 9 to 1, capacity 5,430 c.c., 250 S.A.E. bhp at 4,600 rpm, 345 lb/ft. torque at 2,800 rpm. TRANSMISSION: Hydramatic automatic. OVERALL DIMENSIONS: Wheelbase, 10' 9"; length,, 18' 5.3"; width, 6' 8"; height, 4' 11.7"; clearance, 6.17".

The Cadillac Coupe de Ville has been converted to right-hand drive to meet local traffic requirements. The upholstery is two-tone dark green and light green leather and cloth.

the 1956 cadillac

HIGHLIGHTS: top of 305 hp, new sedan de ville and Eldorado Seville body styles, redesigned Hydra-Matic, aluminum grilles

IN KEEPING with its policy of gradual refinement and evolutionary development, rather than sweeping overnight changes, Cadillac for 1956 is offering a line of cars that have a lot of new features but aren't so different that you can recognize them as Cadillacs at first glance.

There are styling changes and innovations. Engines are bigger, more powerful. Two entirely new body styles have been introduced. The Hydra-Matic transmission has been completely redesigned. Many detail improvements have been made.

Big news in the engine compartment is a displacement increase from 331 to 365 cubic inches, brought about by a boost in the bore from 3.81 to 4 inches. Stroke is still 3.625 inches. This, plus higher compression and improved breathing, has raised horsepower from 250 to 285 horsepower on regular Cadillacs and from 270 to 305 on Eldorado models. Torque is up from 345 to 400 foot pounds on all models.

To go with the bigger engine, Cadillac has the redesigned Hydra-Matic, of which GM is very proud. (It reportedly cost some $35 million to develop and ready for production.) It features a controlled fluid coupling and sprag clutch arrangement, with a new fluid cooling system and oil-submerged gear units.

Big advantages of the new transmission, standard on all Caddies, of course, are smoother, quieter operation, improved acceleration and easier maintenance.

Styling is characteristically Cadillac. Grilles are slightly different, with a finer "egg-crate" cellular texture. A new idea is the anodized aluminum grille with a gold finish available as an option. Hoods have been lowered and front fenders widened.

Rear fenders now have fairings flowing rearward to new oval exhaust outlets at the outer ends of the restyled rear bumpers. New fluted chrome wheel discs are standard on all models except the Eldorado which retains the aluminum spoke design.

The interior features a new and seemingly more functional instrument panel arrangement. The speedometer, something those who have to run performance checks on cars notice particularly, is very readable. The glove compartment has been moved to the center for greater convenience.

Performance, particularly in low and middle speed ranges, has been improved due to the new engine-transmission combination. Zero to 60 times of just over 10 seconds are claimed for the new models.

The two new body styles are the Eldorado Seville, a two-door hardtop introduced as a companion to the Eldorado Biarritz convertible, and the sedan de ville, a four-door hardtop. The Seville has styling features similar to the Biarritz. The roof panel, however is covered with a padded material resembling leather (Cadillac call the material "vicodec").

One detail feature that impressed in a pre-introduction peek at the cars was a side view mirror that is controlled from inside the car—like a spot light.

New power seats which permit the angle of the seat back to be adjusted in addition to the fore and aft and up and down movement is a comfort improvement also.

Brake pedals are much bigger, permitting right or left foot operation, and are supported by two arms instead of the single arm formerly used.

Incidentally, although an Eldorado Brougham was displayed at the press preview of the new Cadillac line, word is that it will be some months before this $8500 model will be in production. Tooling has been released for its production on a limited basis, however, so it definitely will appear later this model year.

Cadillac is backing its optimistic outlook for 1956 by expanding facilities to enable it to build 15,000 more cars than during the '55 model year. (That would boost production to 156,000—and there will probably still be a waiting list.) This move is not much of a gamble, since Cadillac sales manager, Jim Roche, claims to have orders already on hand for the first seven months' production. •

Sedan de Ville (four-door hardtop) is one of two new body types; other is Eldorado Seville, similar to Eldorado Biarritz convertible but with padded top. Rear end changes include inset plates and integral exhaust ports that are oval insteal of round.

Cadillac has 285 hp (Eldorados are 305) from engine with bigger bore that gives 365 cubic inches. Block is new, with more rugged crankshaft on larger journals, redesigned heads that have larger ports, increased intake and exhaust manifolding.

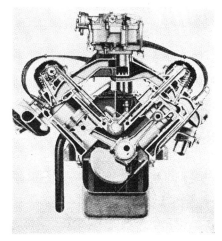

A BARRIS BONANZA

with glittering silver and gold to whet the desire of the most exuberant advocate of "gracious living"

photos by George Barris

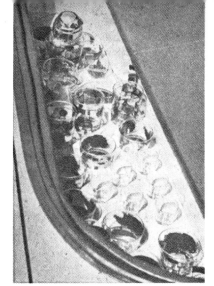

by Bill Babbitt

BOASTING a television set, radio-telephone, tape recorder, and cocktail bar among its many other expressions of all-out individualism, this Cadillac Le Mans by Barris cuts a wide swath anywhere.

Its basic chassis is the experimental Cadillac Le Mans, which was shown over the country in the GM Motorama exhibits of 1953. This modification (by Barris Kustom Autos, 11054 Atlantic Blvd., Lynwood, Calif.) was submitted to Harry Karl, the shoe store executive, before construction began.

The body is mostly Fiberglas with the exception of the lower fender panels, which are formed of body steel and then blue-white chrome plated. Trim between the lower chromed parts of the fenders and the Fiberglas part of the body is ½-inch steel bar, plated with 24-karat gold. To stop rattles before they start, a strip of ⅛-inch rubber separates the gold-plated trim and the body panels. Hubcaps are done in a combination of gold and chrome; the 30 individually inserted "spokes" and the protruding center are gold, with the remainder in chrome. Paint is 30 coats of "platinum dust" sprayed over a polychromatic base sealer.

The rear window and top are trimmed with chrome-plated steel. The whole top assembly including the rear window can be removed, or the window may be left in place and the top removed (photo at right below).

The engine is the 300-horsepower Cadillac with dual 4-throat carburetors set up by the factory for the original Le Mans model. All engine accessories, valve covers, etc., are chrome plated, of course.

A dynamotor, installed by Ernie's TV (8133 Compton Blvd., Paramount, Calif.) converts power from the 12-volt system to the proper voltage for the television, tape recorder and radio-telephone. The TV, wired thru the ignition switch, can be played only when the engine is not running.

C. & C. Bar Specialists (6826 Crenshaw Blvd., Los Angeles) styled the bar in Formica, inlaid wood, and gold leaf. It hides under a red leather panel, which matches the upholstery.

YOUR CHECK LIST
☑ ☑ ☑ ☑ ☑ means top rating

PERFORMANCE ☑ ☑ ☑ ☑ ☑
New Hydra-Matic with second fluid coupling for gear change is exceptionally smooth under all conditions. Teamed with a 285-hp engine, it delivers outstanding performance.

STYLING ☑ ☑ ☑ ☑ ☐
Typical Cadillac; long, low and massive. Graceful sweeping curves of wraparound windshield, roofline and rear window are its most outstanding style features.

RIDING COMFORT ☑ ☑ ☑ ☑ ☑
The combination of long (129") wheelbase, 5000-lb weight, excellent suspension design plus lavish cushioning makes for most all around comfort. Some well-damped body shake sometimes crops up on rough roads.

INTERIOR DESIGN ☑ ☑ ☑ ☑ ☑
Everything that could be wished for with the possible exception of extra headroom. Vision all around is superb, and deep, firmly-padded adjustable front seat most comfortable.

ROADABILITY ☑ ☑ ☑ ☑ ☑
Excellent, particularly at high speeds when the car gives an unusually secure feeling even in sharp curves.

EASE OF CONTROL ☑ ☑ ☑ ☑ ☑
Somewhat less than perfect because power steering "off-and-on" effect requires close attention and an unusual amount of tiresome small corrections. Power brakes and transmission are extremely satisfactory.

ECONOMY ☑ ☑ ☑ ☐ ☐
Was disappointingly less than Cadillacs of previous years which used phenomenally little gas for their weight and performance. Car tested gave less than 15 mpg, which is average for the luxury class but poor for Cadillac.

SERVICEABILITY ☑ ☑ ☑ ☑ ☐
Engine accessibility is neither better nor worse than any medium or high-priced car where the engine compartment is filled with power-assist units. Multitude of power-operated gadgets may need expensive repairs later in car's life.

DURABILITY ☑ ☑ ☑ ☑ ☑
Gets top rating on the basis of record of past Cadillacs with similar engineering features and high-quality manufacture.

WORKMANSHIP ☑ ☑ ☑ ☑ ☑
At a uniformly high level throughout the car. Interior fittings and upholstery are particularly outstanding.

VALUE PER DOLLAR ☑ ☑ ☑ ☑ ☑
Exceptionally low rate of depreciation plus traditional mechanical longevity make Cadillac the "buy" in the high-priced field. An excellent transportation investment for those who can afford it.

CAR LIFE CONSUMER

SPECIFICATIONS
Model:	Sedan DeVille
Wheelbase:	129"
Length:	221.9"
Engine Displacement:	365 cu. in.
Bore and Stroke:	4.0" by 3.625"
Compression Ratio:	9.75:1
Brake Horsepower:	285 @ 4600 rpm
Torque:	400 ft. lbs.
Electrical System:	12 Volt
Factory Delivered Price with standard equipment:	$4569

ALTHOUGH A sizeable amount of money has been spent on the 1956 Cadillac for essentially minor styling changes the car still looks typically Cadillac, with the sweeping rear fender line topped by its much-copied fin. Cadillac still retains its rather high, squared-off hood line, the twin "bombs" on the front bumper and the vertical "leading edge" on its rear fender.

Thus Cadillac protects the investment of last year's buyers by continuing its gradual style change rather than making sweeping changes that would make all preceding models obsolete from a styling viewpoint.

The most important change in the current model is the redesigned Hydra-Matic transmission which matches the overall smoothness of Cadillac's ride and performance. Gone forever are the power "surges" long-associated with the automatic transmission's upshifts and downshifts. Acceleration from a stand-still is one long, smooth increase in speed. Even moving the selector lever from "D-3" range to "D-4" at near full throttle merely increases the rate of acceleration with syrupy smoothness.

The famed Cadillac ride, which has long separated this car from the rest of the large cars, is better than ever. The suspension and insulation have virtually eliminated sound or feel of rough pavement. There is some evidence of well-absorbed body shake on the four-door hardtop "Sedan de Ville," a model added to the line this year. However, this is not noticeable on the conventional four-door sedan.

Cadillac's body designers have not made the mistake of

ANALYSIS:

1956 cadillac

CADILLAC IS THE CAR FOR YOU

If . . . You want a luxury car that you can trade frequently without heavy depreciation loss.

If . . . You want "The" prestige car of the American market and one that will remain fashionably in style for more than just a year or two.

If . . . You can't quite afford a top luxury car for private use but use a car for frequent long business trips.

If . . . You want a combination of unparalleled comfort and high speed travel.

If . . . You've been turning in one of the upper medium-priced cars every year or so and are looking for a more powerful, comfortable and luxurious car for roughly the same expenditure.

SEDAN DE VILLE

putting overly-soft padding into the deeply upholstered seats.

More than ever the car is supremely comfortable on long trips at high speeds. Money has been well spent on sound-deadening insulation and noiseproofing of the traditionally quiet V8 and its large-bore dual exhaust system. Cruising at 85 in the Cadillac is less tiresome than riding in smaller cars at 55.

Roadability is better than ever, with no roll and very little tire squeal evident even in sharp turns at considerable speed. The car has rocklike stability on undulating, high-crowned blacktop roads that often prove the undoing of softly suspended cars.

There is still room for some improvement in handling on the open highway. The "off-and-on" action of power steering can be annoying at road speeds. Starting a turn, the driver exerts a certain amount of force on the wheel, then the power assist "takes over." Until the driver gets used to it, the action seems too abrupt. This makes the wheel turn just a bit more than necessary and the driver must compensate with an increased pull in the opposite direction. Thus steering becomes a continuous series of minute "adjustments" when traversing the gentle curves of a superhighway.

Parking or handling the car in congested traffic is effortless despite its size and weight. The excellent rear vision and prominent rear fender fins (tail lights are visible from the driver's seat), make backing the car nearly foolproof. The power brake (standard on all models) is now operated by a broad pedal suspended from the firewall by two rods, one on either side of the steering column. This change makes left-foot brake operation a natural.

The instrument panel is little changed from last year, with its sweeping, hooded speedometer dial directly in front of the driver; other controls and gages are neatly grouped around it. Readability of all instruments, including the Hydra-Matic quadrant, is equally easy day or night.

Interior accessories leave little to be desired; there are two cigar lighters and two ash trays, an optional six-way power-adjusted seat, a powerful fresh-air heating system with ducts leading through the doors into the rear compartment, and of course power windows. When fully equipped (including air conditioning), there are 13 small electric motors scattered about the car, including one to operate the trunk latch.

One highly desirable feature of the air conditioning enables the blowers to draw in fresh air through the scoops located on the rear deck and "de-mist" the rear windows without operation of the cooling system. The air-conditioner blowers and cooling coils are neatly stowed on a shelf at the forward end of the trunk leaving more usable space than most cars without such installations.

Summing up: Cadillac offers a well-nigh unbeatable package of high performance, unequalled riding comfort and handling ease coupled with high prestige value and low depreciation. For anyone who can afford upwards of $4000 the Cadillac is unquestionably the buy. ●

Bill Holland Tests......

THE CADILLAC 60 SPECIAL

The car furnished by Cadillac Division at Detroit for this driver test turned out to be one of their regular courtesy cars, in use every day and driven by anyone that can get the O.K. from Mr. Gillespie to use a car. I mention this so you'll know it wasn't a special car, or a finely tuned one for this particular occasion. It was a Sixty Special, four-door sedan, with the works on it. By that I mean it had just about all the equipment the factory can supply, such as, power steering and brakes, which are now standard equipment, as is the all new Hydramatic transmission. There was also a six-way power seat, new electrically controlled radio antenna, air conditioner, and many other features I'll mention later. This car delivers as equipped in Detroit for about $6,200 plus taxes.

Ted O'Hearn of the Public Relations Department took me to the garage and checked me out in the car; then I drove around the downtown area of Detroit for awhile to see how it handled in the heavy stop-and-go traffic. I can't say that I was surprised that it drove so beautifully; you just naturally expect a Cadillac to be tops in every way, and this '56 Cadillac is not a disappointment. It's wonderful how easy the power assists make this big 5,000 pound automobile drive.

In only a few blocks I discovered one of Cadillac's firsts. It is no longer necessary to put the window down and put your arm out in the cold or rain to adjust the side view mirror. The mirror is fully adjustable from inside the car by a small handle located near the front of the door, just forward of the power-window control switches.

This is the kind of engineering I think all the car manufacturers should turn to, instead of concentrating so much on increased horse power. In my book 300 or 350 hp is enough for any amateur to be loose with on the highway. There are so many of these little things to be worked out that would make driving for the average person much more pleasant.

Having been in the automobile air conditioning business, I was very interested in the 1956 Cadillac unit. Believe me, this air conditioner is a honey and don't let anyone tell you they have one just as good for less money. The only independent unit that is even comparable to this factory unit, in my opinion, is the A.R.A. unit made in Ft. Worth, Texas.

I couldn't get definite figures regarding the percentage of Cadillacs now being delivered with air conditioners by the factory, but it is estimated to be at least 20% of production and increasing very rapidly. For solid comfort in the hot sticky summer weather we have in most parts of the country, brother, this is it.

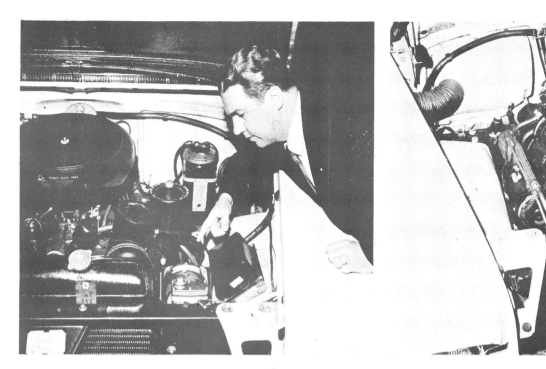

It takes a lot of engine to run this 2½-ton car with all its power equipment. Holland feels that this 365 cu. in. job has nearly reached its capacity, expects to see a new, bigger engine in the near future. Compression ratio is up to 9.75:1.

EASE OF HANDLING, LUXURIOUS FEATURES

IMPRESS MOTORSPORT'S CHIEF TEST DRIVER

Holland points out large running lights on new Cadillac. Style changes this year affect hood, bumpers, new aluminum grille.

Cadillac's system of distributing the cool air through built-in ducts in the roof is the best I've seen. There are four distributor outlets, one over each door. Each distributor outlet has three vents that can be adjusted for both the volume and direction of air desired, or can be shut off entirely. With this system each passenger can regulate the amount of cooling desired.

The compressor is made by Frigidaire and is quite unique, having five cylinders and pistons, but no crankshaft, making it an axial type. The pistons are forced up and down by a wobble plate. It is extremely smooth in operation and uses very little power. In fact I checked the top speed with the air conditioner on, then checked it again with it off and got the same answer both times: 110 mph.

The interior trim of this car is, as expected, both beautiful and serviceable. The dash is new and combines beauty with the utmost in functional arrangement of instruments and driving controls. It isn't necessary to be an engineer to operate the heating system either; there are only two levers to operate: one for heat on the left side of the instrument panel, one for defrosting on the right.

The glove compartment location is center dash, with a drop-down door. If too much junk is collected in this type compartment, not only does the door drop down, but everything in it drops down onto the floor. I have no idea why it was there, but in the compartment was a Decca record #9-29721 by Connie Boswell. I think someone was needling me: the titles were "I Compare You" and "No Other One."

The door latches are the so-called safety type that most of the cars are using now. The safety feature consists of a little piece of thin metal that laps over the "white metal" striker plate. This is a step in the right direction but I question their effectiveness in a fast end-for-end flip. Engineers certainly will come up with something better in the future.

After driving around in the city for awhile, I drove out the Edsel Ford Expressway to the open spaces. The concrete on the expressway is very rough and I noticed considerable body shake between 50 and 60 mph, caused, I think, by the shock absorbers trying to stop the wheel bounce caused by the rough concrete. Cadillac uses two sets of valves in their shock absorbers to control the ride. One set takes care of the small bumps at slow speeds in city driving and gives a nice soft ride. The other set takes over on the big bumps and at higher speeds. One setting is much stiffer than the other; in fact, they are a little stiffer than on the '55 models. Under certain conditions this has a tendency to transfer the jolt through the shock absorbers to the frame and body. However, this also gives a much safer ride when cornering at high speeds. On this subject, I'll note here that there is quite a bit of body lean when cornering fast, but this big sedan is built for the boulevards, not for the race tracks.

The noise level is good except for the noise made by the engine fan. The extra power packed in the engine evidently needed a little more cooling, thus requiring a larger fan. This noise, I think, could and should be lessened.

The engine in this '56 model has so many improvements it could be called a new engine. To begin with they have added 34 cubic inches by boring the block to four inches, making the displacement 365 cubic inches this year. The horsepower is up too, from 250 to 285, and the torque (that's what gives the acceleration) is up from 345 pounds-feet at 2800 rpm to 400 at 2800 rpm.

I have read that the block is entirely new in the '56, but this is not true. It's the same block pattern altered slightly, and the foundry is using a slightly different method of casting. The crankshaft is a little heavier (a pound, to be exact) than the '55. All forged V-8 crankshafts when they are first forged are 180° jobs and look like four-cylinder crankshafts. Then they are heated and twisted until the crankpins are 90° apart instead of 180°.

There are also new cylinder heads, exhaust manifolds, main bearing caps, camshaft, valve springs, valve guides, exhaust valves and pistons. The rods are the same as in last year's models.

The breathing of the engine has been improved by opening up the intake and exhaust manifolds and ports. The intake valves are the same size, but stay open longer due to the new cam. The exhaust valves are a little bigger (1/16-inch), making them 1-9/16 inches. The compression ratio is higher too. It is now 9.75 to

SPECIFICATIONS
1956 CADILLAC SERIES 60 SPECIAL

ENGINE

Type: OHV V-8
Displacement: 365 cu. in.
Bore & stroke: 4" x 3.625"
Compression ratio: 9.75 to 1
Brake horsepower: 285 at 4600 rpm
Torque: 400 ft. lb. at 2800 rpm
Piston travel per car mile: 1334 ft.

BODY & CHASSIS

Wheelbase: 133"
Height: 62"
Length: 225.9"
Width: 80"
Minimum road clearance: 6.1"
Turning circle: 45'
Transmission: Hydramatic
Steering ratio: 19.5 to 1 (power steering standard)
Rear axle ratio: 3.07 to 1 (3.36 to 1 optional)
Tire size: 8.00 x 15

1, and was 9 to 1. The combustion chamber is machined, giving the head a smooth interior surface. It is of the "squish" type, and gets its name because about one-third or more of the piston is covered by the head, when the piston is at top dead center with practically no clearance. This makes the gas that was in that part of the cylinder "squish" into the space left for combustion in a very high state of turbulence, making it possible to use a higher compression ratio, get better fuel consumption and smoother performance.

There are also new spark plugs, a new sealed voltage regulator, a higher torque starting motor, new easily adjusted distributor, an improved fuel pump and improved hydraulic valve lifters which prevent power loss at high engine speeds.

The Hydra-Matic transmission is entirely new, both in principle and mechanical parts. The four-speed design is retained, and a new so-called "controlled coupling" has been added. This hydraulic unit softens the grab that was so noticeable in the old Hydra-Matics, while shifting. The new unit retains the reliability of the old transmission, I'm sure. Don't try to convert one of the old ones; very few of the parts, if any, will be interchangeable.

In smoothness of operation the new transmission is very comparable to any of the other type transmissions on the market. The only fault I could find with it was a slight noise at about 35 mph while it was shifting, but it wasn't enough to be objectionable. A new park position which may be used when the engine is running is included on the transmission quadrant, providing positive lock against car movement when engaged.

Although this is not a high-performance sports-type car, especially with all the power-consuming accessories on it, I put it through the usual acceleration and top speed tests, with the following results. The readings were taken from the uncorrected speedometer.

Using low drive range:
0-30 mph: 3.6 seconds
0-60 mph: 10.7 seconds
Using high drive range:
0-30 mph: 3.7 seconds
0-60 mph: 10.7 seconds
30-60 mph: 7.1 seconds
50-80 mph: 10.3 seconds

Top speed: 110 mph (same with air conditioner on and off)

I call this very satisfactory performance for this big car.

Although the engineers at the factory would say nothing about the future plans of the engine department, I think they are almost to the limit of the present engine. They can bore the block out another ⅛-inch safely, but that's about it. The cam is just beginning to be a little rough at idle now. So don't be surprised to see a completely new and bigger engine in the '57 Cadillac, with the horsepower about 350 to start with and a possible 450 when the competition starts pushing them.

It's even possible we'll see real fuel injection on some models in '57. Who knows?

THE 1957 CADILLAC

Rear of 62 series coupe has relatively simple styling of standard Cadillacs. Bumper is massive, but very straight, with enlarged exhaust outlets. Taillights resemble earlier Eldorados.

Sedan de Ville of 62 series. The 60 Special looks much the same, except aluminum panel on rear fender over wheel well.

STYLING—New body that averages three inches lower, revised fins, all coupes and sedans are now hardtops, new interiors.

PERFORMANCE—Slight boost in engine output likely to shave some time off 1956 figures, but no sensational changes.

ENGINEERING—Biggest news is a unique frame, previously unknown in contemporary U.S. production. Ball-joints added.

BODY TYPES—All series about the same as in '56. Radically new Eldorado Brougham due later with fuel injection setup.

TAKE A LOOK at a '57 Cadillac. Be it a 62, 60 Special or Eldorado model, it has ties with the past. In fact, it's amazing that so many changes could be made in a car and still retain those ties. This doesn't mean the new Cads aren't different; the look you took a second ago told you they are!

The front view has been changed a lot —but is still definitely Cadillac. The hood height has been reduced so there is practically a single flat plane from fender to fender. The grille (it's still anodized aluminum) and bumper arrangement has been changed, but the gull-wing half-bumpers with protruding pods are a link with the past.

No attempt has been made at a dual headlamp setup, but this trend is recognized in the use of two small lamps under the bumperettes—parking and turn signal lights.

The 62 and 60 Special models have rear quarter panels which are a development of Eldorado designs of the past few years. Eldorados have a treatment reminiscent of GM dream cars of similar vintage—and may, to some extent, be previews of the forthcoming Brougham.

Tail lights set into the rear part of the fins have been discarded in all models. In 62 and 60 Special cars they straddle the trailing edge of the rear quarter panels—which extend back of the deck— much like last year's Eldorados. The new Eldorado has three lights, two set in the short bumperettes and one in the quarter panel directly under the fin.

Those are just a few of the detail highlights, of course. The pictures tell more of the story. What you can't tell from the pictures is that standard Caddys have been lowered three inches (59 vs. 62 inches last year). Eldorado models are proportionately lower. Nor can you detect the half-inch increase in wheelbase (from 129 to 129.5 inches).

(Incidentally, both 62 and 60 Special Cadillacs use the new GM "C" body shell, of course. Major difference is that 62 Specials have a 5-inch longer rear deck— plus different interior and exterior trim.)

An interesting example of Cadillac's awareness of trends is that there are no center pillars on *any* 1957 model. All coupes and sedans are so-called hardtops. This will be true throughout the industry before long. •

CADILLAC BODY TYPES

62 SERIES
 Two-door hardtop
 Four-door hardtop
 Convertible

60 SPECIAL SERIES
 Four-door hardtop
 Eldorado Biarritz
  (convertible)
 Eldorado Seville
  (two-door hardtop)

75 SERIES
 Four-door sedan
  (eight-passenger)

Note—All Cadillac standard sedans and coupes are now hardtops.

Eldorados are the hardtop (Seville) above and similar convertible (Biarritz), with a Brougham due later. The exterior styling is especially good, particularly at the rear where the sloping lines recall some masterful roadsters of the 1930's.

CADILLAC ENGINEERING

CADILLAC'S STYLING, though actually changed very much, can still be termed evolutionary. There are certain phases of its engineering, however, which can't be called anything but revolutionary.

The frame is the backbone of a car and it's right there we find the most drastic change in Cadillac for 1957. The conventional ladder-type or X-member designs have been discarded completely.

Instead, Cadillac is using a frame that might be best described as two wishbones superimposed on each other.

Most engineers in their efforts to get lower overall heights for 1957 stuck pretty much with conventional frame designs, only they brought the side rails out closer to the edge of the body. Cadillac engineers have *eliminated* side frame rails!

This means the body, at most points, is secured to outriggers or hangers which extend out from the central frame. An important point that might be overlooked by a layman is that this allows a lot of flexibility for the future. Just by juggling the size of the frame's central section—at the crossover point of the X, or where the two "wishbones" overlap—it can be adjusted to accommodate various body sizes and wheelbases. (This is particularly important to Cadillac, since it builds limousines, ambulances and other special-bodied cars—or is used by custom builders for such purposes.)

This naturally meant that Cadillac engineers had to change their whole approach to frame construction to insure the necessary rigidity. Just as naturally, that's exactly what they've done. (And many of them will tell you privately that they expect the entire industry to come to a related type of frame design in the future. Especially since there are so many rumors about unit construction being not too far off.)

There are not earth-shaking suspension changes in Cadillac for '57 . . . some that have been made were dictated by the new frame. Rear springs obviously had to be mounted outside the frame, but they are still conventional semi-elliptics. And other than the expected switch to ball joints, there are no basic changes to front suspension.

As far as engines are concerned there are no big changes either. Horsepower has been boosted to 300; largely as a result of higher compression and other detail modifications. Displacement is same as 1956—365 cubic inches. Carburetors are still used, although this is something that could change before the year is over.

To get the extra 15 horse, compression was raised from 9.75 to 10-to-1 and a larger diameter—but still wedge-shaped—combustion chamber incorporated. Intake ports have been modified while intake valves have an eighth of an inch larger and exhaust valves are just that much smaller!

Shoe-and-drum brakes essentially the same as last year are retained and Cadillac is still using 15-inch tires and wheels.

Thus, you can see that the 1957 Cadillac is a blend of the old and new. And it's a better-than-even bet the result is one which will keep Cadillac firmly ensconced in the same comfortable position it's enjoyed these many years. •

Revolutionary for Cadillac is its new frame which incorporates highly unconventional feature of stressing entirely through central wishbones and abandoning siderails entirely. The design probably will be extremely adaptable for future changes.

CADILLAC SPECIFICATIONS
Wheelbase: 129.5 inches
Height: 59 inches
Transmission: Hydra-Matic
Horsepower: 300
Cubic Inches: 365
Compression Ratio: 10:1

LONG-AWAITED BROUGHAM FINALLY APPEARS, BUT WITHOUT THE RUMORED INJECTION OR REAR-END AUTOMATIC TRANSMISSION.

AIR SPRINGS, one on each wheel, hold car level and keep the overall height at 55½ inches regardless of the load of passengers.

BROUGHAM CHASSIS is the same new X-frame layout used on all 1957 Cadillacs, except for the addition of air suspension. The engine utilizes two four-barrel carburetors, is rated at a maximum of 325 hp with a "standard" compression ratio of 10-to-1.

Eldorado Brougham for '57

CADILLAC'S Eldorado Brougham, the first American car to use a true air suspension system, has finally reached production reality.

The super-luxurious four-door hardtop made its debut at the National Automobile Show in New York. Public introductions will be held in key cities throughout the United States after February 1.

Although it contains several industry "firsts," the Brougham does not have several of the features expected. It uses conventional carburetors rather than fuel injection, for example.

(The decision to stick with carburetors was a last-minute one. Cadillac engineers have been working frantically to ready an injection system, but were not fully satisfied with test results. It would not be surprising to see Cadillac make a running changeover to fuel injection later in the year, however.)

Only 55½ inches high at the top of its stainless steel roof, the Brougham has a 126-inch wheelbase and is 216 inches long overall. This makes it a compact car by Cadillac standards. (It has a shorter wheelbase and is narrower, but about the same overall length, as current 62 Series models.)

The 325-hp engine is the same one used by other 1957 Eldorado models. It uses two four-barrel carburetors, displaces 365 cubic inches and has a 10-to-1 compression ratio.

The Brougham's frame is similar to the one used by other 1957 Cadillacs. It has a tubular backbone and is shaped roughly like a big "X."

The air suspension system features air spring units at each wheel. Air is supplied to the spring units thru leveling valves so the car remains level with varying loads and road conditions. This contributes to easy handling and exceptionally smooth riding qualities.

Anti-dive characteristics are built into the ball-joint front end to keep the

CONTINUED ON PAGE 128

NEW X-FRAME AND FRONT SUSPENSION, LOWER, AND STILL MORE POWER FOR '57

Cadillac

What's New

Unusual X-frame with tubular backbone . . . Body styling patterned after Eldorado Brougham show car . . . Fenderless, finned rear deck for regular Eldorados . . . Instead of sedans, four-door, four-window hardtops . . . Spherical joint front suspension . . . Top of 325 horsepower.

Your Choice

Cadillac produces cars for pocketbooks ranging from fat to mink-lined. Actually, there are many models of theoretically cheaper cars like Chrysler New Yorker and Buick Roadmaster, not to mention T-Bird and Corvette, that *can* cost you more than a basic Series 62 coupe.

These come in plain and de Ville form, as do the Series 62 four-door hardtops. The difference lies mostly in luxury of interior trim. Next in the price line is the elongated (by nearly nine inches overall) Series 60 Special sedan, newly converted to hardtop form and distinguishable by masses of chrome on the lower reaches of the rear fender.

In addition to the $12,500 Eldorado Brougham, described separately on page 58, there are two versions of what must now be called "standard" Eldorados. Considerably cheaper, relatively speaking, production is limited but there should be enough to go around. Cars are easily recognized by totally different rear end styling where the deck is flush with the quarter panels and fins are inset in a manner reminiscent of GM's Firebird II turbine car. At approximately the same price, you have a choice of the Biarritz convertible or Seville cloth-covered hardtop.

Cadillac Power

Cadillac's under-hood contents cube out to about the same displacement as Buick, considerably less than the top Chryslers. A 15-horse jump in power (to 300) is derived mainly from redesigned combustion chambers; a slight increase (to 10 to 1) in compression ratio; a new, lower carburetor with larger secondary bores and wider bore spread; and larger intake valves.

Optional on Eldorados (and actually, in practice, on other models too) is a twin four-barrel carburetor and manifold set-up that raises horsepower to 325, equal to the industry's top for regular production cars. However, torque, the real performance factor, does not seem to benefit from the changes, remaining the same as last year's 400 pounds-feet at 2800 rpm (3300 rpm for the optional engine). Therefore, although performance will be adequate, do not expect your new Cadillac to show its taillights to '56 models.

Hydra-Matic, standard on all models, is left almost as was, since its big revamping happened last year. This is the one with the second fluid coupling and two sprag clutches replacing the former friction clutch and bands. Gear changes blend into an almost continuous flow of power, but imperceptibly less smoothly than either Dynaflow or Chevrolet's new Turboglide mainly because these do not change gears as such. Big Hydra-Matic advantage is minimum power loss.

Lowered Cadillac silhouette required a switch to a two-piece driveshaft, but still of the Hotchkiss type. A 3.07 ratio gearset is standard, but specify the 3.36 option if you want best performance at a slight cost in economy.

Cadillac on the Road

Most remarkable Cadillac advance is the new "X" frame with tubular center. The body is mounted on outriggers instead of the usual side rails. Advantages can be shown by using an extreme example: The 150-inch wheelbase version for the Series 75 limousine weighs 3½ per cent less, yet has 18 per cent more resistance to twist and is 16 per cent stiffer. Actually, biggest advantage stems from beefing up hardtops and convertibles. Disadvantage is weakened body-side, more vulnerable to damage in a mid-ship collision, despite strengthened rocker panels.

Already excellent Cadillac handling is further improved by adoption of spherical joint (same as ball joint) front suspension, offering better geometry while cornering as well as greatly reduced maintenance requirements. As in other GM makes, much successful attention is paid to the elimination of brake dive.

Further road stability comes from spread-out rear leaf springs mounted parallel to the centerline of the car plus equalized treads (61 inch) fore and aft. Power steering and brakes, 15-inch tires are standard on all models.

Inside Your Cadillac

It is hopeless to try and describe the almost infinite number of interior designs available, not to mention the 500 exterior color combinations possible. Suffice to say, they are all tops in glamour if not in practicality.

Instrument panel is more readable especially because there is not a single item not marked by a lighted placard. Crash safety requirements are newly acknowledged by recessed knobs, standard panel padding, dished steering wheel, floor-mounted parking brake, and left-of-center glove box. A thoughtful feature is thick padding on the rear facing of the front seats.

Your new Cadillac will seem more lithe, easier to drive although the reasons are inexplicable since dimensions, inside and outside, are about the same except for overall height. Maybe it's that lean Brougham styling.

Why Buy?

Prestige, as measured by low depreciation, at top . . . Fine quality control during manufacture . . . Most silent car inside . . . Excellent for both handling and driving ease . . . Close to top performance.

S P E C I A L !   1 9 5 7   S H O W   I S S U E !

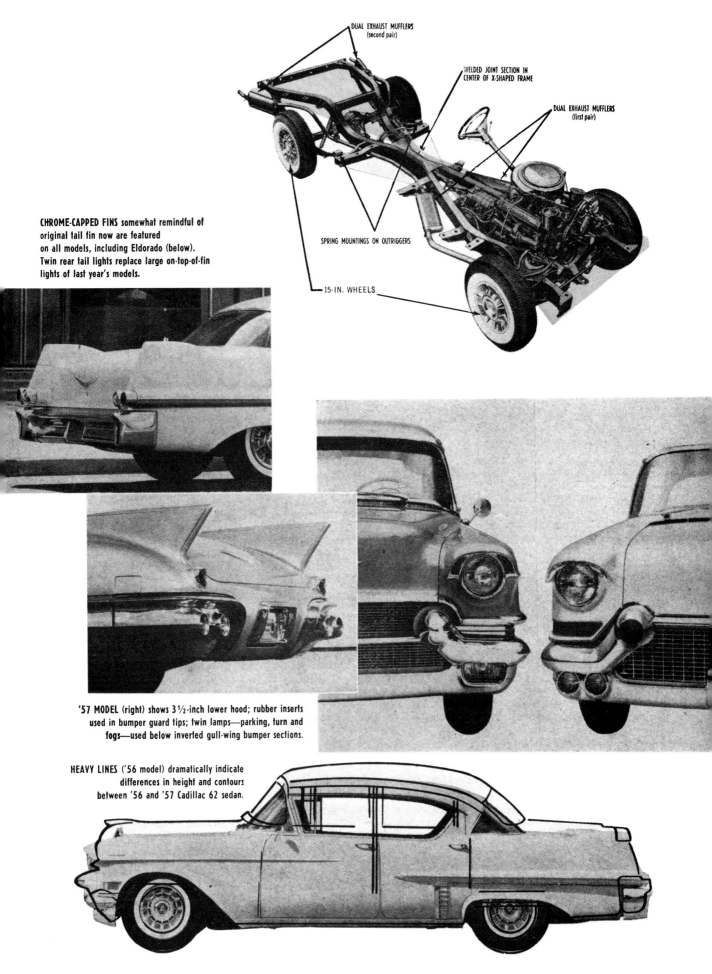

CHROME-CAPPED FINS somewhat remindful of original tail fin now are featured on all models, including Eldorado (below). Twin rear tail lights replace large on-top-of-fin lights of last year's models.

'57 MODEL (right) shows 3½-inch lower hood; rubber inserts used in bumper guard tips; twin lamps—parking, turn and **fogs**—used below inverted gull-wing bumper sections.

HEAVY LINES ('56 model) dramatically indicate differences in height and contours between '56 and '57 Cadillac 62 sedan.

CAR LIFE 1957 CONSUMER ANALYSIS

CADILLAC

By JAMES WHIPPLE

THE year 1957 was one of the big change for Cadillac. All models got new frames, suspension systems and bodies not to mention bumpers, grilles, hoods, tail-lights and instrument panels.

The engine has been given a conservative boost from 285 to 300 horsepower on the 60 Special, 62 and 75 models. The increase is due to a higher compression ratio of 10.0 to 1 and larger intake and smaller exhaust valves.

The Eldorado coupe and convertible are powered with a 325 bhp engine, basically the "standard" engine with the exception of carburetion by two four throat units instead of the single four barrel unit used on the 300 bhp engine.

One of the first things we noticed behind the wheel of the '57 Cadillac was the improved vision due to a 3½-inch lower hood which is now lower than the fender line. Short-statured drivers will welcome this change particularly in maneuvering their Cadillacs in close quarters.

The new windshield provides noticeably better vision than the one on last year's Cadillac because it is deeper (i.e. continues further into the roof panel), and because it wraps further around at each side.

Driving the new Cadillac both in traffic and out on the highway we were less conscious of the windshield corner pillars cutting into our field of vision.

We're glad to report that there was absolutely no distortion in the corners of the new windshield and that the lower corners or "doglegs" of the windshield pillars do not jut into the door opening and interfere with entry and exit.

One of the Cadillac qualities that we've always felt to be particularly outstanding is the seating comfort. The furniture industry could well take some lessons from the men who design and make Cadillac seat cushions. For people who find driving (or even riding) in a car uncomfortable due to back and leg strain, a Cadillac may well be their salvation.

Quite rightly, Cadillac's designers believe that the seat that gives the best support is more comfortable than a seat that is merely deep and soft. The Cadillac's seat backs give firm extra support at the lower part of the spine which is one part of the driver's anatomy most likely to protest at the end of 300 or 400 miles behind the wheel.

Seat cushions have been designed to give especially firm support under the thighs. This eases the strain on the driver's right leg and makes cornering and driving on high-crowned roads much more comfortable, as the driver and passengers do not flounder helplessly in billowy cushions.

Although the entire Cadillac line has been lowered from two to three inches in overall height, there has been no reduction in headroom either in front or rear compartments of the sedan. Retaining a full 35 inches of headroom

Price range (Factory list price)
$4,212 (Series 62 coupe)
to $6,648 (Eldorado Biarritz convertible and Eldorado Seville hardtop)

CADILLAC is the car for you

if... You want the Number One prestige car on the American market.

if... You appreciate the most comfortable seats available in an American car plus a thoroughly soundproof car.

if... You value really excellent workmanship in all details of upholstery, hardware, trim and finish.

if... You want the best investment, dollar for dollar, in the luxury car field.

CADILLAC SPECIFICATIONS

ENGINE	V-8		
Bore and stroke	4 in. x 3.625 in.		
Displacement	365 cu. in.		
Compression ratio	10.1:1		
Max. brake horsepower	300 @ 4800 rpm		
Max. torque	400 @ 2800 rpm		
DIMENSIONS	**SERIES 62**	**ELDORADO**	**FLEETWOOD**
Wheelbase	129.5 in.	129.5 in.	133 in.
Overall length	215.9 in.	222.1 in.	224.4 in.
Overall width	80 in.	80 in.	80 in.
Overall height	59.1 in.	57.9 in.	59.1 in.
TRANSMISSION	HydraMatic		

Eldorado Biarritz convertible is '57 Cadillac version of open-air elegance. Side trim has been reduced, tail fins have been moved inboard.

New Cadillac chassis features tubular center—X frame. Frame has no side rails, permits lowering of car. Body is secured to "outrigger" brackets.

is mandatory for Cadillac whose customers are not inclined to appreciate crushing their fedoras.

The lowering process was made possible by Cadillac's new "cruciform" frame which has a massive "X" member but no side rails. The body itself is supported by frame outriggers. This new design permits lowering of the floor and doorsills as well as the seats.

Thus the relationships of roof seat and floor dimensions remain the same and the owner of last year's (or the year before's) Cadillac will feel comfortably at home in any one of the '57's. He'll be aware of the difference only by means of the increased forward vision, the changed shape of the rear quarter windows and the new instrument panel.

Evidently encouraged by public demand and the expected rigidity of the new frame, Cadillac has scored as the first U.S. automaker to completely drop the conventional center pillar and door frames of the four door sedan.

With the exception of the seven passenger "75" models, all Cadillacs are hardtops (or convertibles). This means a dividend in vision for passengers except for the outside rear seat passengers whose vision is somewhat blocked by the rear window support pillar which angles down from the roofline in a forward dogleg.

We hope that in future models the designers will find a means of eliminating this annoying pillar which seems to have no purpose other than to stabilize the raised rear door glass when the door is swung open or the car is driven with the window half open.

With all windows closed, the new Cadillac hardtop, we tested a "62" Sedan, showed no tendency to rattle or squeak in or around the doors and window frames on rough, cobblestone roads.

This may be more a tribute to a well-designed body than to the stiffness of the new frame because there is more shake on these same rough roads than in last year's model—in fact, a good deal more shake than is to be expected in a car as massive, well-constructed and expensive as Cadillac.

In our opinion, the only real answer to the problem of body shake and vibration is a complete one-piece body and frame structure of extreme stiffness to counteract the absence of center pillars in the four-door hardtops which are by far the worst offenders.

Although body shake is to be expected on almost every heavyweight four-door hardtop made today, it comes as an unpleasant surprise to find it on a Cadillac which in previous conventional sedan models was an exceptionally solid and well-behaved car.

Cadillac's riding qualities are solid and substantial and have improved as far as better chassis stability has reduced swaying at high speeds on rough roads.

As far as interference from surface vibrations is concerned, the '57 Cadillac does not seem to have improved as much you would suspect from an entirely new engineering job. In fact, we felt that the overall riding qualities had fallen somewhat below last year's car which was up to standard for the Cadillac price range.

The two major problems that we found in the Cadillac ride were that the minor bumps caused by rough cobblestones, railroad tracks and the like were not completely absorbed and that sharp bumps such as caused by pot holes and abrupt dips were not sufficiently controlled.

In other words, despite the cushioning of large, low-pressure tires and the coil and leaf springs, and the control of large shock absorbers, the jiggle of minor bumps and the choppy rebound from larger ones got through to the passenger compartment.

Roadability has been much improved by the new chassis and ball joint front suspension layout. Brake dip which used to be a major annoyance in big Cadillacs has almost completely disappeared even in panic stop conditions. The car is no longer the slightest bit inclined to "wallow" or dive when pushed into turns of decreasing radius at high speed. Steering action (power assist is standard) is a

Lowered hood of Cadillac is beneath fender line. Split bumper has rubber tips.

Re-arranged dashboard brings instruments and knobs within driver's easy reach.

CADILLAC CHECK LIST ✓✓✓✓✓
5 CHECKS MEANS TOP RATING IN ITS PRICE CLASS

Category	Comments	Rating
PERFORMANCE	Cadillac performance is smooth and powerful but not sensational. Acceleration rate from standstill to 60 mph 11.9 seconds. Response in D-3 range of HydraMatic is smooth and very fast.	✓✓✓✓
STYLING	In our opinion the restyling of the '57 Cadillac represents a backward step to an overall shell that's less handsome and dignified than the previous models.	✓✓✓
RIDING COMFORT	Undeniably a comfortable car with its large, soft tires and deep, firm, well-designed upholstery. Some jiggling of the heavy unsprung axles and wheels transmitted to body. On very rough going there is some body shake and pitching on sharp bumps.	✓✓✓✓
ROADABILITY	The '57 Cadillac is very stable and roadable for a heavy sedan, with noticeable improvement over last year's car which was better than average. Behavior in sharp curves is good with no plowing or nosing under.	✓✓✓✓
INTERIOR DESIGN	Although Cadillac was lowered from two to three inches this year, excellent interior dimensions are maintained. Doors provide comfortable entry and exit. Seat cushions are exceptionally comfortable on long drives. Vision is considerably improved.	✓✓✓✓
EASE OF CONTROL	Power steering on Cadillac requires somewhat more effort than on other large cars but does not over-control when the steering wheel is moved fast when making a right hand turn. Power brakes are smooth-acting and reliable.	✓✓✓✓
ECONOMY	HydraMatic Drive fourth gear gives Cadillac an edge in superior gasoline mileage over other heavy luxury cars, but more powerful engine which was new in '56 models doesn't give mileage equal to lighter medium-priced cars as was the case several years ago.	✓✓✓✓
SERVICEABILITY	New compact engine compartment with lower hood and a crowd of power accessories makes easy servicing a tough proposition — tougher still with air conditioning piled on top.	✓✓✓
WORKMANSHIP	The continued high quality of paint, finish and trim found on Cadillacs is one of the big reasons for its continued leadership in the luxury field. Body shake was the only flaw in the car we tested.	✓✓✓✓✓
VALUE PER DOLLAR	Cadillac has next to the lowest depreciation rate of all cars at any price. This fact plus Cadillac's reputation for low incidence of repairs makes the car an excellent investment in luxurious transportation.	✓✓✓✓✓

CADILLAC OVERALL RATING... 4.0 CHECKS

good compromise for the average driver—not "quick," not too slow.

There's a nice balance between over-steer and understeer so that the car doesn't tend to "come around after you" in a tight bend, nor does it have the sluggish, plowing tendencies of a car with too much understeer.

For those who do a lot of driving in warm climates, Cadillac has relocated the air conditioning in the front compartment. Cooled air is blown at considerable force from three plastic doors at the base of the windshield which are not connected with the regular defrosting system. Removing the evaporator and blower from the trunk has added much needed luggage capacity to a trunk which is actually smaller than last year's model and smaller than that found on several lower-priced cars.

SUMMING UP: Cadillac is, as always, a very solid, well-built automobile with an impressive look about it. Performance is powerful and incredibly smooth, while handling and control is extremely easy and free from problems. Despite its obvious bulk and length, the Cadillac is easy to maneuver and park if the space is long enough. The quality of manufacture and traditionally low rate of depreciation make it an excellent buy for those who are able to afford the initial investment. ●

CADILLAC FOR '57 IS ALL NEW BUT STILL UNMISTAKABLY CADILLAC. EVOLUTIONARY CHANGE WAS NOT AS RADICAL AS EXPECTED.

CADILLAC ROAD TEST...

THE 1957 Cadillac is paradoxical in many respects. In the first place, it's a brand-new car with practically nothing left over from 1956 except the engine and transmission.

Yet the Cadillac tradition of evoluationary change has been followed so closely that many people won't recognize the real newness of the car!

The Cadillac used for test purposes was a 62 series four-door hardtop. As is true of most Caddys these days, it had a full complement of accessories.

Among them were power brakes and steering and Hydra-Matic, all standard non-extra cost items, plus power seats and windows, signal seeking radio with rear speaker. In short, everything but air conditioning.

With this type of load aboard, a full tank of gas and the driver, the performance turned in was about what you would expect—good, but not outstanding. That's as it should be, since most Cadillac buyers are more interested in the car's comfort and prestige than blinding acceleration.

Performance figures were just about the same as those of the 1956 test car; even slightly slower at the low end of the range, in fact. This is due to the fact that the engine displacement was unchanged and, although 15 hp was added, there was no increase in peak torque. In addition, rear axle ratio went from 3.36 to 3.07. This shows up in slightly better economy and top speed, but hurts acceleration.

Ride and handling of the '57 Cadillac are noticeably better than last year, however. Riding comfort isn't actually much smoother under straight-ahead, smooth road conditions—Cadillac has long been outstanding here.

Major ride improvement is noticed in turns; the current model feels more stable and sway has been reduced, adding to passenger comfort.

Credit for this can go to the new chassis design and resultant lower center of gravity.

As everyone interested in cars should know by now, Cadillac has ditched the traditional side-member-type frame in favor of a huge X-shaped affair. Outriggers extending from this frame help support the body.

Elimination of side frame rails permits floor height to be lowered and Cadillac claims the X-shaped design has more pound-for-pound rigidity than the "cow-belly" frames with swept-out side rails used by most other makes which were lowered drastically for 1957.

If Cadillac had any important quality problems with its all-new car this year they were licked by the time the test car was produced. All switches, gages and accessories did their job properly and finish details, interior and exterior left nothing to be desired.

Two accessories the car had which were especially appreciated were the six-way power seat and the side view mirror controlled from inside the car.

The first is the only type of power seat which really makes sense. It seems ridiculous to go to the extent of adding power just to move a seat fore and aft a few inches. The six-way seat, which can be adjusted to an almost infinite number of positions, is a different matter.

It is of particular benefit on a trip of any length because the driver can change his seating position—up, down, forward or back—easily and quickly. And it's surprising how slight variations every so often will help reduce fatigue and muscle strain.

The side view mirror is nearly a necessity with a seat of this type since it permits the outside mirror to be adjusted easily to conform to the new driving position. In fact, this type of mirror is a boon in *any* car and, since it can be adjusted without opening the window, is always at the correct angle for providing optimum vision to side and rear.

A driver getting into a new Cadillac for the first time will likely have trouble locating all the instrument switches immediately. Not all are in the conventional position directly in front of the driver.

Light switches are in the corner angle where the left side

INTERIOR features are very lush and somewhat dazzling to many people. Instruments are grouped in front of the driver and hooded to prevent glare. Radio speaker is mounted below dash in the center.

WARM AIR for rear seat heater is ducted through the doors, as can be seen here. This is making the most of waste space, in the lower portion of the doors, which is most generally left unused.

of the cowl wraps around—directly under the left wraparound section of the windshield.

Windshield wiper and washer controls are even more around at the left side; just a few inches from the separation point between A-post and door, in fact.

These controls are all easy to reach, however; easier than when in the conventional location, actually, once you get used to them.

Cadillac uses flashing generator and oil pressure warning lights, following the current trend. A feature retained from the past which is useful surprisingly often is the trip mileage indicator.

This gadget is helpful not only on long trips, but in checking gas mileage, etc. Salesmen and others paid expenses on a per-mile basis should find it especially valuable!

Speaking of gas mileage, the Cadillac turned in averages just about on a par with other cars in its class. City driving under varied traffic conditions resulted in an 11 mpg average. Highway cruising average was about 16-17 mpg at steady speeds of 50-65 mph. Overall average was just under 14 mpg.

Another point noted about the '57 Cadillac was that its radio was up to the consistently excellent standard of recent years. The test crew hi-fi fan remarked that few test cars have equalled Cadillac in this respect since 1955.

As far as styling is concerned this year, about all you can say is that it's still definitely Cadillac! You would never confuse this new model with any other make, even if you were seeing a '57 Caddy for the first time.

This was demonstrated by the number of people who asked: "Is this the 1956 or 1957 model?"

This surely proves the success of Cadillac's efforts to be evolutionary rather than revolutionary.

How much longer it can hew so closely to this policy is problematical, however. It appears even now that the radically re-styled 1957 Chrysler is taking away a few Cadillac customers. All of the new customers Lincoln was won in the past year and a half can't be former medium-priced buyers moving up a notch, either.

On the other hand, Cadillac's policy is one of the big reasons for the terrific resale value of its cars. This has become one of its most important sales weapons.

When you combine Cadillac's almost unequalled prestige value, the comfort it offers, relatively low depreciation, high quality and very acceptable all-round performance, it isn't hard to figure why the car has been so successful. •

CADILLAC TEST DATA

Test Car: 1957 Cadillac 62 four-door hardtop
Basic Price: $4780.96
Engine: 365-cubic-inch ohv V-8
Compression Ratio: 10-to-1
Horsepower: 300 @ 4800 rpm
Torque: 400 @ 2800 rpm
Dimensions: Length 221 inches, width 80, height 59, tread 61 front and rear, wheelbase 129.5
Dry Weight: 4600 lbs.
Transmission: Hydra-Matic
Acceleration: 0-30 mph 4 seconds, 0-45 mph 6.9, 0-60 mph 10.9
Gas Mileage: 13.9 average
Speedometer Corrections: Indicated 30, 45 and 60 mph are actual 32, 45 and 58.5

TAILLIGHTS on all Cadillac models have now been moved down (from their former position at the top of the fender fin) to a spot just above the bumper tip exhaust. Bumper is simple, efficient.

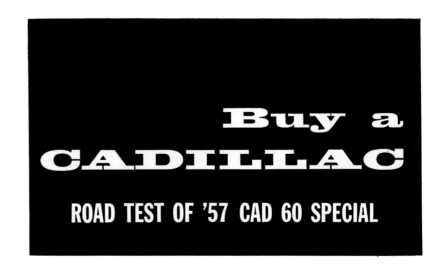

Buy a CADILLAC

ROAD TEST OF '57 CAD 60 SPECIAL

OUR TITLE MAY SOUND STRANGE, but all indications point out the truth of the fact. If you take into consideration that the Cad has the lowest depreciation, percentage-wise, of any domestic car; that repairs should be at a minimum; and that the fuel economy we obtained from our test car without using any gimmicks was the best of any large car tested this year, it all makes sense. Then throw in quality workmanship and materials, practically all the comforts of home, a superb ride, prestige . . . and what have you got to lose?

The Cadillac that we drove was a 60 Special Fleetwood. It has the longest wheelbase (133 inches) and is one of the largest passenger cars overall (224 inches) built in the U.S. Only the Cadillac 75 limousine and the Lincoln are longer. The engine is the same as in the series 62 and 75, with 365 cubic inches developing 300 horsepower. Total weight, with a full tank of Mobilgas, is 5140 pounds.

THE RIDING QUALITIES are just about the best found on any present day automobile: super soft with but very little pitch and roll. Recovery after hitting a bad dip is quick and, even on washboard type roads, vibration can hardly be felt. The car does lean quite a bit in sharp turns, but this characteristic is hardly felt by the passengers.

HANDLING IS EASY, though not as good as on some other domestic cars. The great weight makes itself felt when driving through sharp corners, where the car heels over noticeably, and generally has an adverse effect on performance. The power steering gives enough road feel and is very easy, but at higher speeds on rough roads it needs frequent correction. And, if you're unfamiliar with this car, it's wise to keep an eye on the speedometer, since the absolute silence of operation can be deceiving.

PAINT, FINISH AND TRIM are very good, with body panels and chrome strips meeting where they should—in line, which can't be said for all makes. Interior materials and workmanship are excellent, giving the impression of a custom-made car; and, certainly, with the wide variety of fabric and color combinations offered, it can easily be suited to the individual's personal taste. From the leather-padded dash and leather-covered window sills to the rich upholstery, it spells sheer luxury. Every detail has been worked out for the comfort of the owner.

As a matter of fact, Cadillac would seem to be stressing workmanship, quality, and comfort even more than in previous years. Aside from the consistently fine calibre of the overall craftsmanship, a very successful effort to eliminate the small annoyances and to anticipate passenger and driver wants has been made. The extra large glove compartment, for instance, besides being located amidship, has the release button located far left, within easy reach of the driver. The same is true of the radio, both the volume and tuner knobs being on the left side. All levers, as a matter of fact, have either been recessed or located behind the dish-type steering wheel.

The instruments are well grouped, large, and highly legible. There is no need to squint, squirm, check the road, then squint some more. One glance should do the job. And speaking of glancing, the side view mirror is adjustable from an inside lever.

TIRED OF OPENING THE TRUNK LID? It's now power assisted. Insert the key, turn, and an electric motor will free and partly raise the lid, with the manual effort being reduced to a minimum. It works the same in reverse, both operations being a boon to ladies, children and those who like to play "Open, Sesame." You can also unlock the trunk with a button located in the glove compartment. A red light reading "trunk" will flash on, signifying a successful disengagement and warning you not to drive with the lid open. It is, incidentally, commodious, to say the least.

FUEL ECONOMY WAS ASTONISHING for a 5100-pound automobile. Our tank average for 332 miles was 14.0 mpg, and at steady speeds of 30 mph we averaged 24.1 mpg and at 60 mph, 16.9 mpg. It proves that good fuel economy *is* attainable from a high compression, modern engine, *provided* it's coupled to the right rear axle ratio. In the case of this particular car, the high-speed axle (3.07 to 1) gave good economy, but lessened its acceleration qualities.

PERFORMANCE IS NOT the highest on the list, but don't hold that against the car. It was not, after all, designed to be a hot rod—anything but!—and its 300 horses can move you from place to place very,

PHOTOS BY WORON

ACCELERATION FIGURES compiled with the aid of the fifth wheel indicated that despite size, weight of car, performance was more than adequate.

AN MT RESEARCH REPORT
by Otto Zipper

FOR ECONOMY?

REVEALS FANTASTIC FUEL ECONOMY

very quickly, indeed. Acceleration through the gears is smoothness itself and top speed is well over a hundred.

CADILLAC'S TWO MAIN DOMESTIC competitors in this price-class range have some fine offerings; and, in certain categories (e.g., performance, handling and, some might say, styling) Cad is short of being tops. But in an overall analysis it would be difficult to say that another make is better.

We do know this: while coming back to Los Angeles from our testing site at El Mirage Dry Lake, we drove through an area called Mint Canyon. Maybe it was that magical, just before dusk, time of day —maybe it was the splendidly buoyant semi-desert air—or maybe it was a combination of those natural phenomena and a fine mechanical achievement that made us think we had never before so much enjoyed an automobile ride.

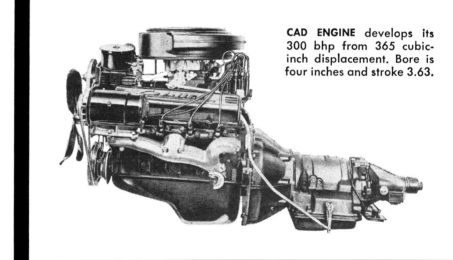

CAD ENGINE develops its 300 bhp from 365 cubic-inch displacement. Bore is four inches and stroke 3.63.

PERFORMANCE
(300-bhp engine, 3.07 rear axle)

SPEEDOMETER ERROR
Read 31 at true 30, 45 at 45, 52 at 50, 62 at 60, 78 at 75, 84 at 80.

ACCELERATION
From Standing Start
0-45 mph 7.7   0-60 mph 12.4
Quarter-mile 18.6 and 75 mph
Passing Speeds
30-50 mph 5.0   45-60 mph 4.7
50-80 mph 12.1

FUEL CONSUMPTION
Using Mobilgas Special
Steady Speeds
24.1 mpg @ 30   19.7 mpg @ 45
16.9 mpg @ 60   14.0 mpg @ 75
Stop-and-Go Driving
14.0 mpg tank average for 332 miles

(285-bhp engine, 3.54 rear axle)

Read 34 at true 30, 49 at 45, 64 at 60, 78 at 75

From Standing Start
0-45 mph 6.6   0-60 mph 11.4
Quarter-mile 17.8 and 78.5 mph
Passing Speeds
30-50 mph 5.3   40-60 mph 5.0
50-80 mph 11.0

Using Mobilgas Special
Steady Speeds
21.4 mpg @ 30   20.2 mpg @ 45
17.4 mpg @ 60   14.7 mpg @ 75
Stop-and-Go Driving
12.8 mpg tank average for 512 miles

RETROSPECT

'57 CADILLAC ELDORADO BROUGHAM

WHEN A CADDY COST MORE THAN A ROLLS

by Don Sherman
PHOTOGRAPHY BY JIM FRENAK

Occasionally, a great notion inspires the auto industry to forge ahead full-throttle against incredible odds. During the fearless '50s, Cadillac launched various flights of fancy, one of which went into production as the '57 Eldorado Brougham. Though it was by no means a financial success, the Brougham is a significant event in automotive history because it is *the* modern-day Duesenberg: the last cost-no-object, limited-production, largely handmade automobile produced in America for sale to the public.

General Motors warmed up for the Brougham production run with several dream cars. At the 1953 GM Motorama (where the Corvette was born), Cadillac presented the Orleans, the industry's first four-door hardtop. The public's interest in this exercise convinced GM's design boss, Harley Earl, that a spectacular four-seat four-door sedan was the way to go.

At the 1954 Motorama, Earl checked his hunch with a luxurious four-door called the Cadillac Park Avenue. Then, at the first stop of the 1955 Motorama in New York City, Cadillac rolled forth its Eldorado Brougham showpiece to more rave reviews. Two months later, when the Motorama stopped in San Francisco, Cadillac announced the Brougham would go on sale during the '56 model year.

Harley Earl's chutzpah wasn't the sole driving force behind the Brougham. In 1952, Ford commenced efforts to resuscitate the Lincoln Continental with hopes of unseating Cadillac as the luxury car king. The Continental Mark II was unveiled in the fall of 1955 with a pricetag of $9517. Various delays beset the Brougham, but when it finally went on sale a year and a half later, its price was a heart-stopping $13,074. A Rolls-Royce Silver Cloud cost $12,700 in 1957.

Other than a 126-inch wheelbase and precious pricetags, the Lincoln Continental Mark II and the Cadillac Eldorado Brougham had little in common. While the Mark was a clean, classic reflection of prewar glories, the Brougham rocketed design aesthetics and engineering capabilities into the '60s.

Regular Cadillacs were growing larger each year, but the Brougham was, in Earl's words, "a compact, personalized automobile." It rode on a wheelbase 3.5 inches shorter than the standard model's and its roof was lower by some 4 inches. Every body panel was unique to this low-volume model. Standard Cadillac powertrain components, such as a 365-cubic-inch V-8 breathing through two four-barrel carburetors, went through a rigorous inspection and selection process to qualify for Brougham use.

The '57 Brougham's custom Fleetwood bodywork was rich-

ly adorned with every stylistic and technological advancement that could be mustered: a low front-hinged hood, quad headlamps, brushed stainless steel roof, narrow-whitewall low-profile tires on composite steel-and-aluminum wheels, air suspension, and a compound-curved windshield. Of course, there were power accessories galore. An electric motor raised and lowered the trunklid at the touch of a button. When a front door opened, the seat moved back and down for entry, then automatically returned to one of two memory positions. If the ignition key was on, the engine started automatically as soon as the shift lever was moved to the park or neutral position.

Shifting into gear locked the doors and disengaged the inside rear door handles. An "autronic" eye watched for oncoming headlamps before automatically selecting low beams.

Luxury touches graced the four-place interior. Sunvisors were laminated from clear and opaque plastic for a polarizing effect. A large glovebox was packed with amenities including six magnetized refreshment tumblers, cigarette case, compact, and tissue dispenser. The fold-down rear armrest housed a notepad with mechanical pencil, beveled mirror, and a one-ounce atomizer of Arpége Extract de Lanvin perfume.

Glen Durmisevich, a member of the General Motors advanced design staff and resident of Rochester, Michigan, owns the Eldorado Brougham featured in this Retrospect. A mere toddler when the Brougham came to be, Durmisevich later discovered the Cadillac of his dreams in a vintage copy of *Popular Science* and purchased this car—actually, his second Brougham—in 1983.

Durmisevich is an excellent guide to the weird but wonderful delights of the Eldorado Brougham because he knows so well that cars *aren't* built this way today. The show begins with a four-horn fanfare loud enough to blast aside a Peterbilt. Durmisevich points out a cast-aluminum front bumper that makes Madonna seem flat-chested. He draws attention to the seamless prow, achieved by welding both front fenders to a finish panel above the grille.

The Brougham's door system is bizarre, to say the least. Suicide rear doors swing out and up on compound hinges. Both doors latch into a half-height B-pillar and seal against each other. Access to the two-place back seat is surprisingly good in spite of the short rear door opening and the two-door-hardtop roofline.

During a test drive granted by our gracious host, we listened for telltale signs of chassis flex. There are the usual old-car creaks and rattles, but the pillarless door system feels solid and secure. The air suspension helps this 35-year-old Cadillac glide over broken pavement with slightly less than the usual amount of impact harshness. Pitch-and-roll motion also feels more damped than in coil-sprung cars of this period. The steering is slow, over-assisted, and imprecise by today's standards, allowing the bias-ply front tires to follow pavement grooves and road crown instead of minding the driver's hands. High-angle visibility through the wrapover windshield is exemplary.

Flooring the accelerator opens eight hungry throttle bores. A polite moan from the engine room is accompanied by a methodical gain in momentum. With 5400 pounds of custom-crafted coachwork and power accessories to tote around, the 325-horsepower (gross rating) engine has its work cut out. Contrary to popular opinion, the fuel-level needle doesn't fall faster than the speedometer needle rises.

Cadillac built 400 Eldorado Broughams in 1957 and sold them to such celebrities and potentates as Bob Hope, Frank Sinatra, and David Rockefeller. Lincoln abandoned the ultra-luxury field at the end of that model year after building 4660 Mark IIs. In 1958, Cadillac sold 304 more Broughams, then handed body manufacturing over to Pinin Farina in Italy for another 200 greatly simplified '59-'60 models.

While the buying public capriciously shifted its attention to tiny European imports and America's first compacts, GM tallied its losses: approximately $9 million for the Brougham affair or $10,000 per car. Considering the fact that it bought absolute luxury-class supremacy, that was a mere pittance.

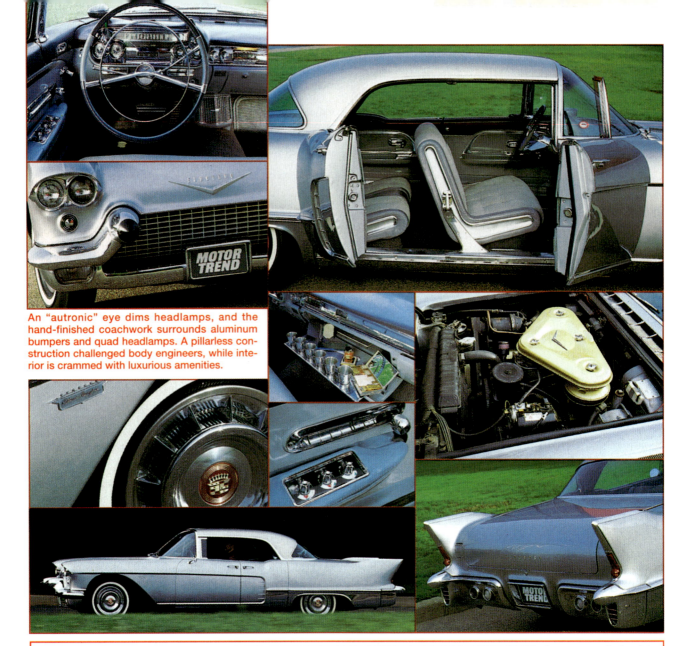

An "autronic" eye dims headlamps, and the hand-finished coachwork surrounds aluminum bumpers and quad headlamps. A pillarless construction challenged body engineers, while interior is crammed with luxurious amenities.

From the Archives

"How It Feels To Ride in a $13,500 Car" was *Motor Trend*'s headline for the July '57 test of the Cadillac Eldorado Brougham. Bigger than a Tokyo apartment, and more luxuriously furnished, the Eldo Brougham amazed and delighted *MT*'s staffers with its gilded upholstery and world-of-tomorrow gadgets.

"When you enter this semi-custom beauty, you find yourself enveloped in an aura of luxury," the description began. "The interior is distinctive and luxurious beyond any production car made in this country."

On the road, the giant Brougham ran "smoothly and almost silently," but it was noted that "performance is not highest on the list." No acceleration runs were timed on the highly guarded test car *MT* drove, but in the June '57 issue, a full-boat Fleetwood 60 Special (weighing "only" 5100 pounds) registered 0-60 mph in 12.4 seconds. Figure about a second slower for the Eldo.

The land yacht's air-suspension was labeled as "super soft," but with "some road feel." In closing, *MT*'s reporter effluviated that he'd "never before so much enjoyed an automobile ride."

—*C. Van Tune*

SPECIFICATIONS
'57 Cadillac Eldorado Brougham (July '57)

Base price	$13,074
Engine	365 ci V-8
Horsepower	325 (gross) @ 4800 rpm
Induction	Two 4-bbl carburetors
Transmission	3-speed auto.
Curb weight	5400 lb
0-60 mph	13.5 sec (est.)
Quarter mile	19.0 sec/75.0 mph (est.)

NOTHING BUT THE BEST

Is this the cleanest 1958 Cadillac Series 62 convertible in Britain? Sarah Bradley checks behind its ears (metaphorically speaking, of course) to find out.

These days buying a brand new car is pretty simple: Walk into your local friendly tin box dealer's office, talk deals, finance, special offers and part-exchanges for your present model, get them to throw in a higher spec stereo and a driver's airbag for free and away you drive, pleased as punch, posing in your new wheels. Easy.

But what about the other side of the coin? By the time you've driven it half a mile down the road your latest status symbol has depreciated by about a quarter of what you paid for it, loosing value at a rate of as much as £10 a yard. So to prevent it from loosing any more of its tentatively held value, over the next few years you can only have it worked on by 'approved' garages at extortionate hourly rates, using 'genuine' parts which cost a fortune, and must keep the service booklet so up-to-date that it hurts. Just so you can repeat the whole palaver in three years time. All that hassle and expense, and nobody even *looks* at you driving it!

It's just not logical, in fact it's a mug's game, but I guess some people never learn. And they have the cheek to think that *we're* the oddballs. I don't know; today, it seems, to be different is to be frowned upon.

So what if you do want to stand out from the crowd? What if you do want the attention and excitement that driving an old and unusual vehicle brings? But what if, at the same time, you don't want the hassle of component failure, or leaking door rubbers, or rusty bodywork which naturally, and quite justifiably, come hand-in-hand with cars which are as old as you are and have probably lived a lot tougher life? What you need is a brand new classic car; something a bit like the machine you see here.

This totally restored 1958 Cadillac Series 62 convertible really is the nearest thing to a new-old-stock classic that you could ever wish to find. From the rubber tips on the front bumpers through to the chrome-encased tailfins, every component has been refurbished, replaced and refined to the extent that it really is very easy to convince yourself that the car has just rolled out of the showroom.

The deep blue paragon of elegance is a showcase for the talents of one particular London-based American car import and restoration company, Dream Cars. Yes, yes, that's right; those infamous Homan brothers of *Channel 4* television fame – Stewart with *that* laugh and Milton with the outrageously dry sense of humour. Those Dream Car chaps who, throughout an eight-year period which has seen the American car scene rise in magnitude practically overnight to outrageous proportions in the late 1980s, only to drop so quickly again with the onset of the recession, have stayed right at the top of their profession, seeing off any opposition while earning themselves a warranted reputation for bringing in first-rate rust-free cars. Facts is facts, guv – to have survived the last few years in this country means you've got to be good at what you do.

The Homans originally located this Cadillac two years ago on one of their frequent undertakings to search through the hot and dry West Coast states of America for the right automobiles. At the request of a client, they had already tracked down and inspected several examples of this sought-after model, but for one reason or another nothing had yet been what they were looking for – a straight, complete but unrestored car.

Then they spied this one. Baby blue with a white hood and cheap, retrimmed white vinyl Mexican interior, it sat on the sales lot of a garage over on Ventura Boulevard in Studio City, California. The car was not

specs which begin to mar the chromework, were thankfully absent. However, a receipt from a garage in Utah was discovered in the car during stripdown, indicating that it was there on at least one occasion. Wherever the car spent its previous 34 years, the complete lack of anything other than negligible surface rust indicated the climate sure was warm.

Once taken back to a rolling shell, the true nature of a car is always revealed, but the Cadillac proved to be nothing other than what had been expected. However, after the paint had been stripped, one door was found to have been badly hit sometime in the past, and although it had been well disguised with filler it was decided on closer inspection to have a new doorskin made and fitted. Other areas of the body which showed any signs of damage were easily rectifiable at the hands of a good panel beater.

Next the shell was prepared and repainted. As with all cars, colour is a totally personal choice, and in this case the original Daphne Blue was discarded in favour of stunning dark blue metallic, matched with Cadillac's rarely-seen original Cobalt Blue. A clear lacquer finished the shine off perfectly.

The search had long since begun to find the items needed to restore the Cadillac to a first-class standard. NOS and reproduction light lenses and other cosmetic items were purchased while many existing mechanical components were returned to the States for refurbishment. The distributor, carburettor, brake servo and wiper motor all underwent this treatment, while all the other working units, right down to the thermostat control for the heater, were stripped, cleaned and refitted using parts readily available in the UK.

The interior was the next department to receive attention. The original six-way power seat (which, according to its style plate, was one of the few optional extras this particular car was fitted with) had long since gone walkabouts and been replaced by a bog-standard two-way bench, so a new one was the first thing to be located. The badly cracked padded dash was returned to America where a 'secret' process is used to remold the vinyl over the metal carcass and dye it to colour. The same company also sent over a length of matching vinyl to be used to trim the door cappings.

The finished interior is in fact of a higher spec than original. Leather facings and vinyl sides were standard on the seats – you never found cloth in a convertible Cadillac – but those in this car are fully trimmed in Connolly leather using the exact techniques utilised in the GM trim shop. The specially dyed metallic white and blue leather is imprinted with the closest grain to factory-finish still available. Dark blue Wilton carpet replaces the original synthetic/wool mix tufted floor covering – overkill maybe, but when luxury is at stake, expense is not a consideration.

The cracked steering wheel, self-seeking radio, even the lights in the ashtrays were all returned to their original glory as the brand new wiring loom and dash were put in place. A brand new pump, rams and hoses graced the hood frame. The handsome dark blue cloth top is again not as the factory turned out their convertibles – in the 1950s even Cadillac settled for standard vinyl diced hooding. To go with Cobalt Blue, the original owner could have chosen from black, white or a paler blue material. Contrary to popular belief, the hood boot doesn't necessarily match the hood – it usually carries through the colour theme of the top half of the interior. Hence the choice of white vinyl here. Inside the trunk was completely retrimmed using a period finish vinyl which is easy to keep clean.

Next came the fitting of the exterior trim, along with all new rubbers and E-Z-Eye factory-tinted glass. Luckily, the majority of the car's original stainless and chrome trim had survived its later and apparently less than glamorous life. Although some of it was bent, and even broken, having something to work with is always better than nothing at all. Missing or broken-beyond-repair badges and scripts were obtained from America, where plenty of companies specialise in their reproduction. While all the larger pieces were being rechromed or polished, Dream Cars also uprated the front of the car to include a gold-finished grille – a standard item on top-of-the-range Eldorados, but an optional extra costing $27 for other models. This in itself took two days to reassemble after being anodised.

All that was left was to reassemble the mechanics, brakes, steering and suspension of the car, all using completely new parts. Other than a clean and fluid change, the four-speed Jetaway Hydra-Matic transmission remained untouched – it was the only

unblemished by any stretch of the imagination – the electrics were shot, the power hood and antenna were no more, the gauges on the dash refused to even blink and the servo on the brakes had died long since – but experience looked beneath those cosmetic faults to find a perfect restoration-ripe piece of American steel.

Soon the car was on its way over to England, where it was transported back to Dream Cars' Battersea workshop ready for the stripdown and restoration to commence. So thorough was this labour of love to be, that it was another 18 months before the car set rubber to tarmac again.

Little is known about the history of the car before its appearance on that used car lot back in Studio City, LA county. Stewart told me he'd surmised that the car had not spent too much of its life in the great smog-choked metropolis itself – the usual tell-tale signs of a car which has spent any significant period in a polluted atmosphere, for instance the tiny black

Photography: Garry Stuart

NOTHING BUT THE BEST

item on the car which had been thoroughly rebuilt just before its departure from native soil.

The 365cu.in. 310bhp V8 engine was taken apart and completely balanced and blueprinted from the pan to the rocker covers. It had in its past been semi-customised – the block was painted red instead of the correct Cadillac blue, and fitted with chromed valve covers and air cleaner, but all was returned to original before being shoehorned back into the engine bay. This itself had been completely stripped back and the inner wings shotblasted and stove enamelled along with the rest of the front sheet metal such as the radiator support and all the fixings. Smaller nuts and bolts, hinges and brackets were zinc plated for a clean show finish.

Shunning the easy option of installing electric wipers, the car's vacuum-operated ones were restored to their former working order. In fact the only concession to modernity made was the retaining of the alternator which had been fitted in the place of the original generator to help the car stay totally reliable. All the original parts have been kept in case anyone should wish to return the system to original in the future.

A custom-made dual system exhaust was then fitted, correctly exiting from the bottom of the car rather than through the bumper's louvred inserts (that arrangement only applied to the 1957 model year which shared the same rear bumpers).

Finally the front wings and trim were bolted on. A final fit and finish, a thorough polish here and a few minor adjustments there, and the car was ready for delivery to its new owner.

And there it is. An automobile which may be thirty-four years old, but to all intents and purposes is as fresh as the day it rolled off the production line. This car is going to be used – you may occasionally see it at shows but more than likely will spot it cruisin' the Kings Road for many years to come. And I'd infinitely prefer that to buying an anonymous blob of 'new' metal any day. ∎

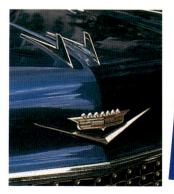

Dream Cars will undertake the complete restoration of any 1950s or 1960 American automobile. They offer every service outlined here, and more, and also cater for general mechanical servicing and can supply hard-to-find new and used parts. Speak to them on 071 627 5775 or visit their showroom at 8/10 Ingate Place, Battersea, London SW8 3NS.

Many thanks to Regents College, Regents Park, London.

DREAM "CADDIE" IS OUT

CADILLAC'S Eldorado Brougham, premiered as a dream-car teaser two years ago, has become reality at last. In the past few weeks a small but steady trickle of these 12,000-dollar (£A5400) luxury chariots has been issuing from the Cadillac Division's Detroit factory to fill orders placed months ago.

I happened to be visiting the General Motors plant when the first five production Broughams were nearing completion and saw the reason for the delay: the cars were almost entirely hand-made — a distinction the Eldorado Brougham shares only with its arch-rival for the luxury trade, Ford's Lincoln Continental.

G.M. officials showed me Broughams in various stages of construction, and also the test car for the series, which has covered thousands of miles. I was suitably impressed.

In contrast to the ordinary Cadillac's juke-box vulgarity, the Brougham has sleek, extremely graceful lines, accentuated by its pillarless four-door styling and the soft sheen of its hardtop, made of brushed stainless steel.

Australian Ken Tyas visits Cadillac factory, sees first Eldorado Broughams take shape

X-FRAME chassis with tubular backbone has outriggers to carry the body, mounts a massive V8 developing 325 b.h.p. White hoods near rear wheels cover Brougham's air springs; similar units mounted forward are obscured in photo. They are claimed to keep car always level.

Interesting engineering features include an X-frame chassis with tubular central backbone, a new type of air suspension and a four-headlight system (pioneered on the Eldorado prototype but since copied by several other car-makers).

The chassis allows a very low floor, at the same time increasing torsional rigidity. The body is secured to sturdy outrigger mountings, and the rigidity of the whole structure is such that it permits the use of pillarless four-door styling on a 126-inch wheelbase, in a car that's 18 feet long and 6½ft. wide. Overall height is only 4ft. 7½in. There's a penalty in the form of 5¼in. road clearance, but this won't be much of a worry on America's super-highways.

Use of air springs is probably the most daring innovation. The system incorporates an individual hemispherical air chamber at each wheel; the car from nose-diving when you hit the power-assisted brakes (which have a lining area of 220 sq. in.).

In the "four-eyed" headlight system, the two outer lamps incorporate high and low beam and are used for city driving, while the inner pair are bright spotlights for use on country roads. Twin fog lamps are also provided, built into the front bumper assembly (incidentally, those dark tips on the front bumper projections are replaceable rubber inserts). The rear bumpers contain backing lights and direction indicators, in addition to twin exhaust ports.

Power plant is a formidable 365 cu. in. (6-litre) overhead-valve V8, with 4in. bore, 3.625in. stroke and 10 to 1 compression. It churns out 325 b.h.p. at 4800 r.p.m. and develops a maximum torque of 400ft./lb. at 3300 revs. Fuel is supplied through twin four-barrel carburettors, and an

Inside, there's literally everything that opens and shuts. Windows and air vents are power-operated, and even the boot-lid can be unlocked, raised and lowered again by means of a control in the glovebox, without the driver leaving the car.

The front seat has a "built-in memory" (now also offered as an extra on some Ford Mercury models). The driver selects and sets the seat adjustments that suit him best. When he opens the front door, the seat moves down and back for easy exit; when the driver returns to the car and all doors are closed, the seat automatically returns to the desired driving position, as before.

There is a special heating system with individual controls for each occupant (the Brougham is described as a five-seater, although it can easily carry six on its five-foot-wide bench seats). In summer, an air-conditioner

LOW bodywork, spread of tailfins, enormous rear window make Brougham look much wider than its 78 inches.

levelling valves control the supply of pressurised air to the rubber hemispheres, providing a constantly level ride over any road, and with varying load conditions. Roll on corners is minimised and correct steering geometry is preserved on rough surfaces. The levelling controls are so sensitive that they spring into action the moment a door is opened, and G.M. claim the air springs should never need repairs. Correct pressure is supplied automatically by a pump working off the engine.

An anti-dive control built into the spherical-joint front suspension keeps improved form of hydraulic transmission carries the power to a 3.36 to 1 ratio rear axle.

G.M. originally planned to produce the Brougham with a fuel-injection engine, but their engineers struck some problems which couldn't be ironed out in time for the production deadline — so meanwhile customers will have to make do with a mere 325 b.h.p.

The 15-inch road wheels are beautifully forged aluminium and carry 8.40 by 15 tubeless tyres. Steering is power-assisted, of course, and turning circle is a very moderate 42ft.

cools the whole interior of the car.

The transistor radio, fitted as standard, has an aerial which rises automatically as the set is switched on and retracts when it is turned off.

Minor luxuries include a host of personal accessories fitted into the spacious glovebox — cigarette case, tissue dispenser, four gold-finished magnetised tumblers, compact and lipstick, a bottle of cologne, and a metal-backed vanity mirror which can be folded out to form a shelf.

Add a choice of 45 color schemes to all this, and what more could you possibly want for your 12,000 bucks?

first feel behind the wheel CADILLAC

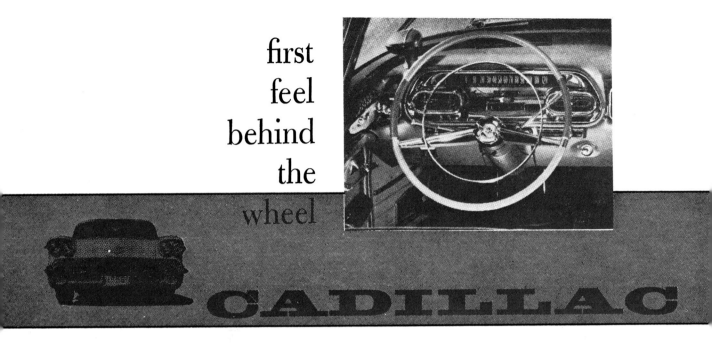

by Joe Wherry
Detroit Editor

WHEN YOU HAVE a good thing," the Cadillac people are prone to say, "why change?"

They have a point and Cadillac's firm hold on the prestige market may prove the point. Of course several changes are evident, but they are definitely in the face-lift category. Take our introduction model for instance, a luxurious Series 62 Coupe de Ville; it's scarcely an inch longer than the '57 counterpart. The wheelbase is unchanged, and the overall width is the same. The height overall, too, is unchanged.

Under the hood there are few changes. The compression ratio has been stepped up, slightly, to 10.25 to 1 on all models. Advertised horsepower, therefore, now stands at 310 bhp at 4800 rpm with a single four-barrel carburetor. This engine is standard on all models except the ultra-luxury jobs—the Eldorado Biarritz and Seville and the Brougham. The latter have the otherwise optional "Q" engine which shares the same block but has triple-two-barrel carburetors with ratings of 335 bhp at 4800. Regardless of carburetion, the torque of each is stated at 405 pounds-feet at 3100 and 3400 rpm respectively.

Dual range Hydra-Matic transmissions are standard on all, of course, as are power steering and power brakes. Steering has been improved, unspecified details having enabled even more effortless steering, and response is quick with only 3⅔ turns of the wheel being required from lock-to-lock. The wheel size and effective brake lining area are the same as last year.

Cadillac's new tubular center section X-type frame, introduced in '57, is little changed except for modification necessary to accommodate air suspension, an option on all models except for the Eldorado Brougham where *air* is standard. A new four-link-type trailing arm rear suspension is used across the board. Our steel-sprung *first feel* car was equipped thusly. A trailing arm attaches, on each side, to a crossmember extending far outboard of the wasp-waisted frame forward of the rear wheels. These two arms precisely position the rear axle. Another trailing link, actually two links in one and shaped in outline like an asymmetrical circle, attaches to the differential cage, in the rear, and is hinged to the rear frame crossmember.

Take a new Cadillac, one with coil springs, through a fast series of S-bends and you'll gain new respect for the roadability that *can* be built into a large and heavy car. Solidly positioning the rear axle in this manner prevents torque and road-induced misalignment of the rear axle. The big car holds firm at speeds at least 50 per cent greater than could formerly be held. On fast corners there is still considerable heeling over, but no longer is this accompanied by as much rear end sway as formerly. Rear end breakaway is less likely, there's more warning, and correction is easier and less violent.

STARTING OUT from scratch, with the Hydra-Matic selector in top DRIVE range, our 310-horsepower Coupe de Ville made the following acceleration times: 0 to 30 mph, 3.9 seconds; to 45, 7.4; to 60, 11.7. The 50-80 time was 11.8 seconds.

A cold rain hampered these acceleration tests; despite this, however, rear wheels did *not* hop; they stayed put under maximum torque, slipped remarkably

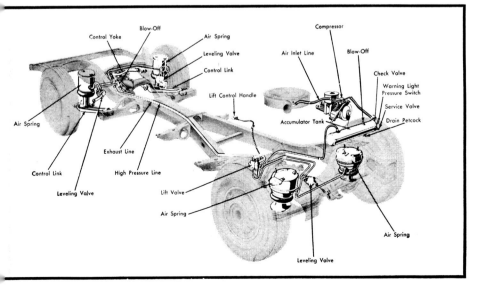

FRAME has only slight modifications to accommodate air suspension system.

little, and evidenced the benefits of the trailing links in the rear with better traction and less squat.

On a high-speed test track this heavy car snuggled down in the curves and, though the road was wet, it was solid and unaffected by a moderate crosswind that blew all day. It gave excellent feel of the road. The optional air suspension would, theoretically at least, give a softer ride. How this could be, or better yet how the air bags could improve ride and driver feel and control proportionately, is difficult to imagine since the new rear suspension now allows a more violent type of driving with increased road adhesion.

But Cadillac buyers are not usually so concerned with handling approaching that expected of sports cars as they are of the quality evidenced and the appointments. There are no less than 55 interior trim and color combinations available on all series below the Brougham; the latter has 44 available interior trims. The power window controls have been extended, in scope, to include the front vent windows. All four-door models now feature rear vent windows as well. Stylish and just as practical is a new molded Fiberglas headliner for the hardtop models. Easy to clean, this headliner has sound-deadening properties as well. The buyer can choose conventional two-way power seat controls or six-way controls; the latter are now controlled from the driver's armrest. Also optional is power operation for the rear deck lid—a switch in the glove compartment does the trick. Electrical door locks are also optional on any model with power windows.

Passenger comfort in the front seat has been improved by relocation of the radio speaker in the dashboard—it was in the center of the floor. The instrument panel now includes, at the right side, the clock. Vacationers will find that their '58 Cadillac, regardless of model, will hold more luggage than formerly. The trunk has a new floor that is perfectly flat.

OUR TEST CAR was a run-of-the-mill job and so we noted, particularly, that assembly and workmanship generally were excellent. In '57 we experienced drafts, in one hardtop, caused by badly out-of-line doors and weatherstripping. We have been told that Cadillac is tightening up on quality control. Even fine car manufacturers have to watch final assembly; the new models should show improvement to the point where they will undoubtedly be the best assembled high-priced cars made domestically.

Cadillac has not released the percentage of air-suspended cars they expect to build, but the ratio will probably be the highest in the industry. This system is refined over that introduced on the Brougham last spring but is technically the same. Incorporated in the air suspension system is a lift valve actuated by an under-dash handle which forces the air bags full of air, puts the car at full-jounce position to enable the driver to clear obstructions, high road centers in an emergency, or to back out of steep driveways without damaging bumper guards, etc.

Distinctive styling in the Biarritz and Seville models in the Eldorado series is maintained by rear quarter panel trim, by a different bumper bar, and by vertical strips between the outer bumper sections. The Biarritz features Cape Buffalo leathers with both grained and metallic finishes, or one may optionally choose combinations of leather and metallic-threaded nylon materials.

The 133-inch wheelbase Fleetwood Series 60 Special is distinguished by an extruded aluminum panel across the lower portion of the rear quarter panel—this grooved decoration is matched on the rear deck between the backup lights. Stainless steel gets a new nod from Caddy on the Fleetwood 60 with a rocker sill molding beneath the doors. /MT

BODY STYLING for '58 (below) is not greatly changed from '57 (above) except in front end.

CAR LIFE 1958 CONSUMER ANALYSIS

CADILLAC

By JIM WHIPPLE

IN THE FACE of the first serious competition in many years, Cadillac has stepped down off its Rolls Royce-like pedestal and, with the '57 and '58 models, commenced to make really worthwhile improvements in riding qualities, handling and roadability.

Having the uncontested leader of U.S. luxury field for so many years, made Cadillac management feel that it was enough just to come forth with a large, quiet-running, beautifully-made luxury package year after year.

The fact of the matter is that they were right. Until 1957, when the eye-stopping new Imperial and a vastly upgraded Lincoln caught the luxury buyer's eye, Cadillac's conservative, massive good looks and high prestige was enough to give each and every Cad salesman a happy backlog of potential customers, not only for new cars but for well-kept trade-ins too!

In 1958, Cadillac is still the sales leader although the margin of sales supremacy has been cut down. For those who may be waiting for a new Caddy or making a choice between the big three we've got good news; the engineering progress that did much toward winning Cadillac its crown is under way in earnest once more.

The '58 Cadillac is more than just an elegantly facelifted new edition of a perennial favorite; it is a very noticeably improved automobile. When we got behind the wheel of the Series 62 Sedan DeVille test car, we were once again impressed by the deep, firm comfort of the upholstery which is second to no other U.S. car.

The driving position is as comfortable as ever and vision through the wrap-around windshield is nearly distortion-free. For short-statured drivers, the '58 Cad's 5-inch longer hood is no help as it cuts down view of the road immediately ahead of the car.

Whether the owner's pleasure in a longer, more massive-looking car (wheelbase remains 129 in.) will counteract the annoyance of groping blindly into narrow driveways or bumping into curbs is for him to judge. Happily, the longer hood and fenders and the longer backslanted tail fins do not impair safe vision on the open highway.

The familiar Cad instrument panel is, as always, an irritating paradox. The instrument dials are wonderfully readable white on black, perfectly placed so that they can be read through the steering wheel, softly lighted yet surrounded by dazzling chrome trim as thick as whipped cream. The glitter from this needless frosting manages to be equally annoying in daylight and after dark and makes you think seriously of spending an hour or so working it over with a small brush and some lusterless enamel.

Cad's power steering is as good as ever. It has just the right balance of gradually increasing boost and true feel of forces reacting between front wheels and road surface. This doesn't mean that Cadillac steering transmits

Series 62 four-door hardtop snows Cadillac's returning to high, swept-back tailfins and longer hood of '56. Its 310-hp engine is standard throughout the line.

CADILLAC is the car for you

if... You want the top prestige car in America today.

if... You liked everything about last year's Cadillac, yet found its ride and roadability inferior to its '57 competition; the '58 solves your problems.

if... High quality of finish and workmanship are important to you.

if... The lowest rate of depreciation in the luxury field makes economic sense to you.

CADILLAC SPECIFICATIONS

ENGINE	V-8	ELDORADO "Q" V-8	
Bore and stroke	4 in. x 3.625 in.	4 in. x 3.625 in.	
Displacement	365 cu. in.	365 cu. in.	
Compression ratio	10.25:1	10.25:1	
Max. brake horsepower	310 @ 4800 rpm	335 @ 4800 rpm	
Max. torque	405 @ 3100 rpm	405 @ 3400 rpm	
DIMENSIONS	**62 SERIES**	**60 FLEETWOOD**	**75 FLEETWOOD**
Wheelbase	129.5 in.	133 in.	149.7 in.
Overall length	216.8 in.	225.3 in.	237.1 in.
Overall width	80 in.	80 in.	80 in.
Overall height	59.1 in.	59.1 in.	61.6 in.
TRANSMISSION			
Hydra-Matic			

CAR LIFE 1958 CONSUMER ANALYSIS

Cadillac's air-suspension system illustrated below is a '58 option.

Eldorado series is available only in convertible, below, and two-door hardtop.

road shock because it is completely free of it.

The steering on Cadillac's competition is good but we give Cad the edge for best "feel" under all conditions.

One of the first things that we noticed out on the road was the greater stability of the car. On a rough high-crowned rolling macadam road the '58 Cad seems to knife through the uneven sections rather than roll over them or sway to one side.

Cadillac engineers attribute the improvement to the new rear suspension set-up in which the car is supported by coil instead of leaf springs and the axle is precisely positioned by three rubber-cushioned links rather than flexibly shackled by leaf springs.

This new set-up raises the car's "roll center" or point of lateral oscilation some 5 inches which cuts down sway very considerably and makes the car feel much closer to the road even though its center of gravity is no lower than on last year's model. This new rear suspension has done a lot to improve ride as well. There is noticeably less pitching (now almost none) than last year and even less vibration from surface roughness is transmitted. Cadillac's ride with standard all-coil spring suspension compares very favorably with Lincoln's similar system and Imperial's torsion-bar, leaf-spring set-up. It is hard to say which is more comfortable. The three cars are very close. In the final accounting we'd give Lincoln a slight edge because of the shake-proof rigidity of its one piece body and frame.

Cadillac's frame, a tubular-backboned X-shape has been changed slightly in respect to body mounting and the body sills which bridge between the open sides of the X have been beefed up. As a result of these fairly minor changes there is a great reduction in body shake on rough roads. The amount of shake on last year's Cadillac was, in our opinion, barely excusable in a car costing $5000 and up. The '58 Cadillac has as little shake as any car with conventional separate body and frame construction.

Handling has improved on the '58 Cad, and it's an important item to be upgraded on a car of the size power potential of a Cadillac. There's nothing that will make a big car seem elephantine more quickly than sloppy handling qualities. The new, precisely positioned rear suspension is again responsible for the improvement.

You can snake the '58 Cadillac down narrow winding dirt and macadam roads at 50 and 60 mph with ease and security never known before. The car is steered, not aimed as was the case with many luxury cars of the past which were not only bargelike in dimension but equally clumsy in maneuvering.

Probably few of the sedate and successful middle-aged buyers of '58 Cadillacs will fully appreciate the improvements in ride, handling and roadability over previous Cadillacs, but they may take our word for it that these changes have made trading in the old Cadillac more desirable than perhaps ever before.

Performance of the '58 Cadillac is just about the same as last year. Engine horsepower has been raised from 300 to 310 (325 on the Eldorado models) which has made no measureable difference. However, those accustomed to reading higher figures on smaller, lighter and lower-priced cars (e.g. 345 on Chrysler and Edsel, 400 on the top Mercury engine) shouldn't come with the impression that the '58 Cadillac is a laggard in acceleration. Moving a 4800-lb. sedan from 0 to 60 mph in 11.5 seconds is no mean feat and should raise few legitimate complaints. Much of the responsibility for Cad's brisk performance goes to the excellent four-speed Hydra-Matic transmission. Coupled with a 3.07 to 1 rear-axle ratio, this transmission makes the best use of the Cadillac engine's

Fleetwood Sixty Special four-door hardtop has an advertised delivered price of $6,232.

Eldorado Brougham is basically unchanged from '57, rates as most expensive car built in U.S.—$13,074.

Dashboard arrangement holds big, bold speedometer, transmission indicator.

405 lbs. ft. of torque which is developed at 3100 rpm. Only hot rodders, and Cadillac doesn't angle for their business, would be discontent with performance. Hydra-Matic's top ratio corresponds to an overdrive ratio and makes Cad one of the quietest cars on the road at high (80 mph) cruising speeds.

Summing up: Cadillac is, as usual, an extremely well-built and well-finished car with a roomy and comfortable interior and traditionally rich General Motors styling. This year's models offer top notch riding comfort and roadability to match quiet, powerful performance. ●

CAR LIFE'S overall rating for the '57 Cadillac was 4.0 checks. The following car in Cadillac's price range has already been tested by CAR LIFE. The issue in which it appeared may be obtained by sending 35¢ to CAR LIFE, 41 East 42 Street, New York 17, N. Y.: Lincoln, January, 1958.

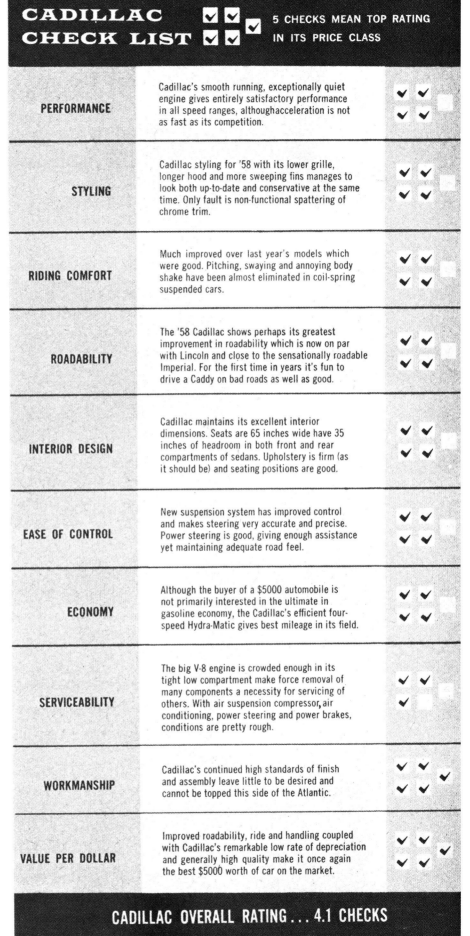

CADILLAC CHECK LIST

5 CHECKS MEAN TOP RATING IN ITS PRICE CLASS

PERFORMANCE — Cadillac's smooth running, exceptionally quiet engine gives entirely satisfactory performance in all speed ranges, although acceleration is not as fast as its competition.

STYLING — Cadillac styling for '58 with its lower grille, longer hood and more sweeping fins manages to look both up-to-date and conservative at the same time. Only fault is non-functional spattering of chrome trim.

RIDING COMFORT — Much improved over last year's models which were good. Pitching, swaying and annoying body shake have been almost eliminated in coil-spring suspended cars.

ROADABILITY — The '58 Cadillac shows perhaps its greatest improvement in roadability which is now on par with Lincoln and close to the sensationally roadable Imperial. For the first time in years it's fun to drive a Caddy on bad roads as well as good.

INTERIOR DESIGN — Cadillac maintains its excellent interior dimensions. Seats are 65 inches wide have 35 inches of headroom in both front and rear compartments of sedans. Upholstery is firm (as it should be) and seating positions are good.

EASE OF CONTROL — New suspension system has improved control and makes steering very accurate and precise. Power steering is good, giving enough assistance yet maintaining adequate road feel.

ECONOMY — Although the buyer of a $5000 automobile is not primarily interested in the ultimate in gasoline economy, the Cadillac's efficient four-speed Hydra-Matic gives best mileage in its field.

SERVICEABILITY — The big V-8 engine is crowded enough in its tight low compartment make force removal of many components a necessity for servicing of others. With air suspension compressor, air conditioning, power steering and power brakes, conditions are pretty rough.

WORKMANSHIP — Cadillac's continued high standards of finish and assembly leave little to be desired and cannot be topped this side of the Atlantic.

VALUE PER DOLLAR — Improved roadability, ride and handling coupled with Cadillac's remarkable low rate of depreciation and generally high quality make it once again the best $5000 worth of car on the market.

CADILLAC OVERALL RATING... 4.1 CHECKS

QUALITY, prestige and comfort are three big reasons for Cadillac's continued success in the luxury car field. That's been true for some years, and it's true again in 1958.

Originally, however, the make established itself on the basis of continued engineering advances and progress. There have been concrete reminders of this in the past two years.

Cadillac introduced the X-type tubular center frame for 1957 and pioneered air suspension on its Eldorado Brougham.

The 62 series hardtop sedan tested was equipped with this type of suspension (standard only for Broughams, but optional for all other 1958 Cadillacs) and it showed up in the form of more comfort than ever!

Cadillac riding qualities have always been considered excellent, so the advantages of air suspension might seem only like frosting on the cake. That isn't completely accurate.

While it's true that Caddys of recent years have offered a ride that was extremely soft and smooth under most conditions, it's equally true that compromises made to obtain this softness have resulted in some adverse effects under less normal conditions.

They had a tendency to bound slightly on adverse surfaces and were not exceptionally well controlled over really bad bumps. In short, boulevard ride was outstanding, but there were a number of situations in which Cadillacs didn't react so favorably.

The air-suspended 1958 test car was quite different. Degree of ride improvement on smooth roads was difficult to measure, true. On rough surfaces or over bumps, however, this car was noticeably better than previous Cadillacs tested.

Admittedly there probably are few Caddy owners who drive their cars through the boondocks, but our road system is far from being so perfect that there is no advantage in having an automobile which furnishes a stable, controlled ride over both smooth and beat-up highways.

Even more important in many respects is that 1958 Cadillacs have far better handling qualities than those of several years back. Improvements in this area were noted when 1957 models were checked and it was encouraging to note that even more progress had been made for 1958.

A major reason for both the better ride over rough surfaces and improved handling is the new four-link suspension arrangement.

Introduced on Broughams (and new Chevrolets are using a similar setup), this design has resulted in Cadillacs having a roll center almost six inches higher than in 1957. This makes for increased stability and better cornering characteristics; body heeling and side sway is reduced markedly as compared to Cadillacs of the middle and early 1950's.

CADILLAC ROAD TEST

CADILLAC STYLING has retained its basic look for a number of years. As father of the fin it must continue the tradition. The jewel-like grille was hailed immediately by car customizers and can be seen today incorporated into a number of their productions.

BEAUTIFULLY finished interior revealed no flaws in the paint, trim or fitting. The quality throughout appeared extremely high.

IT'S STILL NOT SOLID GOLD BUT IT REMAINS THE COIN OF THE LUXURY REALM

Again, it's obvious that Cadillacs aren't built, or billed, as sporty-type automobiles and their buyers normally don't plan to drive them with abandon. The effortless way in which these cars cruise at high road speeds makes the extra margin of controllability in 1958 models a praiseworthy step forward, however.

This improvement, incidentally, holds true for both air-suspended Cadillacs and those with standard steel springs. (Caddys with steel springs now use coils at all four wheels; in previous years coils were used at front and semi-elliptics at the rear.) The basic suspension is the same, only difference being that air bags are substituted for the normal coil springs; the design permits easy interchangeability between the two suspension media during production.

Another virtue of air suspension as compared to steel springs, well-known by this time, is that car height remains constant regardless of amount of positioning of load. Another benefit is that a lift control handle near the steering column permits the driver of an air-suspended Cadillac to raise his car an additional five inches.

This height control is handy when tires have to be changed, when driving up steep ramps or driveways and when additional road clearance is needed for a short period.

One factor in which Cadillac has fallen behind somewhat recently is performance. One of the first makes to adopt the modern short-stroke, overhead valve V-8, Cadillac was deservedly known as one of the "hot ones" up until a couple of years ago. This isn't the case anymore.

When the first 331-cubic-inch Caddy V-8's were introduced they were regarded as big engine. Displacement went up to 365 cubic inches in 1956 and has stayed there. Meanwhile, many newer engines have appeared and now a number of lower priced cars than Cadillac have larger, more powerful engines. Even the so-called low priced Big Three now sport powerplants of only slightly small size, either as standard equipment or extra-cost options.

The result is that Cadillacs have dropped from their former status as hot performers to the strictly mediocre class —which disturbs its makers not at all.

"We aren't building cars for drag racing," as one engineer put it last fall. "We feel our cars offer all the performance their drivers need—and can use with safety."

The point is well taken. Acceleration from a standstill is far from blinding in today's terms, but it's plenty adequate for any type of day-to-day driving. Mid-range punch is good, offering ample surge for highway passing. Top speed is well above the maximum most drivers ever use.

The current Cadillac V-8 is a much-modified version of the original 331-cubic-incher. Compression is up to 10.25-to-1 (compared to 10-to-1 in 1957) due to a redesigned combustion chamber shape, which utilizes a depression in the piston head, incidentally. Valve sizes were increased this year and a different cam grind is now used. This has resulted in a modest 10 hp increase from last year, plus a slight torque boost (405 vs. 400 lb.-ft.).

(All Eldorados have essentially the same engine as this one, but it uses three two-barrel carburetors and is rated at 335 hp at 4800 rpm.)

Despite Cadillac's apparent unconcern about the falling prowess, relatively, of its V-8, it would not be surprising to see a new one appear in the not too-distant future.

Quality was mentioned in the beginning as a Cadillac strong point and the test car was proof that there has been no letdown.

This is just about what the test crew has come to expect, however. Cadillac is one of the few makes which, over the years Motor Life has been testing cars, has been remarkably free of the petty and annoying defects often found during the test period. This has invariably been the case with Cadillacs checked and such a record is rare enough to be worth mentioning!

Add all these things up and you begin to understand why Cadillac has maintained an even sales pace this year in the face of reduced demand. Latest figures available show the make to be less than 2,000 sales under 1957 and that it is firmly perched in the number nine sales spot—well ahead of competitors in its price class, even in front of many cars which sell for considerably less! •

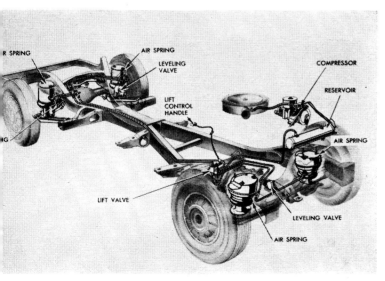

AIR SUSPENSION system was pioneered by Cadillac in its 1957 Eldorado Brougham. Although the Cadillac ride has always been good, the introduction of the air system did away with a few compromises retained for ride which had harmed handling in the past.

Test Data

Test Car: 1958 Cadillac 62
Body Type: four-door hardtop sedan
Basic Price: $4891
Engine: ohv V-8
Carburetion: single four-barrel
Displacement: 365 cubic inches
Bore & Stroke: 4 x 3.675
Compression Ratio: 10.25-to-1
Horsepower: 310 @ 4800 rpm
Horsepower per Cubic Inch: .85
Torque: 405 lb.-ft. @ 3100
Test Weight: 4874 lbs.
Weight Distribution: 53% of weight on front wheels
Power-Weight Ratio: 15.7 lbs. per hp
Transmission: Hydra-Matic, four-speed planetary incorporating fluid coupling
Rear Axle Ratio: 3.07-to-1
Springs: Air
Steering: 4.5 turns lock-to-lock
Tires: 8.00 x 15 tubeless
Gas Mileage: 11.7 mpg average
Speedometer Error: Indicated 30, 45 and 60 mph are actual 28.5, 43 and 56.8 mph, respectively
Acceleration: 0-30 mph in 4 seconds, 0-45 mph in 6.8 and 0-60 in 11 seconds

It's everyone's dream – to travel to the States, find a classic convertible, bring it back home and restore it. But for Mike Dochree, the whole experience was not without its problems

SOFT TOP, HARD WOR

WORDS & PHOTOGRAPHS: COLIN GLANVILLE

TWENTY FEET OF TOTALLY BAD TASTE or the pinnacle of dream car design? Whether pretty in pink or beautiful in blue, the late Fifties Cadillacs certainly had style, a style that reflected the confidence of a nation that saw itself as the most technologically advanced in the world. On the other side of the cold war, the Commies couldn't even afford can, and the few that were available to the Party Elite were slab-sided, ugly boxes. Late Fifties fins and chrome may not appeal to everyone, but if you're going to make a statement, then why not make it an overstatement.

One person who certainly likes the styling of the Cadillac is Mike Dochree from Berkshire. He has owned several American and British classics over the years, including the loudest pink Chevrolet Impala ever seen, but the '58 Cadillac Series 62 Convertible Coupe de Ville in the pictures is his first restoration. His previous car was a '58 Caddy two-door hardtop, so he felt he should know every nut and bolt of a convertible when he decided to buy one for restoration.

Mike likes to buy his classics from the States, and organises his holiday trips around the car he is looking for. Using Hemmings, cars can be located and enquiries made before the trip. But not everything goes according to plan ...

Having chosen model and make, found a car and seen photographs of it, Mike flew out to Florida in the summer of 1992 to see the '58 Cadillac Convertible that he fancied. When he got there, the car bore no resemblance to the photographs. It was a complete wreck, with hardly any body panels on it and totally rusted through. He says it simply wasn't recognisable as a Cadillac. Having flown the best part of 4000 miles, Mike understandably felt very cheated.

Chatting with people about his disappointment, Mike heard of another convertible near St Louis, Missouri, saw some photographs and decided to take a look. He took an internal flight, then drove the 250 miles to Colombia, Missouri. Here, in a back yard, he found exactly the car he had been looking for: very clean, straight, all there and no damage to any of the panels. Okay, so it wasn't perfect – the seats were just on the floor, the dashboard was laid across the back seat and it had a frame but no hood for the rag top – but after the disappointment of the Florida car this one was beautiful.

What Mike first thought was rust turned out to be red oxide paint, and the only damage the metal moths had managed to wreak was to the floorpan (although that could soon remedied with replacement parts). So there it was – all ready to ship back to Blighty. A parts car came in the deal too, a two-door hardtop, so both were containerised and shipped out of Miami to Stanstead via Felixstowe.

Putting the cars on a trailer at Stanstead caused a great deal of 'What on earth have I done' to be muttered, the rosy glow of the excitement of buying promptly turning to the cold reality of the forthcoming restoration.

The restoration plan was relatively simple. Take the car to pieces, refurbish, repair or replace every single part of it, then put it all back together again. Well, maybe not quite that simple. Two years of evenings and weekends, stripping the car down, labelling and bagging all the parts, learning new skills on the way and then reassembling the myriad of parts is what really happened. But even the longest task has to begin somewhere, and that point was degreasing the mechanical parts, a job Mike describes as 'disgusting'. But it's not until all the muck has been shifted that the real work can begin.

The engine had seized solid, so that needed freeing and then dismantling. Almost everything was renewed following a rebore, and when finished Mike had an engine that was essentially new, showing not a trace of its previous 100,000 miles.

The steering and suspension were all good, so Mike just replaced all the ball joints and bushes and nothing else needed to be touched. Very little has been necessary in the way of spares, and what didn't come from the spares car was generally brought in from the States. Mike says that the service he's received from the various mail order suppliers has been very good.

One tip worth passing on to other owners of classic American hardware concerns changing the oil in the Cadillac's differential. Most 1950s cars didn't have drain plugs in their diffs, so changing the oil usually means splitting, with the attendant problem of getting an absolutely oil-tight seal on reassembly. But Mike used a very large syringe to draw the oil off and to suck out any sludge. The result is a clean oil change and no worries about the seal. Clever stuff.

Mike's Cadillac required a new windscreen as there were two bullet holes in the original one, plus another in the front

ABOVE: A fairly understated interior compared with some of the Cadillac's cheaper 'imitators' of 1958. It simply oozes style, don't you think?
BELOW: Poetry in motion! The folding hood in all its glorious action

SOFT TOP HARD WORK!

quarterlight. Since there was no bullet damage anywhere else in or on the car, how the holes got there was a little puzzling to say the least! The new screen came from a coupe that was being broken for spares and Mike did a swap for some parts from his second car. The quarterlight was also replaced via the parts car.

One of Mike's new skills learned on the Cadillac was welding, replacing the original floor panels that had rusted through. One important point that Mike stresses is that when carrying out a restoration, one's eyes must be fixed firmly on the end result. When the car is completely stripped and in pieces, then is not the time to get disheartened and take up fishing instead!

The Cadillac's external brightwork has obviously been rechromed – and rechromed properly using a copper dip followed by a layer of nickel before the actual chrome plating. The internal chrome just needed a clean and polish to restore the superb original finish.

Cadillacs were made for a very select market in 1958, the Series 62 Convertible costing $5454 when new – exclusive enough for just 7825 of them to be made in total. Weighing in at well over two tons, the Series 62 needed every one of the 310 horses from its 361cu.in. V8 to provide it not only with easy speed but also the wherewithal to drive the powered everything – steering, brakes, seats, windows, even the quarterlights. One anomaly is that even in a top model luxury car, the windscreen wipers were vacuum operated, albeit with fewer problems

Although basically sound, Mike Dochree's '58 Cadillac Series 62 needed extensive restoration work

than, say, Ford's old Zodiac set-up as the vacuum was taken from the oil pump rather than the manifold.

Back in 1958, there were plenty of Cadillac options to choose from and Mike's convertible seems to have its fair share of them. Tinted glass, powered front seat adjustment, fog lamps, automatic heater and an automatic headlamp dimmer. All the power for the rear wheels was delivered through a four-speed Hydra-Matic gearbox, giving the smooth ride expected from a Cadillac. It's the creature comforts that make a Cadillac a cut above the rest too, including this one's heavenly plush leather upholstery, finished in white and metallic blue.

As well as welding, Mike also learned the skill of spraying whilst renovating his Caddy, restoring the paintwork with a spray gun that cost him just £5 from an autojumble. But the old paint had to come off first ...

After buckets of stripper and wet and dry, the Cadillac's bare metal shell was finally revealed. The seams were all leaded, so anything disturbed in the stripping was put right before the first layers of new paint were applied: a simple etch primer followed by four coats of primer filler. These layers were flatted, two top coats of paint were then sprayed and, again, these were flatted before being finished off with four final top coats. The result is a beautiful sheen on the Daphne Blue paintwork, computer matched against a sample of original Cadillac paint taken from a showroom paintcard.

To give his car that final finishing touch, Mike bought a continental kit from Continental Enterprises in Canada and had it delivered to the hotel he was staying in whilst on holiday in the States! With all the pieces wrapped separately, it was possible for him and his wife to bring it home as hand luggage ...

Mike's house is a real treasure trove of bits and pieces of Fifties' Americana. Little nooks and crannies reveal models and photographs, and the conservatory boasts a Wurlitzer jukebox and number plates from almost every state. The jukebox is echoed in the kitchen door, where a friend in the window business has made a stained glass copy of it. Also in the kitchen, close by the Wurlitzer window, is the large and growing display of trophies won by the Cadillac at shows around the country.

And this Cadillac has certainly done well for itself since its thorough restoration at the hands of Mike Dochree. Such is its attention to detail that was awarded the accolade of being a runner-up in the *Classic American*/Hill House Hammond Car Of the Year 1995 contest.

As dream cars go, Cadillac's 1958 convertibles are arguably the dreamiest around. These were great cars to drive and to be driven in, with beautiful flowing lines from chrome laden front to aeroplane-finned back. The way car design progressed from the mid-Fifties must not be seen as happening in isolation – everything the Americans were doing was on the grand scale and the jukebox styling influenced many designs, from toasters and wireless sets to the new jet airliners. Some (though not many) may dismiss this styling as lacking in refinement and taste, but the world of the American automobile would be much the poorer without them. **CA**

Summer posin'! Find the right road, wait for the right weather and, even in Britain, a Cadillac Convertible makes the ultimate sunshine cruiser

'Late Fifties fins and chrome may not appeal to everyone, but if you're going to make a statement, then why not make it an overstatement'

Big, bold, beautiful, and loaded with 310 horsepower under the hood, Cadillac's Fleetwood Sixty Special is one of the most affordably priced Fifties-era dream machines you can buy today. It offers irresistible finned styling, outstanding build-quality, and that distinctive four-door look that's becoming increasingly popular with old car enthusiasts on a budget.

Sliding behind the big wheel, I was more comfortable than on any seat in my own living room. Support to the lower back is particularly good, and leg room is ample. Upholstery fabrics and carpeting—all original in this low-mileage car—are of exceptional quality, and the level of fit and finish is very high.

The dash panel includes, in addition to the speedometer/odometer, gauges for temperature and fuel level, though warning lights are used for both oil pressure and generator. Personally, I much prefer gauges to lights, but there is something to be said for the argument that a red warning light might be more likely than a gauge to attract the driver's attention, should something go wrong.

There had been a time, back around 1950, when Cadillacs had posted some creditable speed records; but by the time this car was built, the emphasis was clearly upon luxury rather than high performance. Still, the Sixty Special is no slouch. *Motor Life* magazine, road-testing a 1958 Series 62 sedan, made the zero-to-sixty run in eleven seconds flat. Not quick enough to send anyone to the chiropractor with whiplash, to be sure; but not too shabby, either. (Now, let's admit it: this is not a fair comparison, for the Sixty Special is considerably heavier than the Series 62 tested by the magazine. But *Motor Trend*, in an earlier road-test of a '57 Sixty Special—a car with ten fewer horses under the hood than the '58 model—recorded a time of 12.4 seconds in a similar run. Not bad for a big, heavy luxury barge.)

The Dual-Range HydraMatic transmission shifts smoothly, with hardly a trace of the "surge" that characterized early editions of this fine automatic. In "highway" range, with an overall ratio of 3.07:1, the car cruises quietly and smoothly, even at speeds well above the legal limit. Corners are taken with aplomb; there is very little leaning, no bobbing, no weaving. Steering, while light, preserves just enough "road feel" to add to the driver's sense of confidence. And the ride is notably smooth, even over rough surfaces. In fact, the difference between Cadillacs equipped with air suspension and those with steel springs is particularly evident when the car is traveling over uneven terrain.

The air suspension, designed by Cadillac staffers Lester Milliken and Fred Cowin, was standard equipment on the

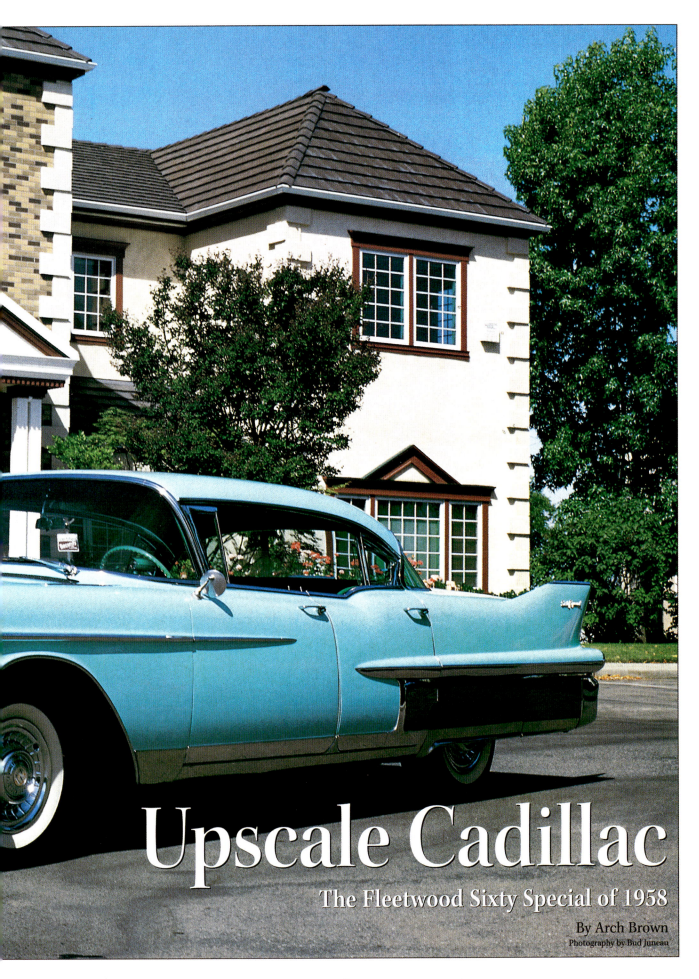

Upscale Cadillac

The Fleetwood Sixty Special of 1958

By Arch Brown
Photography by Bud Juneau

Eldorado Seville, Biarritz and Brougham models, and available for an extra $214 on other Cadillacs. It offers a further advantage: Should the driver find himself out in the boondocks, he can reach for a little handle near the steering column, thus raising his car by five inches for additional ground clearance.

To be sure, there were problems with the air suspension. Air leaks sometimes left the car sitting abruptly on its axles. Even our drive/Report car had to be carefully regulated as to air pressure before we undertook our test drive. This intriguing and seemingly promising feature was retained for only four years. Ed Cole, former Works Manager at Cadillac and later, GM President, explained why: "As far as the system was concerned it gave outstanding capability (in) ride leveling and damping. The only problem was with air leaks, usually around the fittings or valves, which let the car's suspension relax and bottom out. Further, it became quite complicated and costly for the benefit it provided in leveling and riding comfort. Therefore it was abandoned."

The Cadillac's power-assisted drum brakes are excellent, bringing the car to a smooth, straight stop. We note, however, that the Cadillac carries nearly 16 percent more weight per square inch of effective braking area than either the 1958 Continental Mark III or the Imperial LeBaron. One is compelled to ask whether this might have some negative effect on fade resistance under hard use.

The original Sixty Special, introduced twenty-years prior to the '58 model, was designed by 23-year-old Bill Mitchell, then Cadillac's newly appointed styling chief, was undoubtedly the most distinctive automobile of its time, and the most influential as well. Standing nearly three inches lower than any previous Cadillac, it was the first American production car to feature an extended deck, making the trunk an integral part of the over-all design. All four doors were front-hinged, an unusual practice at the time. Running boards were eliminated, and "pontoon" fenders created the illusion of greater length. Belt moldings were likewise eliminated, and slim pillars gave a hint of the "hardtop" design that the industry would adopt in later years.

But the American public was notoriously fickle when it came to styling—probably even more so in those days than today; and after four years it was time for something new. So commencing with the introduction of the 1942 models, in September 1941 the Sixty Special became quite a different automobile. Exterior styling this time was virtually identical to that of the bread-and-butter Series 62, except that the rear deck was extended. The wheelbase was stretched by four inches, overall length (in the case of the '42) by more than six inches, all of the difference appearing behind the passenger compartment.

Which is to say, the Sixty Special, while retaining the luxury and the superb quality of earlier models, lost most of its distinctiveness. The same practice was resumed during the postwar years; the Fleetwood Sixty Special was simply a stretched, upscale version of the Series 62. And this, we suspect, accounts for the fact that when the recession of 1958 hit, while sales of the popular Series 62 dipped by a little less than ten percent, the Fleetwood Sixty Special's volume plummeted by more than 46 percent. The buyer could, after all, get Cadillac's styling, comfort and prestige, along with much of its luxury,

Riding on a lengthy 133-inch wheelbase, the 4-door body is well proportioned for its size.

Exterior details abound, with lots of body protrusions, fender skirts, and lavish chrome trim.

Thick, shapely rear doors feature windows that roll down all the way into the door shell.

Spacious trunk houses spare tire and has a deep opening for easy loading of luggage.

Automatic headlamp dimmer was optional.

Elegantly styled hubcaps cover entire wheel.

Futuristic bullet-shaped lamps in rear.

Vent windows in the rear are a nice touch.

Distinctive fins with classy script lettering.

in a Series 62 sedan, at a savings of $1,341. Even the Sedan DeVille, which offered most of the Sixty Special's distinct features—items such as power windows and seats—cost $735 less.

Yet another threat to the popularity of the Fleetwood Sixty Special came from a new, in-house competitor. Added to the line for 1958 was an extended-deck Series 62 sedan. Employing the same 129.5 inch wheelbase as the balance of the series, it measured eight and a half inches longer than other models in the line, with the stretch occurring entirely in the rear deck. No doubt it was this big, impressive car, which cost only $188 more than the standard sedan, that was responsible for stealing a substantial number of sales from the Fleetwood Sixty Special, for it proved to be the second most popular car in the entire Cadillac line.

In terms of styling, the 1958 Cadillacs seemed little changed. The rear fender fins were sharper and canted to the rear, while up front there was the obligatory new grille, and there were some differences in trim. Engine and driveline were also essentially the same as 1957, although the compression ratio was increased from 10.00 to 10.25:1, raising the horsepower from 300 to 310. But the chassis was re-engineered in a couple of significant ways. The front suspension was modified in such a way that it could accommodate either coil springs or air bags; while at the rear, 1957's longitudinal leaf springs were replaced by coils—again designed to be interchangeable with air bags. Apart from these modifications, the most visible change for '58 had to do with the adoption of quad headlamps.

One of the most original '58 Sixty Specials we have ever come across is this outstanding example owned by Paul Gudmundson, Jr., of Chico, California. With only 28,000 miles on the clock, its history is as interesting as its condition.

Purchased originally by a Southern

SPECIALISTS & RESTORERS

Mastermind Inc.
32155 Joshua Dr.
Dept. SIA-182
Wildomar, CA 92595
909-674-0509
Complete and partial restorations

Piru Cads
402 Via Fustero Rd.
Dept. SIA-182
P.O. Box 227
Piru, CA 93040
805-521-1741
Complete and partial restorations

REPAIR COSTS

Drum brake rebuild (front and rear)	$1,250
Engine rebuild	$4,000-$7,000
Front suspension overhaul	$2,000
New exhaust system installed	$1,035
New U-joints installed	$240
Transmission rebuild	$1,400
Tune-up	$225

ASKING PRICES

With 12,900 Fleetwood Sixty Specials built in 1958, the level of difficulty you might expect in finding such a luxurious and elusive automobile is quite surprising. Examples with the optional triple-carbureted Eldorado V-8 will tend to dramatically increase the car's value. In the last four issues of *Hemmings Motor News* we located three cars for sale. You can also search our extensive database of vehicles and parts for sale at www.hemmings.com.

1958, painstaking restoration including NOS upholstery, 90% complete, original rust-free desert car, $10,000.

1958, Eldorado Tri-power engine option, air suspension, a/c, 53,000 miles, no rust or repairs, newer paint, nice driver, $15,000.

1958, white with a black interior, restoration completed, 46,000 miles, $17,500.

WHAT TO PAY

Low	Avg.	High
$3,000	$8,000	$14,000

Ribbed trim with integral backup lamps adds to the Fleetwood's upscale appearance.

"Made by Fleetwood" badges and courtesy lamps fitted to bottom of interior doors.

California bank president named Wesley Dumm, it was chauffeur-driven by Paul Gudmundson, Sr., ferrying Mr. Dumm back and forth between his home in Pasadena and his office in La Jolla. Mr. Dumm evidently had powerful political connections, for the younger Gudmundson reports that he had a "red phone," a direct line to President Richard Nixon. Occasionally, Paul, Sr. chauffeured Mr. Dumm to the San Clemente White House.

Some time around 1969 or '70, Mr. Dumm evidently began to drop the hint that he might replace the Cadillac. Chauffeur Gudmundson asked if he could have first refusal on the Sixty Special, in the event that it was to be sold. Dumm's reply was to ask him for a dollar. And with that the bargain was sealed; the car belonged to the elder Gudmundson.

Paul Jr., who runs a fine automotive upholstery shop, reports that when his father retired he moved to Kentucky. The Cadillac was shipped to him there; and the elder Gudmundson retained it until his death in 1988. At that point his son fell heir to the car, though he didn't truck it home to California until 1992. In the meantime, for reasons that Paul Jr. cannot explain, during 1986 the car was repainted in its original color. The car deserves a better paint job than the Kentucky shop gave it, though it's quite presentable. The worst of it is that the engine was painted black. And so it remains, for the present. Paul fully intends to pull the engine and repaint it, along with the engine bay. Eventually he'll refinish the entire exterior, but the press of business at his shop has left Paul with little time for restoring his own car—a familiar dilemma among collectors.

The Cadillac had only about 23,000 miles on it upon its return to California. It hadn't been run in four years; yet with a new battery installed and with its fuel system thoroughly cleaned out, it started up readily. It's not a daily driver; one wouldn't expect it to be. But Paul has put about 5,000 miles on it over the past eight years; and he and his family expect to enjoy driving it this summer. Sharp-eyed readers will have observed that the compressor for the air conditioner is missing. It's in the shop under-

PARTS SUPPLIERS

Caddy Central
11117 Tippett Rd.
Dept. SIA-182
Clinton, MD 20735
301-234-0135
NOS bumpers and body parts

Cadillac International
32 Kinney St.
Dept. SIA-182
Piermont, N.Y. 10968
914-365-8290
Chrome, interiors, moldings, and sheet metal

Cadillac Parts and Cars Limited
46 Hardy St.
Dept. SIA-182
Sparks, NV 89431
775-826-8363
Extensive supply of body parts

Ed Cholakian Enterprises
12811 Foothill Blvd.
Sylmar, CA 91342
800-808-1147
NOS and reproduction weatherstripping

Holcombe Cadillac Parts
2933 Century Lane
Dept. SIA-182
Bensalem, PA 19020
215-245-4560
NOS and used body and trim parts

Mahoning Auto
11110 Mahoning Ave.
Dept. SIA-182
North Jackson, OH 44451
330-538-3246
Interior and trim parts, wheels skirts, and engine parts and accessories

Sam Quinn Cadillac Parts
Dept. SIA-182
P.O. Box 837
Estacada, OR 97023
503-637-3852
Engine accessories, body trim, and sheet metal

specifications

illustrations by Russell von Sauers, The Graphic Automobile Studio
© copyright 2001, Special Interest Autos

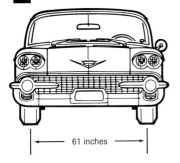
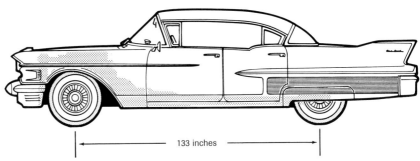

61 inches

133 inches

1958 Cadillac Sixty Special

Base price	$6,232 f.o.b. factory, federal excise tax included
Std. equipment	HydraMatic transmission, power steering, power brakes, power windows, power seat, heater
Options on dR car	Air-conditioning, automatic headlamp dimmer, air-ride suspension, lap blankets, radio

ENGINE
Type	90-degree OHV V-8
Bore x stroke	4 inches x 3.625 inches
Displacement	364.4 cubic inches
Compression ratio	10.25:1
Horsepower @ rpm	310 @ 4,800 (gross)
Torque @ rpm	405 @ 3,100 (gross)
Taxable horsepower	51.2
Valve lifters	Hydraulic
Main bearings	5
Fuel system	1 4-bbl carburetor, mechanical pump
Exhaust system	Dual
Electrical system	12-volt battery/coil

TRANSMISSION
Type	HydraMatic 4-speed automatic planetary
Ratios	1st: 3.97:1; 2nd: 2.55:1; 3rd: 1.55:1; 4th: 1.00; Reverse: 3.74:1
Overdrive	0.72:1

REAR AXLE
Type	Hypoid
Ratio	3.07:1
Drive axles	Semi-floating, Hotchkiss drive

STEERING
Type	Ball nut and sector, power-assisted
Ratios	17.5 gear, 19.5 overall
Turning diameter	48' 3" (wall/wall)
Turns lock-to-lock	4.5

BRAKES
Type	4-wheel hydraulic, drum type, power-assisted
Drum diameter	12 inches
Effective area	210.3 square inches

CHASSIS & BODY
Construction	Body-on-frame
Frame	Tubular center rigid X-type, no siderails
Body construction	All steel
Body type	4-door hardtop sedan
Layout	Front engine, rear wheel drive

SUSPENSION
Front	Independent, coil springs
Rear	Rigid axle, coil springs
Wheels	Pressed steel
Tires	8.00/15

WEIGHTS AND MEASURES
Wheelbase	133 inches
Overall length	225.3 inches
Overall width	80 inches
Overall height	59.1 inches (unloaded)
Front track	61 inches
Rear track	61 inches
Min. road clearance	6.4 inches
Shipping weight	4,930 pounds

INTERIOR DIMENSIONS
Head room, front/rear	34.9/34.9 inches
Shoulder room, f/r	59.0/56.5 inches
Hip room, front/rear	65.2/65.0 inches
Leg room, front/rear	44.8/45.2 inches
Cushion height to floor	13.5/12.6 inches (front/rear)

CAPACITIES
Cooling system	20.7 quarts (with heater)
Engine oil	5 quarts
Fuel tank	20 gallons
Transmission	23 pints (refill)
Rear axle	5 pints

CALCULATED DATA
Stroke/bore ratio	0.906:1
Hp per c.i.d.	.851
Weight per hp	15.9 pounds
Weight per c.i.d.	13.5
Lb. per sq. in. (brakes)	23.4

PERFORMANCE
Acceleration: 0-30 mph	4.0 seconds
0-45 mph	6.8 seconds
0-60 mph	11.0 seconds

Left-side taillamp housing hides gas cap.

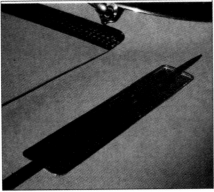

Chromed grille vents reside atop each fender.

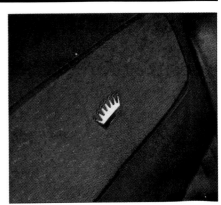

Cadillac crown emblems fixed to seat backs.

Power steering and brakes and HydraMatic four-speed transmission were all standard.

PROS & CONS

Pro
Very affordable
High build quality
Excellent parts supply

Con
Not very desirable
Marginal acceleration
Troublesome air suspension

Rear seating for three is deep and very couch-like; wide armrest increases comfort for two.

Interior headliner ribs run front to rear.

364.5-cu.in. V-8 makes 405-lb.ft. of torque.

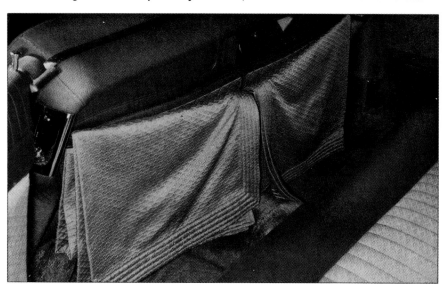
Optional lap blankets hang from front seat backs, providing added warmth to rear occupants.

Air lift handle raises car.

going repairs in preparation for the hot weather.

There are a number of interesting features on this car worth mentioning. For instance: there's a neat, chrome-plated fresh-air intake on the top of each front fender. A monogrammed lap robe hangs from a strap in the rear passenger compartment. The original spare, still with plenty of tread showing, is in the trunk; and lighting the Sixty Special's way are four rare T3 sealed-beam headlamps, all in operating condition.

CLUB SCENE

Cadillac Drivers Club
5825 Vista Ave
Sacramento, CA 95824-1428
916-421-3193
Dues: $17.50/year; Members: 115

Cadillac LaSalle Club Inc.
P.O. Box 1916
Lenoir, NC 28645-1916
828-757-9919
Dues: $30/year; Members: 6,200

Classic Cadillac Club Deutschland e.V.
Windmuehlenste 49
50129 Bergheim
Germany
Email: cccd@classiccars.de
Dues: 150 DM; Members: 185

1958 Cadillac Owners Association
P.O. Box 850029
Braintree, MA 02185
781-843-4485
Dues: $22/one time; Members: 260

For a complete listing of the nearly 50 regional Cadillac clubs located nationwide, visit Car Club Central at www.hemmings.com. With nearly 10,000 car clubs listed, it's the largest car club site in the world!

PARTS PRICES

Distributor cap and rotor	$40
Fuel pump	$49
Inner and outer front wheel bearing set	$240
Front shocks	$55/each
Heater core	$150
Idler arm	$110
Oil pump	$148
Power steering box	$340
Power steering pump	$160
Power window motors	$100
Rear coil springs	$240/pair
Reconditioned 4-row radiator	$400
Set of spark plug wires	$46
Stainless Steel brake lines	$190
Tri-power carb rebuild kit	$175
Upper and lower radiator hoses	$35
Water pump	$200

With the return of better times, and the coming of a fully restyled line of Cadillacs for 1959, one might have expected that sales of the Fleetwood Sixty Special would once again boom. This was not to be, however. Production for 1959 came to just 2,250 units, down from 12,900 the previous year. Sales rebounded somewhat for 1960, however, with 11,800 Sixty Specials finding buyers; and by 1965, with another brand new body to attract customers, the total came to 18,100 units. But never again would the Fleetwood Sixty Special achieve the sales success that it had enjoyed in 1957, when 24,000 examples were produced.

1958 CADILLAC PRICES, WEIGHTS AND PRODUCTION

	Price	Weight	Production
Series 62 (129.5" wheelbase)			
Hardtop Sedan, 4-door, 6-pass.	$4,891	4,675	13,335
Export Sedan, 4-door, 6-pass.	4,891	4,675	204
Extended Deck Sedan, 6-pass.	5,079	4,770	20,952
Sedan DeVille, 4-door, 6-pass.	5,497	4,855	23,989
Hardtop Coupe, 2-door, 6-pass.	4,784	4,630	18,736
Coupe DeVille, 2-door, 6-pass.	5,231	4,705	18,414
Convertible Coupe, 6-pass.	5,454	4,845	7,925
Chassis only	n/a	n/a	1
Total production, Series Sixty-Two:			103,556
Series 62 Eldorado Specials (129.5" wheelbase)			
Seville Hardtop, 2-door, 6-pass.	7,500	4,910	855
Biarritz Convertible, 2-door	7,500	5,070	815
Seville Sedan, 4-door	n/a	n/a	1
Total production, Series Sixty-Two Eldorado Specials:			1,671
Series Fleetwood Sixty Special (133" wheelbase)			
Hardtop Sedan, 4-door, 6-pass.	6,232	4,930	12,900
Series 70 Eldorado Brougham (126" wheelbase)			
Hardtop Sedan, 4-door, 6-pass.	13,074	5,315	304
Series 75 Fleetwood (149.7" wheelbase)			
Sedan, 4-door, 9-pass.	8,460	5,360	802
Imperial Sedan, 4-door, 9-pass.	8,675	5,475	730
Commercial Chassis*	n/a	n/a	1,915
*156" wheelbase			
Total production, Series 75 Fleetwood:			3,447
TOTAL MODEL YEAR PRODUCTION:			121,878
TOTAL CALENDAR YEAR PRODUCTION:			125,50

THE SIXTY SPECIAL VS. THE COMPETITION

Here's how our featured Cadillac stacked up against other luxury cars.

	Cadillac Sixty-Special	Imperial LeBaron	Continental Mark III
Price, 4-door hardtop	$6,232	$5,891	$6,072
Wheelbase	133.0"	129.0"	131.0"
Length	225.3"	225.8"	229.0"
Width	80.0"	81.2"	80.1"
Height (unloaded)	59.1"	58.7"	58.2"
Shipping weight (lbs.)	4,930	4,940	4,965
Tread, front/rear	61.0"/61.0"	61.8"/62.4"	61.0"/61.0"
Leg room, front/rear	44.8"/45.2"	48.0"/45.0"	44.4"/42.0"
Shoulder room, f/r	59.0"/56.5"	64.0"/62.0"	63.1"/67.0"
Hip room, front/rear	65.2"/65.0"	61.0"/60.2"	61.0"/65.1"
Head room, f/r	34.9"/34.9"	35.4"/34.2"	35.0"/34.1"
Engine cid	364.4	392.7	429.6
Horsepower @ rpm	310/4,800	345/4,600	375/4,800
Torque @ rpm	405/3,100	450/2,800	490/3,100
Compression ratio	10.25:1	10.00:1	10.50:1
Carburetor	1-4 bbl	1-4 bbl	1-4 bbl
Auto. Transmission	HydraMatic	TorqueFlite	Turbo-Drive
Transmission speeds	4	3	3
Torque converter	na	Yes	Yes
Final drive ratio	3.07:1	2.93:1	2.87:1
Steering	Ball nut/sector	Rack/sector	Recirc. ball
Turning diameter	48' 3"	51' 1"	47' 4" (est.)
Braking area (sq. in.)	210.3	251.0	262.0
Drum diameter	12"	12"	11"
Tire size (original)	8.00/15	9.50/14	9.00/14
Horsepower per c.i.d.	.851	.879	.873
Weight per hp	15.9	14.3	13.2
Weight per c.i.d.	13.5	12.6	11.6
Weight/sq. in. (brakes)	23.4	19.7	19.0

"Handles well in city traffic. More like a small car."—Louisiana Chevrolet dealer.

"Easy handling. Easy to park, power steering greatly improved."—California property owner.

"Styling. The car draws many glances and comments from people. When stopped for gas, drivers of other cars start asking questions. Neatest and best-looking car on the road."—New York physician.

"Long, smooth profile, beautiful colors."—Illinois housewife.

"No excessive flares."—Michigan foreman.

"Each line and feature reflect expert craftsmanship."—Michigan executive.

But Cadillac Is Not Perfect

Although a high percentage of Cadillac owners make no complaints at all about their cars (44.6 percent), the majority mention a few bad features. First on the complaint list is poor workmanship, followed by poor gasoline economy and body noises. Here are quotations describing these troubles:

"Not meticulous in final inspection. There is always a series of minor adjustments. Nothing serious, just annoying."—California executive.

"My first Cadillac. It should have been a dream car, especially for the price. But, alas and alack, it wasn't put together as well as the car I traded."—Maine salesman.

"Low gas mileage. It averages 9 miles per gallon in city (I got 11 and 12 on previous Cadillacs)."—Ohio chemical research director.

"I would like more gas mileage. I wish I could get two more miles per gallon (I get 14 on long trips)."—Texas salesman.

"No gas mileage. Have had it in the shop one third of the time since December 15th. They can't seem to do anything about it. I get 8 miles per gallon in the city."—Oregon club operator.

"A car costing $7000 should be engineered for quietness. All my Cadillacs (this is the 4th) rattle like a truck."—Texas investor.

"Car is not prechecked for body rattles and squeaks. It must be brought in time and again on the same complaints."—Illinois lawyer.

CADILLAC PIPES HOT AIR INTO REAR SEAT VIA A DUCT INSIDE DOOR AND A CENTER-POST GRILLE

Always the same complaint! Certainly some way can be found to catch production faults on a $7000 car before the customer finds them.

For years Cadillac owners bragged that they got more miles per gallon than small-car owners. The honeymoon seems to be over at last.

Test car had no rattles. In fact, its main virtue was its absolute quietness. It was much quieter, both in engine and road noise, than either of the other two cars. He must use his Cadillacs to round up the cattle.

SUMMARY OF CADILLAC OWNERS' OPINIONS:

OVER-ALL RATING: Excellent 80.9% Average 17.3% Poor 1.8%

Best-liked features	
Riding comfort	46.4%
Handling ease	40.2%
Exterior styling	21.4%
Power, performance	20.5%
Heavy, safe feeling	8.9%
Quiet, smooth running	6.3%
Prestige	5.4%
Most-frequent complaints	
None at all	44.6%
Poor workmanship	14.3%
Poor gas economy	13.4%
Body Rattles, squeaks	11.6%
Engine noise, trouble	3.6%
Rear-view mirror location	3.6%
Poor acceleration	3.6%
Had trouble with engine?	
No trouble	89.1%
Some trouble	8.2%
Considerable trouble	2.7%
What was engine trouble?	
Carburetor	2.7%
Valve trouble	1.8%
Oil leaks	1.8%
How is dealer service?	
Excellent	60.7%
Average	30.4%
Poor	8.9%
Would buy from him again?	
Yes, would	36.6%
No, would not	8.0%
Undecided, no answer	55.4%
Have optional air suspension?	
Yes, have it	16.1%
No, do not	76.8%
No answer	7.1%
Is air suspension worth it?	
(asked of those with it)	
Yes, it is	3.6%
No, it is not	1.8%
No answer, undecided	10.7%
What make was traded?	
Cadillac	73.3%
Other GM make	8.0%
Ford Motor make	7.1%
Chrysler Corp. make	1.8%
No trade, no answer	9.8%
What make will buy next time?	
Another Cadillac	75.9%
Other GM make	6.3%
Ford Motor make	3.6%
Chrysler Corp. make	1.8%
Undecided, no answer	12.5%
What other car now owner?	
Another Cadillac	8.0%
Other GM make	14.3%
Ford Motor make	42.9%
Chrysler Corp. car	5.4%
Other U.S. car	3.6%
Foreign car	2.7%
None, no answer	30.4%

AN ENGINEER'S ANALYSIS
By DALE KELLY, SAE
Registered Professional Engineer

1958 CADILLAC TEST DATA

MODEL TESTED: 1958 Cadillac Series 62 four-door hardtop with four-barrel carburetor, dual exhausts, automatic transmission, power brakes, steering, seat and windows, air conditioning. Rear-axle ratio: 3.36 to 1. Wheelbase: 129.5 inches. Tires: 8.20 by 15. Weight: 5128 pounds with gas tank half full (55½ percent on front, 44½ percent on rear). Mileage on car at time of test: 4350 miles. Barometer: 28.98 inches. Temperature: 80 degrees F. Payload: 200 lb.

ACCELERATION TIME FROM STANDING START (in seconds)

	0 to 20	0 to 40	0 to 60	0 to 80	¼ mile
Ignition timed for:					
Regular gasoline	3.4	7.3	13.3	21.9	19.9
Premium gasoline	3.2	6.6	12.4	21.2	19.4
Super-premium gasoline			No improvement		

Gasoline used had the following octane ratings by Research method: Regular 90; Premium 97; Super-premium 105.)

FUEL ECONOMY (miles per gallon)

	Steady 30 m.p.h.	Steady 50 m.p.h.	Steady 70 m.p.h.	Traffic Route
Ignition timed for:				
Regular gasoline	19.1	15.4	13.2	7.7
Premium gasoline	20.2	15.1	12.55	7.8
Super-premium gasoline		Not tested (see Observations below)		

(In traffic test, car makes 10 full stops per mile and is driven just enough to average 15 miles per hour.)

ESTIMATED AVERAGE ANNUAL GASOLINE BILL: $245 for 10,000 miles
(Based on all cars using premium gasoline)

SPEEDOMETER ERROR (miles per hour)

Speedometer reading	20	30	40	50	60	70	80
True speed	21	31	40	50	60	69	79

ODOMETER ERROR (miles traveled)
Odometer registered 101 miles for an actual distance of 100 miles.

DRIVER'S VISION
Driver could see part of road 20 feet in front of car, full width of road 23 feet in front of car.

GROUND CLEARANCE (unloaded car)

Worst dip that could be crossed....26-ft. radius*
Worst hump that could be crossed 24-ft. radius*
Deepest rut that could be negotiated......7.0 in.
Curb clearance for door opening...........13 in.
* See Observations below

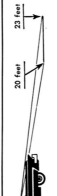

MISCELLANEOUS

TRUNK CAPACITY
13 cartons (one cubic foot each)
WATER RESISTANCE: Fair
Splash-pan test: No leaks. Brakes only slightly affected.
High-pressure test: Leakage at tops of all doors.

OBSERVATIONS

Because no acceleration improvement was noted with the spark advanced for super-premium fuel, there is no reason for using this extra-cost gasoline. Therefore, no fuel-consumption test was made with it. During full-throttle acceleration above 60, there were signs of vapor lock on two different commercial gasolines. The time to 80 m.p.h. might have been a little better in cooler weather or with a less volatile gasoline. In spite of poor gasoline mileage in traffic, the over-all gasoline bill was no more than the average for the Chevrolet, Ford and Plymouth cars tested a few months ago.

Power-brake reserve vacuum was enough for three full applications with the engine dead. Gasoline tank holds 20 gallons. When the car was allowed to run out of gas, a little more than a gallon was required to move the pointer.

STEERING:
Steering-wheel turns for 100-ft. circle..0.80 turn
Curb-to-curb turn-circle diameter............47 feet
Wall-to-wall turn-circle diameter..............49 feet
Steering-wheel turns, lock-to-lock............3.7 turns
CENTER OF GRAVITY: 19 inches

Speedometer scale has been straightened out and as a result the five-mile-per-hour intervals in the middle range (where most driving is done) are very small. Excessive chrome impairs visibility of entire panel.

With air suspension at maximum height (a separate control is used to elevate it above normal height) the radius of the worst dip drops to 19 feet, and the worst hump drops to 14 feet. This is excellent clearance. With air suspension at normal height, clearance was fair under rear overhang and relatively poor amidships. Deepest rut clearance is normally determined by the differential housing and cannot be increased by changing air-suspension height. However, with the engine dead and the air bags deflated, the front end dropped so low that a rut deeper than four inches would have stopped the car.

126

Cadillac Owners Rate Riding Comfort First

Fourth on the complaint list is engine noise, although it is mentioned by only 3.6 percent. The same number complain about brake trouble, principally with the parking brake. Other complaints involve mirror location and poor acceleration. Here, in order of frequency of mention, are these additional owners' complaints:

"Excessive roar in exhaust system at high speeds and when taking off."—Iowa dairy farmer.

"Engine too noisy. Suspect it is because r.p.m. is away up. Noise commences at 60 miles per hour. Sounds like a truck going by in 7th gear."—California owner.

"Poorly placed parking-brake release. Could be operated more efficiently by hand knob on dash."—Maine general contractor.

"Brakes require 1000-mile attention. Won't release. Engine must be tuned every 1500 miles."—Tennessee owner.

"My only complaint is that the rear-view mirror is too low. It makes a blind spot which is very hazardous."—Wyoming retired owner.

Suggestions to Industry

Cadillac owners offer some interesting answers when asked to make one suggestion to the entire automobile industry (not just to Cadillac):

"Don't go any lower to satisfy styling at the expense of seating position."—Michigan engineer.

"Make it look like an automobile again."—New Jersey funeral director.

"Don't make the cars any longer or wider."—Pennsylvania bakery owner.

"Cut back on horsepower to increase gas mileage."—Minnesota businessman.

"Make more distinction between different cars."—Texas funeral director.

"Build a quality American car. I saw some foreign makes that seemed better built."—Pennsylvania salesman.

"Get off the emphasis on tails."—New Mexico engineer.

"For higher-price models, stop changing to cheaper styling."—Florida school principal.

"The industry tries to create a car 'out of this world' to beat its competitor, rather than to create the kind of car the average motorist really wants. The extreme fins, the wrap-around windshields, increase the cost of the car and are not what the public really wants. The average American businessman would prefer a car on the conservative side."—Kentucky contractor.

More Best-Liked Features

Fourth on the best-liked list is power and performance, followed by that heavy, safe feeling of the big car. After these come roadability, quiet operation, prestige and others described in the following quotations (given in order of frequency of mention):

"Engine seems to respond promptly when power is needed."—Pennsylvania salesman.

"I like the safety factor of a heavy, well constructed car. Also it gives me prestige away from home."—California real-estate investor.

"It has a solid feeling. It's the safest feeling car on the road I have driven."—Oregon contractor.

"Well balanced. Hugs road on curves."—North Carolina executive.

"I like its absolute quietness on the road."—California retired owner.

"The name 'Cadillac' has the sound and feel of prestige due to good propaganda advertising."—Pennsylvania owner.

"Cadillac prestige."—Texas investment executive (and to prove he's most interested in prestige, he adds a complaint that there is "not sufficient identification of Cadillac on the side of the car").

"The Cadillac is not as good as the reputation it has. It is better than most cars, but you pay for this in a number of ways. I would say that the best thing about a Cadillac is that it builds up one's ego."—Louisiana sales engineer.

"Dollar for dollar, the least expensive car to own."—Arizona sales engineer.

"I find now that I can trade Cadillac for a Cadillac about as cheap or cheaper than when I drove a new Dodge or new Buicks. My 1955 Cadillac I sold outright for cash within $950 of what I paid new at end of one year."—Michigan real estate dealer.

"Gives a durability that I have been unable to get in any other car."—Wisconsin real estate man.

"Starts good in cold weather."—Idaho farmer.

"The car has a nice view from every seat inside. Instrument panel is excellent with everything at your fingertips. The car is built solid."—Illinois motel manager.

And the Other Complaints

Mentioned by a small percentage of the total, but still by enough to be of interest are the following:

"Too much slippage in Low. Motor races and car barely moves off. Pickup speed too slow. Dangerous in heavy traffic."—Oklahoma owner.

"There is something wrong with the transmission, I think. A heavy noise that we don't like and the garage can't detect the trouble. We have been waiting two months to get it fixed, if and when a factory representative gets here."—Illinois decorator.

"Body slightly too long."—North Carolina surgeon.

"Nice car, but price much too high. Everything but the four wheels, body and steering wheel is extra cost."—Washington, D.C., executive.

"Rear springs are too soft. Car sags in the rear with very little luggage in trunk."—Ohio businessman.

"Poor paint job. Many spots are bare where body panels meet."—New Jersey housewife.

"Front grille is a car-washer's nightmare."—Ohio mechanical engineer.

"Dust fogs in the trunk and back seat when driving on country roads."—Colorado farmer.

"Window cranks are in awkward position. Difficult to use."—New Jersey executive.

"Door opener is hard to reach. Foot parking brake hard to release. I prefer a hand release."—Connecticut physician.

"Hands on the clock and the pointer on the gas gauge have little white dots on them and are very hard to read."—Texas housewife.

"I certainly don't like that 'seven minute warmup,' racing period to warm up the engine in cold weather."—Illinois publisher.

That is the story of the 1958 Cadillac as told by the owners themselves—owners from all over the country who know the car best.

Most cars have gone to a foot-operated parking brake. Now comes the foot-operated release. It's just another skill to be learned and it's hard to see the advantage.

CADILLAC MOUNTS ITS BATTERY IN FRONT FENDER BEHIND HEAD-LIGHTS — A VULNERABLE SPOT

When Cadillac owners talk like this, it is time for Detroit to get on with it!

It feels so heavy that its inertia is a bit frightening. There seem to be tons in motion. Braking requires an unusual amount of pedal pressure even with power assistance.

Balance is something you can't measure — you have to feel it. Railton ranks Imperial best in this department. You should drive all three and make your own judgment.

There's no sin in buying a car to build up your ego. The error comes when you buy it for this reason, but justify it on other grounds.

He must have latched onto a live one!

CADILLAC'S FRONT DOOR HAS A CLUTTER OF HANDLES, NOT ALL OF WHICH ARE WELL POSITIONED

Added comments: Seats of excellent height and comfortable. Very good speedometer dial. Vent and heat controls simple and convenient. Ash trays handy, lighter location not in the other two cars, seems to have less road sense too. Front end shakes on washboard. Ride too soft on undulating roads. Fuel-gauge needle a masterpiece of uncertainty. A huge dot on end of needle covers almost a quarter of the scale. Heater blower runs all time heat is needed. Extreme display of chrome on dashboard seems out of place in a top-drawer car. Some windshield reflections at night. Vacuum wipers slow down on acceleration, just when most needed. High-beam indicator lamp almost invisible, as are the hands of the clock.

CADILLAC ROAD TEST
(Continued from page 73)

of engine quietness, the mileage benefits of top gear are lost. It would not be surprising if GM shortly produced some kind of visual reminder for forgetful motorists in this respect.

Cadillac's heat and ventilating system employs the cowl intake, with warm air conducted through the vented front door panel to the rear seat area. The arrangement is an elaborate one, but is simply controlled and highly functional. Unlike many modern cars, it can be mastered without undue study of the owner's manual furnished by the division.

Today's wrap-around windshields have created an annoying situation caused by wipers which are inadequate for the curved glass. On Cadillac, a cam guides the blades effectively around the curve, wiping cleanly to within two inches of the corner posts. The windshield washer-wiper system is fully automatic—touch of a button puts both into operation and the cutoff takes place a few seconds later without further attention.

Additional evidence of manufacturing care can be found inside the vast trunk, which is upholstered more luxuriously than the passenger compartments of many other automobiles. Cadillac provides its owners with a rubber covered lug wrench, jack is fixed to the floor in a non-rattling position by a spring, while a triangular piece of wood (painted black) is included for blocking the tires while jacking.

Cadillac likes to point out that some of its models cost no more than comparable cars in other makes. This is true, but in order to enjoy many of the features commented upon here, you will have to pay a high price. As of this moment, a fully equipped Cadillac is one of the costliest American cars on the road.

On the other hand, Cadillac depreciates at a slower rate than almost any other car. This, along with good mileage and dependability, gives the expensive vehicle certain qualities of economy. It's a paradoxical situation, but actually an honest argument which Cadillac salesmen have found highly effective. •

SPECIFICATIONS

TEST CAR: 1955 Cadillac Fleetwood Series 60 Special sedan.
ENGINE: ohv V-8. Bore 3 13/16, stroke 3 5/8. Displacement 331 cubic inches. Compression ratio 9 to 1. Bhp 250 at 4600 rpm. Torque 345 ft.-lbs. at 2800 rpm. Crankcase capacity (with filter) 6 quarts. Fuel tank capacity 20 gallons. Cooling system capacity (with heater) 22 quarts. Electrical system 12 volts.
TRANSMISSION: Hydra-Matic standard on all models is dual-range with four forward speeds and fluid coupling. Ratios: 1st 3.82, 2nd 2.63, 3rd 1.45, 4th 1.0, reverse 4.03. Rear axle ratio: standard 3.36, optional 3.07.
OVERALL DIMENSIONS: Wheelbase 129 inches. Tread 60 front, 63 rear. Length 227.3, width 80, height 62.1. Dry weight 4540 lbs. Turning circle 45 feet. Tire size 8.00 x 15 tubeless.
PRICES: Series 60 Special four-door sedan $4728. Radio $214. Power brakes $47. Electric seat adjustment $53.

'55 Cadillac *(Continued from page 68)* built some five or six Cadillac engines a day. He took pride and a personal responsibility. A progressive assembly line precludes this type of workman, so recourse must be had to posters, more time for a given operation, and most important, quality control. This last starts with the dealer pipeline which funnels in product information reports (PIRs) on manufacturing and design failures. Dealers would soon lose interest in PIRs if they were not acted upon immediately, so they are—religiously. These spot the workman at fault, and if it lies with his methods or machine (and not a chronic Monday hangover), this operation becomes subject to statistical quality control which ranges from a sampling to inspection of every part produced. Cadillac was not the first to do this, but they probably developed the system to a greater degree than any of their competitors. Every machine tool operator in the plant has his production charted. Posted by the machine, these show if he goofed, when, and how often.

CONTINUED FROM PAGE 87
Brougham from nosing down during fast stops.

The Brougham has a four headlamp lighting system like that pioneered by its original prototype, the 1955 GM Motorama show car.

This system uses outer lamps with both high and low beams; these lamps are for city driving. Low beam has more wattage than standard single lamps.

Thus, improved low beam illumination is provided. High beam of the outer lamps gives a soft, general lighting.

Inner lamps have a high beam only; actually, they furnish a kind of spotlight effect. They are used along with high beam of the outer lamps for highway and country driving.

Combined wattage of these four lamps is much greater than two-lamp systems and furnishes better illumination. In addition, the light is so directed that a driver gets maximum vision without creating a glare to blind drivers of oncoming cars.

The Brougham's power train is similar to standard Cadillacs. The Hydra-Matic transmission is mounted conventionally right behind the engine.

There are no center pillars in the Brougham. Instead, locking plates, 14 inches from the floor, provide latching points for rotary-type door locks.

Gadget lovers will have a field day with this new Cadillac. Just about everything that can be power-operated is! This includes seats, all windows (including vents), trunk lid, etc.

Power steering, power brakes and air conditioning are standard equipment. There are special heaters for both front and rear seats and Broughams all will have all-transistorized radios. (Radio antennas are power-operated—naturally—and rise automatically to "city height" when the radio is turned on. They can be raised to full height for maximum range by means of an overriding switch for country driving. The antennas automatically retract into fender wells when radio or ignition is turned off!)

Brougham styling shows its Cadillac relationship very clearly. Such typical identification features as the grille and rear fenders are retained.

An interesting construction note, however, is the one-piece front end. Fenders are made of one piece which is continuous across the front of the car above the grille. It is to this crossover panel that the forward-hinged hood is attached.

The huge compound curved windshield rakes back sharply to the roof line. Both windshield and backlight are made of tinted E-Z Eye glass to cut glare.

The price tag for the Brougham had not been announced at the time this report was written. However, it very likely will exceed $10,000. And, even at these unusual figures, Cadillac undoubtedly will be able to sell all it can make, and will no doubt give Continental a rough time for "Prestige Car" honors in 1957. •